TO THE ENDS OF THE
EARTH

TO THE ENDS OF THE

EARTH

HOW THE GREATEST MAPS WERE MADE

Philip
Parker

IVY PRESS

Quarto

First published in 2023 by Ivy Press,
an imprint of The Quarto Group.
One Triptych Place
London, SE1 9SH,
United Kingdom
T (0)20 7700 6700
www.Quarto.com

A catalogue record for this book is available from the British Library.

ISBN 978-0-7112-8264-3
Ebook ISBN 978-0-7112-8266-7

10 9 8 7 6 5 4 3 2 1

Text by Philip Parker
Design by Ben Ruocco

Printed in Malaysia

INTRODUCTION

This is a book about the making of maps: the maps themselves, the cartographers who made them and the techniques and materials they employed. It covers a vast arc in time, from the first identifiable attempts at map-making contemporary with Stonehenge or the Great Pyramids to the on-demand mapping available in billions of 21st-century smartphones, and also covers the journey of individual maps from conception to completion.

First of all, what is a map? It seems such a simple question, which in turn must have an equally obvious answer. Everyone, after all, can recognize a map. Most people use them daily for navigating around city streets or urban transportation networks, and the majority of us have at some point owned an atlas, either of our own country or the world, with geographical areas neatly packaged in rectangular slices, further subdivided by grid lines to enable the easier location of points of interest.

Yet the wider the would-be map user's gaze extends, the more blurred becomes the concept of what a map is. Etched lines on Neolithic rock-carvings. Clay tablets containing a stylized world view from 7th-century BC Mesopotamia. Medieval world maps teeming with martyrs, manticores and mandrakes. Maps composed on the cusp of the age of European exploration which are shorn of half the world (because no one outside the Americas or Australia yet knew of those regions' existence). Maps of battlefields, with

OBSERVATOIRE DE PEKING
tiré du Pere LE COMTE.

contending armies arrayed behind the dense hatching of sheltering hills or along the blue swirl of rivers to be crossed. Maps of population density, literacy, the distribution of sparrows or the frequency of use of dialect words, colour-coded according to the exigencies of a thousand thematic subjects. Maps of places that only exist in the mind of an author: of Middle-earth, Hundred Acre Wood or Earthsea. Maps of places that do exist, but which we can never reach, such as Mars, Jupiter or, at the extreme end of the mapping scale, the Milky Way or the entire universe.

All this dazzling, breathtaking and somewhat confusing panoply – and much else besides – comes under the heading of maps. Any definition needs to be wide enough to encompass the vast spectrum of cartographic endeavours. Perhaps 'the visual representation of a space' will do, as it includes ideological, cultural and thematic spaces as well as the purely geographical and allows for the creation of maps on media as diverse as bone, marble, vellum, paper and bronze, and intangibly on internet servers, and in both two- and three-dimensional forms.

The word 'representation' is crucial here, as any map involves a conversation between creator and audience. While a conservative definition of mapping might relegate the role of a map to a very practical tool for finding the way from a physical starting point to a destination on the ground and how the user examines it for that purpose, most maps have not been used, and in many cases were scarcely useable, to that end. One of the very earliest maps we have, of part of a field system around Nuzi in Mesopotamia, which dates from around 2300 BC, was not intended to show a route, but to depict property rights. Similarly, the maps of the New

World that proliferated in the wake of Christopher Columbus's first European voyage there in 1492 were not practical guides to following him, but a way of asserting ownership on the part of his royal sponsors and to portray the quite remarkable broadening of Europe's horizons that his and his imitators' explorations heralded. Most world atlases could never in any real sense have been used as a practical means of navigating from one country to another (the scale and level of detail is hopelessly impractical for that purpose).

More generally, maps such as the doctor John Snow's plotting of cases during the London cholera epidemic of 1854 answered a question (of what the cause of the infection might be), but they were not a route-planner, while the whole genre of historical atlases tells us how nations arrived in their current form (often coloured by the historical concerns or prejudices of the compiler), but not how to travel around their modern iterations.

ABOVE

Map of the 1854
Soho Cholera
Outbreak,
Dr John Snow

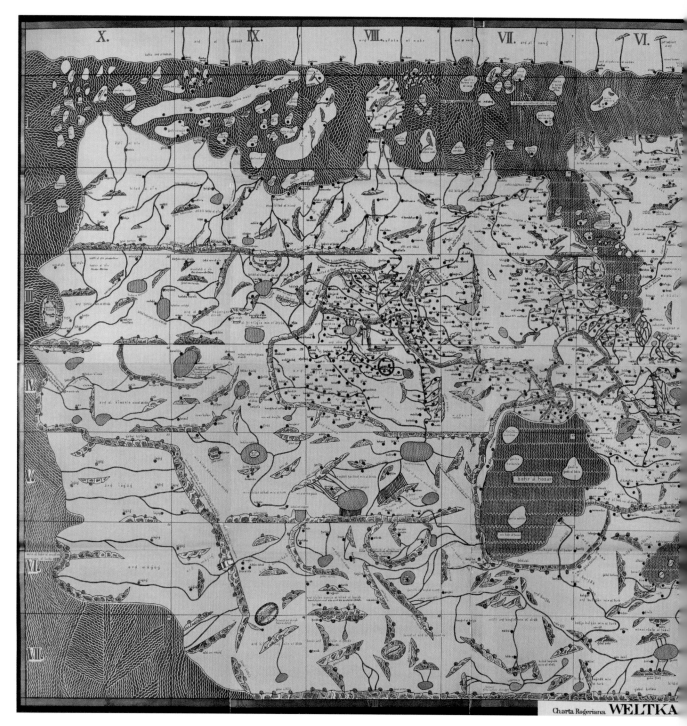

ABOVE

Tabula Rogeriana
world map,
Muhammad
al-Sharif al-Idrisi,
1154

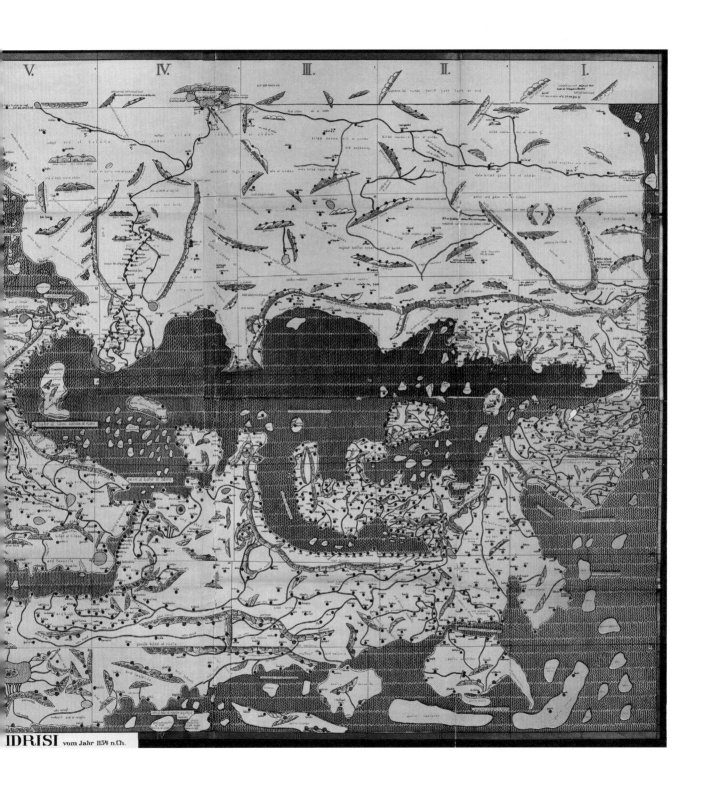

IDRISI vom Jahr 1154 n.Ch.

Cartographer
at work, from
*Methodus
Geometrica*, Paul
Pfintzing, 1598

Of course, many maps did have an entirely
practical function: the portolan charts of the
14th century and onwards – densely packed portrayals
of coastal areas with webs of lines helping to calculate
the most direct way for ships to traverse the seas –
were compiled precisely for that purpose, with pilots'
charts of harbours and maritime hazards even more
obviously so. Ancient itinerary maps, such as the
Peutinger Table, showed roads through the Roman
Empire, and the text that accompanied some of them
gave a wealth of practical information, such as the
best harbours in which to trade in ivory or gems.
Then, from around the 17th century, genuine travel
maps began to appear, which gave their users a good
sense of the amount of time they needed to allow in
order to travel along Britain's patchily maintained
road system. All of these, and even 21st-century
internet mapping, notably that produced by Google,
involve some element of choice and compromise: in
what to show, and in what to leave out to avoid the
map becoming so dense as to be incomprehensible.
In the case of much medieval mapping, what to put
in for those areas where the compiler's knowledge
was partial or completely lacking led to concocted

coastlines, a plethora of fantastic beasts, and the
persistence of mysterious islands such as Antillia in
the Atlantic, whose staying power on maps defied
their entirely fictitious nature.

Mapping, then, is an uncertain science, where
choices in what to portray and how to do it, have
played as much a role as geographical knowledge and
technical expertise. This is hardly surprising. Humans
are a very visual species and mapping has always
been an ideal medium to encapsulate and transmit
information in an immediately appealing and
understandable fashion. A map showing a navigable
channel through low-lying shoals (submerged banks),
one depicting the waxing and waning of an empire
over time, or another with arrows showing the routes
of migrations (forced or otherwise) speak more
directly and clearly than a thousand accompanying
words could do.

Mapping is an art, too, as map-makers have
always been conscious of the appearance of their
products. Lavish cartouches, extravagant scrolls, sea
beasts cavorting in the ocean or the simple elegance
of the lines engraved on the page are all elements
that have been employed by cartographers to create

ABOVE

Cartography in the digital age

objects of sometimes astonishing beauty. Many of them, such as the late 13th-century *Hereford Mappa Mundi*, the 15th-century Fra Mauro map, produced by a monk on a small island close to Venice, or the *Cantino Planisphere*, the product of a judicious exercise in information espionage in the 16th century, are works of art in their own right.

This book is a tribute to all those who have made maps, from the very first anonymous cartographers to their information-age successors. It tells the story of mapping, map-makers and the ways in which maps have been conceived, created and disseminated. From the origins of the first maps, to the reasons for which maps have been crafted through the ages; the ways in which that information has been gathered and selected (which beast to include, which bay to exclude?); the tools and methods the map-maker has used to draw the map and then to reproduce it (by laborious copying before the age of printing, by a variety of printing techniques since then); the characters and careers of the map-makers themselves; and, finally, the uses to which the maps have been put (which were not always those originally intended or even imagined by the cartographers). This book tells the story from the point of view of a hypothetical cartographer (of admittedly unlikely longevity) investigating the means by which to create a map, beginning in the age when maps were a rare and experimental form of knowledge, and ending in the age of the internet, when they are practically ubiquitous. Their work stands testament to myriad ways of understanding the world, a process that is still unfolding into the 21st century.

CHAPTER 1

IN THE BEGINNING

THE FIRST MAPS

There was a time before maps. The need to 'find the way' and even the desire to impose some sense of order on the world almost certainly long predates the emergence 40–50,000 years ago of the first figurative art (found in a cave at Lubang Jeriji Saléh in Borneo – it may depict some form of wild cattle). It required an advanced level of spatial cognition, with an awareness of left and right, inner and outer and an appreciation the importance of symmetry, together with some sense of 'boundary' (one side of this line is 'ours', the other is 'theirs') before the idea of mapping could have any meaning at all.

Equipped with a mental map of their surroundings, and having developed language sophisticated enough to describe their immediate world, its hazards, the best hunting grounds, sites imbued with some numinous quality and perhaps even the migrations of their ancestors, it was only a matter of time before the artistic impulse melded with the linguistic one in early humans and the first map was created. When, though, exactly did that occur?

Much of the earliest evidence and many of the candidates for the earliest map present problems. For a map to be a map, the person who created it must have intended it to be a representation of the relationship of objects in some kind of space, and that the representation should bear some resemblance to a reality (even an imagined one) and not simply be a jumbled set of images. Scratchings found on a bone plaque excavated at Kesserloch near Thayngen in Switzerland in the 1870s, which date from around 13,000 BC, might have been intended as some kind of representation of the local area, but it is hard to relate these with any certainty to the topography around the cave. Only about 10,000 years later do objects begin to appear which more plausibly could be described as mapping (or at least contain elements which come close to it). 'Picture maps' which contain possible images of huts or houses have been found across the southern Mediterranean, from a cave painting at Peñalsordo, near Badajoz, Spain, dating to around 10,000 BC, which may show two figures set inside some form of enclosure, to rock paintings in Algeria's Tassili Mountains that really do look like groups of huts, around which human-like figures are arrayed. The largest of these North African picture maps is the Great Disk from Talat N'Iisk in the Atlas Mountains of Morocco, a colossal stone slab around 1 m (3¼ ft) in diameter. Placed within a bounding circle are markings which could be a valley between two mountain ranges with a river and its tributaries in the middle. Perhaps as early as the late 4th millennium BC, it is a little younger than an earthenware jar excavated at Tepe Gawra in Iraq. The upper portion of this 'Landscape Jar' is divided into 12 panels, each decorated with parallel lines of triangles, which have been interpreted as representations of mountains, and herringbone patterns which may be intended to show rivers.

TOP

Landscape jar, excavated at Tepe Gawra, Iraq, c. 4500 BC

RIGHT

Topographic rock-engraving in Paspardo, Val Camonica, Italy, carved during the 3rd millennium BC

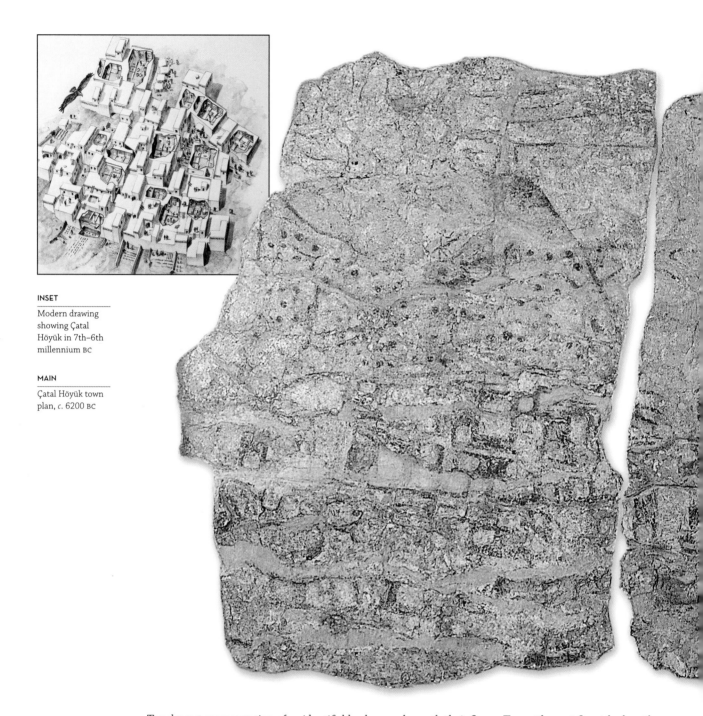

The clearest representation of an identifiable place (though to what extent the artist did so accurately or even intended to do so is unclear) is what may well be a plan of the Neolithic town of Çatal Höyük, southeast of Konya in modern Turkey. Its 6,000 or so inhabitants grew wheat and barley, kept sheep and goats, and engaged in some form of cattle cult. The skulls of the dead animals adorned the plaster walls of their houses, with those of their human ancestors buried – in, to modern sensibility, macabre fashion – beneath their floors. The settlement flourished until around 6200 BC and its prosperity was enhanced by one of the earliest known long-distance trade routes, in obsidian, a razor-sharp volcanic glass which was quarried from the nearby volcano of Nemrut Dağ, worked in Çatal Höyük and then transmitted onwards. The erupting volcano, appearing as a faint cone with a red flame emerging from it, is depicted on a fresco that adorned the wall of one of the rectangular mud-brick dwellings in which the people of Çatal

Höyük lived, stacked on top of each other like a house of cards. At the foot of the fresco, a regular pattern of rectangles is hard to interpret as anything other than a plan of the town. Over 8,000 years old, it has a strong claim to be the very first map.

As well as tentatively beginning to map the land around them, early peoples also started to map the sky. Some attempts may have been purely symbolic and scarcely reach the threshold to be counted as maps: a pottery dish from Egypt's Amratian period

in the 4th millennium BC shows what could be a representation of the Sun's course from east to west, passing over a primeval ocean and two large mountains, but the subject is a generic one. Megaliths such as Stonehenge – its first elements erected around 2500 BC – show a sophisticated understanding of the cycles of the year, key parts of it oriented to align with the summer and winter solstices, but, monumental though they are, these are not maps. Dating from about a thousand years later, a disc or pendant

RIGHT

Sky disc found at
Nebra, Germany,
c. 1800–1600 BC

BELOW

Statue of Sumerian
ruler Gudea of
Lagash with
plan of temple
enclosure,
c. 2100 BC

unearthed in 1999 at Nebra around 50 km (31 miles) north of Erfurt in Germany shows the urge to understand the heavens had been translated into a more tangible visual form. The 30-cm (12-in) diameter circle of bronze is unique: its greenish background is overlaid with golden shapes that probably depict the Sun, the crescent Moon in several phases and a pattern of stars, which have been interpreted as representing the Pleiades. Whether it was an instrument for calculating the phases of the Moon, the pattern of sunsets or simply an outline of the heavens, it is one of the earliest, and certainly one of the most spectacular, celestial maps.

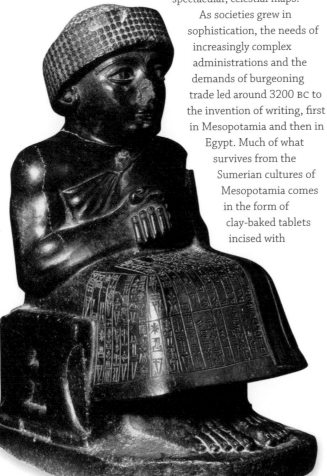

As societies grew in sophistication, the needs of increasingly complex administrations and the demands of burgeoning trade led around 3200 BC to the invention of writing, first in Mesopotamia and then in Egypt. Much of what survives from the Sumerian cultures of Mesopotamia comes in the form of clay-baked tablets incised with cuneiform script – so called because the characters were created by pressing the end of a stylus in the shape of a wedge (*cuneus* in Latin) into wet clay. Before long, Sumerian scribes added compilations of place names to their repertoire – one series survives from the town of Ebla in northern Syria, from around 2500 to 2200 BC – and itineraries, including those of military expeditions. By the late 3rd millennium BC, the scribes had progressed to the occasional inclusion of sketches, showing walls, streets and rivers. One, shown as part of a statue of Gudea, the ruler of the city-state of Lagash from around 2141 to 2122 BC, shows him balancing a table on his knees which has a plan of an enclosure, possibly that of a temple, engraved on it. Created around 1500 BC, a tablet from the religious centre of Nippur may count as the first detailed town plan to survive. It shows the city's main temple, a park and enclosure and the River Euphrates snaking through it, together with the city walls punctuated by seven gates, each of which is named. Earlier than all of these, however, is a small clay tablet found near Kirkuk in the north of modern Iraq. Dating from round 2300 BC it shows an area surrounded by two ranges of hills, with a river or stream running through it. The central portion depicts a field or plot of land, complete with its boundaries and its extent (given as 354 Sumerian *iku*, equivalent to around 12 hectares/30 acres), and even the name of its owner, a certain Azala. An inscription at the bottom indicates the region shown was at Durubla (near modern Yorghan Tepe). Right at the start, ownership rather than navigation was a primary motivation for mapping.

Egypt, too, generated its own cartographic tradition. A unitary state far earlier than Mesopotamia, it was united under the first pharaohs around 3100 BC. Dependent on the life-giving qualities of the River Nile, it was also a land obsessed by death, or at least the provision to the deceased of the means to survive in the afterlife. Drawings on the tombs of many of the rulers and nobility have a map-like quality, showing landscapes of town and country scattered with fertile and idyllic gardens.

Some, illustrating the collection of spells known as *The Book of the Dead*, which equipped the departed's soul with the magical tools to navigate the hazardous path to the afterlife, show idealized fields which the dead person will cultivate in the next world. The rather more detailed illustrations for another funerary text, *The Book of the Two Ways*, which appear on coffins from the Middle Kingdom period, around 2000 BC, show the route the soul must take to reach the Field of Offerings, the paradise presided over by the god Osiris. Along the way, the map-like pictures show points such as the Lake of the Knife Wielders and mystic guardians who must be cajoled or overcome to allow the soul free passage, such as the intriguingly named 'He who eats the droppings of his hinder parts'.

Although mystical maps – and celestial ones such as the star chart painted on the ceiling of the tomb of Senenmut, the chief minister of Queen Hatshepsut around 1470 BC – had a religious role, the Egyptians used them for a very practical purpose, too. Although

the pharaonic administration, ruling over a vast kingdom extending from the Nile Delta to the frontier fort of Buhen south of modern Aswan, must have had just as much need for mapping as its Mesopotamian counterparts, very little has survived. One notable exception is the *Turin Papyrus*, which takes its name from the city in which it has resided, in the Museo Egizio, since the 1850s, but which shows a section of Egypt's Eastern Desert around Wadi Hammamat. The main section, around 40 cm (15¾ in) high, depicts roads, watercourses and colour-coded rock formations. As well as being a main trade route for expeditions to the Red Sea and then south to the Land of Punt (possibly modern Somalia), the area was the source of precious mineral resources, particularly gold (which is indicated by a red shade) and greywacke, a greyish-green stone which was particularly prized by the Egyptians. Greywacke was quarried for over 3,000 years, and provided the material for the Narmer Palette, one of the earliest artefacts to survive from pharaonic Egypt, which shows the – possibly legendary –

ABOVE

Nippur town plan,
c. 1500 BC

first pharaoh Narmer smiting his enemies. Other features on the map include wells, a cistern, a goldminers' settlement and a stele erected to the god Amun by Pharaoh Seti I. Probably compiled as a route map for a stone-cutting expedition under Pharaoh Ramesses IV (*r.* 1152–1145 BC), the papyrus is both the earliest map showing genuine topographical detail we have from Egypt as well as possibly the world's first geological map.

Many subsequent cultures in the Near East and Europe would develop their own cartographic traditions and produce maps (most notably the Greeks and Romans), but these fall long outside the bounds of the search for the first map. Elsewhere in Asia, rock paintings not dissimilar to those found in North Africa and southern Europe (see p.14) depict what might be huts or symbolic plans of settlements, such as those found in sandstone caves in Madhya

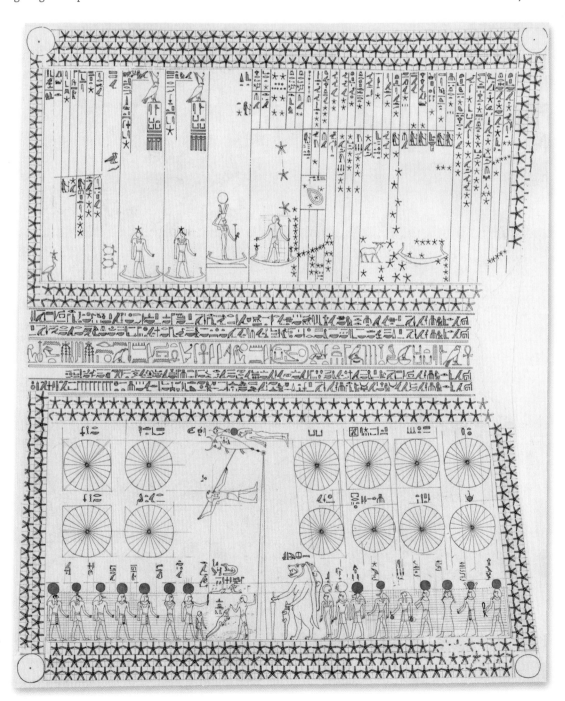

Pradesh, while information embedded in the Vedas, the sacred Hindu texts, the composition of the earliest parts of which date back to around 1500 BC, suggest a detailed geographical knowledge. The first fragmentary survival of mapping from South Asia, however, comes from the Mauryan Empire, founded in 321 BC by Chandragupta Maurya. It should perhaps come as no surprise that the institution by the Mauryans of a land tax, which required surveyors and assessors to determine how much landowners needed to pay, coincides roughly with the same time period in which we find the first cartographic artefacts from India. Fragments of pots containing geographical designs that may represent house plans, and some, such as a dish found at Salihundam in Andhra Pradesh, which dates from the around the 1st century BC or 1st century AD, are inscribed with plans of

monasteries or temples. After this, however, there is a long hiatus, and it is not until the end of the 12th century AD that Indian mapping re-emerges with a stone relief of the cosmos as seen by the scriptures of the Jain religion. Placed in the cloister of the Sagaram Temple at Saurashtra in Gujarat it contained seven concentric circles showing the various continents, culminating in Nandisvaradvipa, the outermost of the Jain middle worlds in which humans were said to dwell.

By then, a tradition of mapping had been flourishing for many centuries far to the east. In China, the early establishment of a centralized state, with a large bureaucracy and the accompanying need to tax subjects (and, of course, to assess their wealth and landholdings as accurately as possible) must have played a role in this. Cities such as Chang'an (modern

ABOVE

Turin Papyrus, 12th century BC. The Wadi Hammamat is the broad line running across the lower third, with 'mountains of gold' to either side.

Xi'an), which became the capital under the Han dynasty in 195 BC, and which by the time of the Tang in the mid-8th century AD would have a population of over a million, already had nearly 150,000 inhabitants shortly after its foundation, making it one of the largest cities in the world. From here, merchants set out on the long trek along the Silk Route through Central Asia down into Persia and eventually the eastern Mediterranean, and so the intelligence-gathering that eventually fed into Chinese geographical awareness was substantial.

The earliest map that survives from China, though, is on a far smaller scale. It was found in 1978 in the tomb of King Cuo of the Zhongshan Kingdom, one of the many warring states which struggled for dominance in the two centuries before China's eventual unification. Dating from around 310 BC and inscribed on a bronze plaque it is a map of King Cuo's mausoleum, with five sacrifice halls, an inner and outer wall and the burial mound of the king himself. Covering a larger area are the four wooden boards inked with a plan of the Fangmatan region (now in Gansu Province), which were buried in the tomb of an officer in the Qin army (which really did unify China 18 years after the maps' interment in 239 BC). Clearly intended to be of some strategic military use, the Fangmatan map shows rivers with black lines, dried-up gullies and even differentiates between the main species of trees in woods (pine, fir or cedar), which are all separately labelled. Even more striking are three maps found secreted in a lacquer box inside a noble tomb at Mawangdui, in the south-east of Hunan province. All three were created around 168 BC with vegetable-dye ink on silk; two of the maps are purely topographic, showing a part of the frontier state of Changsha, which formed part of the Han Empire, including mountains, rivers and the seats of administrative counties. The third is even more extraordinary: about 98 x 78 cm (38½ x 30½ in) in extent, it includes the area of the border with the tributary kingdom of Nanyue, and shows such strategically useful information as military posts (with symbols included for 25 of them, many of them sited on commanding mountain peaks) and the total number of households in each local village, as well as the position of watchtowers and that of main army units. Referred to, for obvious reasons, as the *Mawangdui Military Map*, it is the first complete piece of mapping from China, as well as probably the oldest piece of military cartography to survive.

LEFT

One of two purely
topographic
maps discovered
alongside the
Military Map,
c. 183–168 BC

CHAPTER 2

SURVEYS AND SKETCHES

GATHERING THE INFORMATION

I f there is one thing that is certain about a map, it is that it must contain information (accurate, we hope), and someone must compile or gather that information. And then, to be of any use, this must be transferred onto the map using one of a variety of techniques developed over time.

This chapter is dedicated to the surveyors who trekked through forests, swamps and deserts and up mountains throughout the ages, the instruments they took with them and to those who engaged in the more delicate arts of engraving, illumination and printing to create the physical map which the final customer can use, and later generations can admire.

To make a map, the land must be surveyed, observed and measured, and the information compiled into a form the cartographer can use. Or at least that's the case for those maps that are

purporting to show some realistic image of a place – those maps with a less practical purpose, or which show a purely ideological image of the world, are more surveys of the mind of the creator or his intellectual milieu than of the real landscape (see Chapter 8). The very first surveys, just as some of the very earliest maps, were needed to show the boundaries between plots of land and to resolve disputes between their owners. The Greek historian Herodotus (*c.* 484–425 BC) reported that the Egyptian pharaoh had inspectors who would re-survey the land when the boundaries had been obliterated by the flooding of the Nile, which would both ensure the owners' rights were respected and, more importantly to the ruler, that there would be no quarrel about who owed tax on it. The Egyptians clearly did have practical knowledge of surveying – the Pyramids at Giza are aligned on a strict north–south axis, and on the Great Pyramid the difference in length between the north and east sides is an astonishingly small 6 cm (2½ in). All of this was achieved with fairly rudimentary surveying instruments, notably knotted cords to establish length, and varieties of plumb bobs, boards or frames to which a cord with a round weight was attached in order to establish vertical lines. Egyptian surveyors also employed the *merkhet*, a simple alignment device consisting of one split palm leaf and another plumb line, which could be lined up against the celestial pole or other part of the horizon to establish a consistent direction. One surveyor's board with a tear-shaped limestone bob on an A-shaped frame was found in the tomb of Sennedjem, chief architect to the pharaohs Seti I

and Rameses II; dating to around 1250 BC, it is a stunning demonstration that the art of surveying buildings is a very ancient one.

Knowledge of such devices spread through the Near East to the Assyrians and Persians, and eventually the Greeks. They used a version of the knotted cord, known as the *skoinion*, which was constructed of knotted rushes or flax, and later iron chains (as these were seen as more reliable, and not subject to stretching or fraying). Greek surveyors also used measuring rods, or *kalamoi*, of varying lengths, but normally about 6 cubits (an ancient measure equivalent to the distance between the elbow and the fingertips, or about 45 cm/17½ in). A less sophisticated method of recording distances was simply to document the number of paces, a technique employed by Alexander the Great during his conquests in the 330s and 320s BC, when he designated specialist soldiers to count the number of paces as they marched and the direction in which they went so that these could be compiled and converted into itineraries (and possibly mapped). More complex means were needed to plan those Greek colonies such as Thurii in southern Italy, which were laid out on a regular grid pattern first devised by Hippodamus of Miletus around 479 BC. Instruments such as the *dioptra*, which was certainly in use by the time Hero of Alexandria (a polymath among whose inventions was a very early version of a steam engine) who described it in the 1st century BC, consisted of a gradated column with a circular bronze disc near the top, and a toothed wheel at the base. The wheel could be rotated to change the angle of the disc, which could then be used for sighting and establishing the angles between two points in the distance.

Hero also describes an odometer, a wheeled instrument with another toothed wheel which moved a pointed arm every time the wheel rotated 400 times, a distance of 1 Roman mile (1,480 m/4,860 ft).

VXORI·ET·SVIS·ET
ZEPYRE   LIBERT
V   F

RIGHT

Tombstone of
Lucius Aebutius
Faustus, depicting
the tools of a
Roman land
surveyor,
1st century BC

The Romans took surveying to a new level. Their conquest involved the establishment of new colonies for retired military veterans which were laid out on strict rectangular grids – based on the layout of a Roman legionary marching camp with a central principal street known as a *decumanus maximus* always running as an east–west spine through its centre. All the plots which were handed out to the former soldiers had to be measured and recorded by surveyors, and so by the reign of Emperor Augustus (*r.* 27 BC–AD 14), the profession of *agrimensor*, or surveyor, was well established. They carried out cadastrations, the formal process by which land was measured, recorded and allotted in the new colonies, copies of which were deposited in the Tabularium, a central registry in Rome. We have the remains of only one substantial cadastration, of the area of Arausio (Orange) in southern France, carried out around AD 77 to settle land disputes as the original owners sold or

otherwise disposed of their land, though we know that records of the *subseciva* (government lands) and *beneficia* (private plots) were often displayed on bronze plaques.

To the Romans we owe the first treatise on surveying, the *De aquis urbis Romae* ('On the Waters of the City of Rome'). Written by Sextus Julius Frontinus (*c.* AD 35–103), who combined a career as senior official (including as consul and then governor of Britain, where he campaigned in South Wales in the 70s AD) with that of surveyor, his experience as superintendent of Rome's aqueduct system gave him unique insight into the challenges of urban planning. A more comprehensive surveyor's manual, the *Corpus agrimensorum* was compiled in the 4th century AD, including the work of a number of authors, notably Hyginus Gromaticus (who lived during the reign of Trajan around 200 years earlier). His name is taken from the *groma*, the Roman surveying instrument

BELOW

Illustration of the Greek mathematician Euclid holding a sphere and dioptra and observing the moon and stars; 11th-century German mathematician Hermannus Contractus holding an astrolabe, Bernardus Silvester, late 14th century

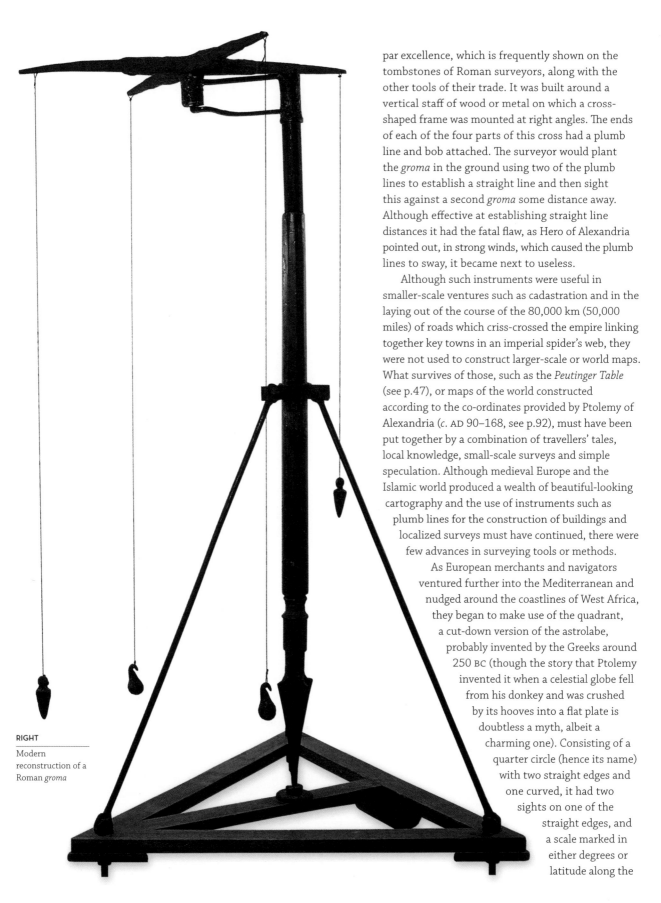

par excellence, which is frequently shown on the tombstones of Roman surveyors, along with the other tools of their trade. It was built around a vertical staff of wood or metal on which a cross-shaped frame was mounted at right angles. The ends of each of the four parts of this cross had a plumb line and bob attached. The surveyor would plant the *groma* in the ground using two of the plumb lines to establish a straight line and then sight this against a second *groma* some distance away. Although effective at establishing straight line distances it had the fatal flaw, as Hero of Alexandria pointed out, in strong winds, which caused the plumb lines to sway, it became next to useless.

Although such instruments were useful in smaller-scale ventures such as cadastration and in the laying out of the course of the 80,000 km (50,000 miles) of roads which criss-crossed the empire linking together key towns in an imperial spider's web, they were not used to construct larger-scale or world maps. What survives of those, such as the *Peutinger Table* (see p.47), or maps of the world constructed according to the co-ordinates provided by Ptolemy of Alexandria (*c.* AD 90–168, see p.92), must have been put together by a combination of travellers' tales, local knowledge, small-scale surveys and simple speculation. Although medieval Europe and the Islamic world produced a wealth of beautiful-looking cartography and the use of instruments such as plumb lines for the construction of buildings and localized surveys must have continued, there were few advances in surveying tools or methods.

As European merchants and navigators ventured further into the Mediterranean and nudged around the coastlines of West Africa, they began to make use of the quadrant, a cut-down version of the astrolabe, probably invented by the Greeks around 250 BC (though the story that Ptolemy invented it when a celestial globe fell from his donkey and was crushed by its hooves into a flat plate is doubtless a myth, albeit a charming one). Consisting of a quarter circle (hence its name) with two straight edges and one curved, it had two sights on one of the straight edges, and a scale marked in either degrees or latitude along the

RIGHT

Modern reconstruction of a Roman *groma*

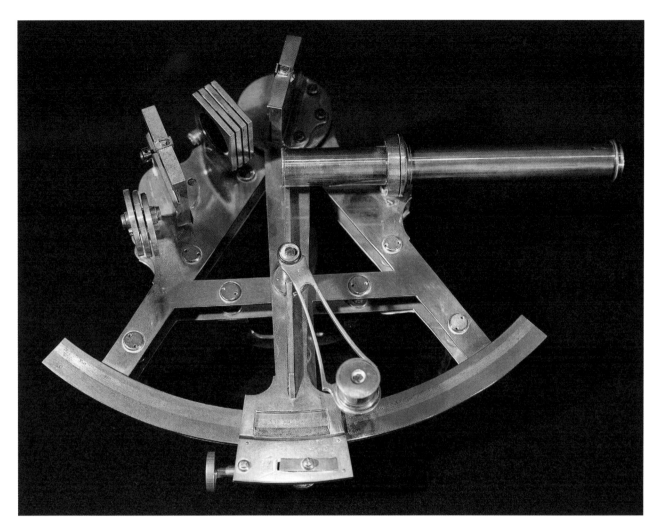

curve. A plumb line whose angle moved when the sights were lined up against a known point (at sea this was usually Polaris, the North Star) would indicate the latitude of the ship. A more sophisticated version was devised in 1730 by the English mathematician John Hadley (1682–1744). It had an index arm to move what was now a fixed line along the scale, and which incorporated a split mirror to allow the user to view both the celestial body being used as a fixed object and the point on the horizon to which travel was intended. In effect a double octant, it evolved into the sextant, which became the standard instrument for taking readings at sea.

By then, the techniques of land surveying had finally shaken off their long torpor, considerably advanced by the work of the Dutch mathematician Gemma Frisius (1508–55), who devised the system of scientific surveying known as triangulation. A man of a considerable breadth of talent, from physician – he studied medicine at the University of Louvain – to mathematics and astronomy, his greatest contribution came in cartography, or specifically in devising a system by which distances could be measured and a baseline grid established for the construction of accurate mapping. His *Libellus de locorum describendum ratione* ('Booklet concerning a way of describing places') published in 1533 used the principles of trigonometry – knowing the two angles of a triangle and the length of one side, the other angle and two sides can be calculated. By measuring out a straight line between two points (the straightness ensured by traditional sighting techniques) and then setting a third stake or similar object to create a triangle and measuring the angle between that and the first two points, the distance between those and the third point can be calculated without actually having to measure it. Once this is done the process can be repeated to create a network of triangles, with all the distances exactly calculated (hence the term triangulation).

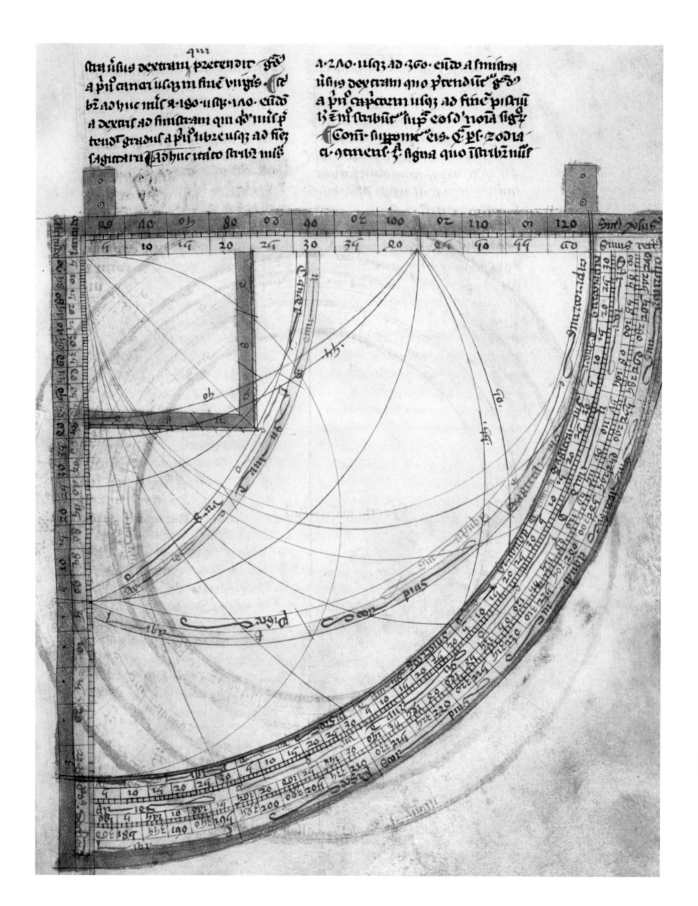

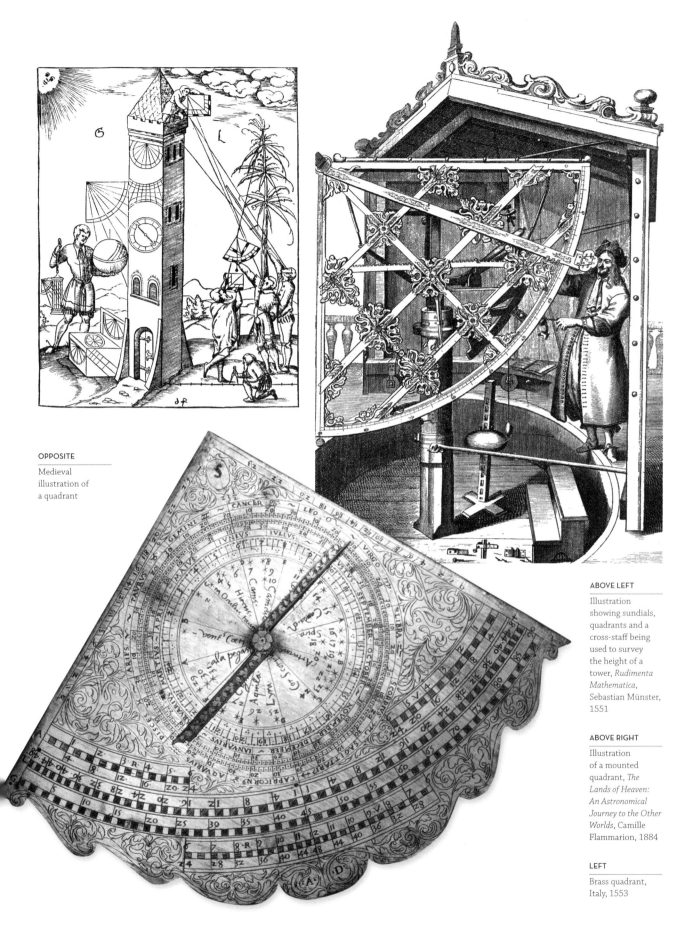

OPPOSITE

Medieval
illustration of
a quadrant

ABOVE LEFT

Illustration
showing sundials,
quadrants and a
cross-staff being
used to survey
the height of a
tower, *Rudimenta
Mathematica*,
Sebastian Münster,
1551

ABOVE RIGHT

Illustration
of a mounted
quadrant, *The
Lands of Heaven:
An Astronomical
Journey to the Other
Worlds*, Camille
Flammarion, 1884

LEFT

Brass quadrant,
Italy, 1553

RIGHT

Portrait of
Willebrord Snell

BELOW

Theodolite,
Jonathan Sisson,
mid-18th century

It was a system popularized by another Dutch surveyor Willebrord Snell (1580–1626), who around 1615 laid out a baseline from the church spire of Leiden, his hometown, to nearby Zoeterwoude, and then used with increasing regularity by the new breed of surveyors who created maps of their nation-states, such as the four generations of Cassinis, whose map of France took a century and a half to complete. The originator of that survey, Giovanni Domenico Cassini (1625–1712), can have had no inkling when the first meridian line was surveyed in 1669-70 that it would only be his great-grandson Jean-Dominique who would see it to completion (or, nearly so, as the French Revolutionary authorities nationalized the whole thing and seized the map plates in 1790, before issuing the final maps in 1815). Nor could he have predicted the hazards some of his surveyors would face, including one who was murdered in the remote Mézenc region of the Ardèche in the

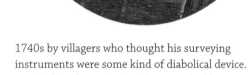

1740s by villagers who thought his surveying instruments were some kind of diabolical device.

By then the mainstay of surveys had become the theodolite, a hybrid between a compass and a telescope, or, in the very earliest version invented by the English surveyor Leonard Digges (1520–59), which was described by his son Thomas in 1571, of a compass and a quadrant. The telescopic versions of 'great theodolites' were first devised by the English instrument-maker Jonathan Sisson (1690–1747) around 1725. His renown was such that when a survey was needed to resolve a long-standing quarrel between the authorities in the colonies of New York and New Jersey as to their mutual boundary, and no suitably accurate instrument could be found anywhere in North America, Sisson was commissioned to build one. His theodolite arrived in 1745, and was found to measures angles with an accuracy of 1/120th of a degree and soon settled the matter of where the 41st parallel lay – the circle of latitude which was supposed to be the line between the two colonies.

The acknowledged master of the theodolite, however, was Jesse Ramsden (1735–1800). Yorkshire-born, Ramsden was originally apprenticed as a clothmaker, but after moving to London in 1755, he changed direction and became instead apprentice to Mark Burton, a London instrument-maker. His attention to the detail of construction of theodolites brought him a steady stream of commissions and election to the Royal Society in 1786. Not everyone was quite so appreciative: when the British East India

Company ordered a theodolite from Ramsden as part of its surveying efforts in India, they found the bill for the 90-kg (200-lb) monster (with a 0.9-m/3-ft diameter horizontal circle) so excessive that they refused to pay for it. Instead, the instrument ended up in June 1791 with the Ordnance Survey, which had just begun its own project for the triangulation of Britain. It remained in their service for nearly seven decades, traversing the length and breadth of the nation on its own purpose-built carriage, being so unwieldy it had to be winched to the top of church steeples to make its observations. It was only finally retired in 1858, by which time its constructor had been dead for nearly 60 years. While Ramsden's mortal remains were put to rest in the churchyard of St James's Piccadilly in London, his theodolite ended up a little further west in what was to become London's Science Museum.

Subsequent surveyors had access to even more sophisticated equipment, such as the transit theodolite, which could rotate in both the horizontal and vertical planes, invented by the American surveyor William J. Young in 1832, and the solar compass, devised in 1835 by another American William Austin Burt to determine the direction of true north in areas where the presence of large quantities of iron ore made regular magnetic compasses useless. Nowadays, though, theodolites are electronic and surveyors go equipped with electronic distance-measuring tools, using laser scanners and

Global Positioning System (GPS) devices for location. For those hard-to-reach places, it is no longer necessary to scale a mountain or become stuck in a swamp or parched in a desert: the 21st-century surveyor can simply send in a drone. The romance of surveying may be dead, but as an occupation it is an order of magnitude safer.

Once the surveyors have delivered their information, gathered by *groma*, theodolite and the hard grind of pacing the land, it must all be written down in visual form. What gets included is to a great extent determined by the purpose of the map (see Chapter 3), but there is the very practical consideration of which tools are used to physically create the map and how, in later ages, it is to be printed. For the first 3,000 years of map-making (broadly from the *Turin Papyrus*, see p.19 to the medieval *mappae mundi*, see p.50), maps had to be drawn by hand. In Europe this was done in much the

same way, and often by the same craftsmen and artists who created the illuminations that graced Bible manuscripts or Books of Hours for aristocratic families and well-appointed monasteries. Maps were largely drawn with feather pens, the quills – if of the best quality – plucked from the wings of geese or swans.

The ink with which to draw the outline of the map (or for plainer productions like many portolans, almost the whole of it) was a serious consideration. It could be made from charcoal, which gave a suitably deep hue, but that was not long-lasting and certainly for those maps likely to be used in the field, over a long time, or at sea, was apt to fade away or flake off. Instead, the best quality ink was manufactured from powdered oak gall, a kind of allergic reaction in the bark of oak trees to the activities of gall wasps. To this was added iron sulphate, which darkened the ink and also made it more permanent, and gum arabic, which was made from the powdered sap of the acacia tree. For the decorative elements, which abound in medieval maps, and for adding colour to areas such as the sea or mountains, other pigments were needed. The sources for these were manifold, such as verdigris, created from copper acetate, which could be used for green, or a deep blue, which was made from powdered lapis lazuli. The most expensive and rarest was gold, in leaf or powdered form, which was reserved for the most luxurious or prestige maps.

The intricate and painstaking world of hand-drawn maps was revolutionized by the invention of printing. Although printing using movable type, a process invented by the Nuremberg printer Johannes Gutenberg some time in the 1440s, did not provide such a short-cut to mass production as it did for purely text-based books (as the map still had to be drawn by someone, while the type for text pages could be made up, broken up and reset into a different page by someone without artistic training), it still speeded up the process and allowed far more copies of maps to be made. Rather than hand-drawing or at best carving a wood block and then inking it and using that to stamp a sheet of paper or parchment, the lever on a printing press could be depressed, pushing an inked

printing plate down onto a sheet of paper and the process repeated many times in an hour.

Most of the maps or plans which accompanied text pages were still at this stage woodcuts. Among the most magnificent are the illustrations of cityscapes which illustrated the *Nuremberg Chronicle* by Hartmann Schedel (1440–1514), one of the runaway best-sellers of the early age of printing. Published in 1493, it had over 600 woodcut illustrations, including a large number of panoramas of cities, in its rapid run through world history from the Creation to (in rather more speculative mode) the Last Judgement. Some of them are believed to be the work of no lesser an artist than Albrecht Dürer (1471–1528), then an apprentice in the workshop of

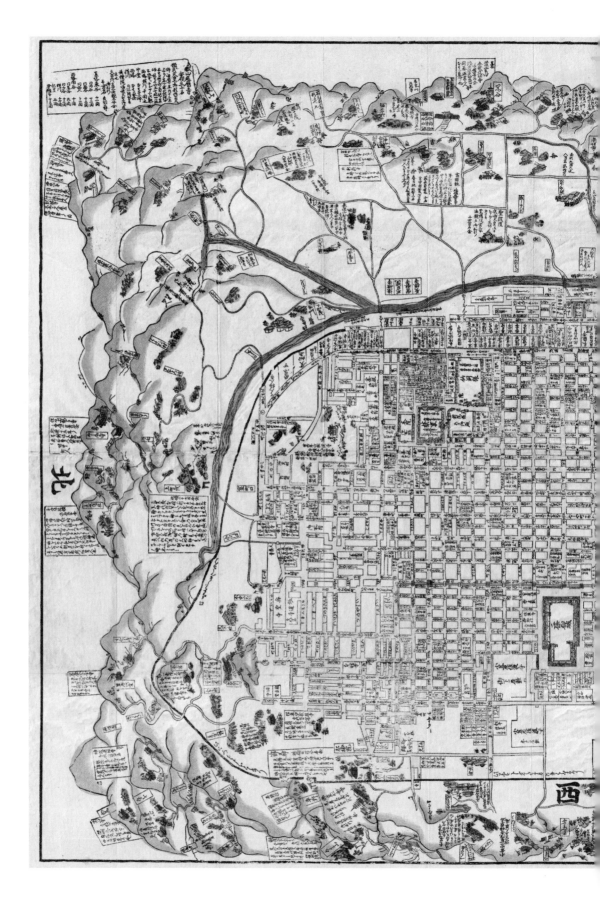

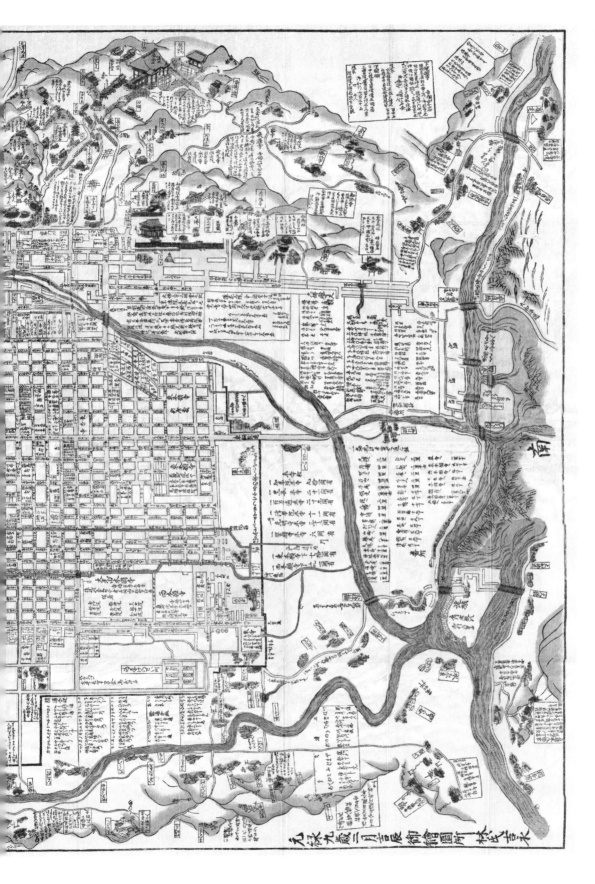

Michael Wohlgemuth, who provided most of the woodcut illustrations. The woodcutting was done by leaving those parts of the surface which will be shown on the map and cutting away the rest (as the raised part of the wood that remains will carry the ink). Originally the text for the maps was cut into the block, but as time went on these were replaced with sections into which movable type could be inserted, although purists argue that this gives the type a rather stiff and formulaic look, unlike the earlier purely engraved type which still has the air of the older style medieval manuscript script.

Engraving on wooden blocks was laborious, and etching illustrations onto copperplates, which were more durable and so more suitable for longer print-runs, was even more so. First used for an edition of Ptolemy's *Geography* produced in Bologna in 1477 – the first printed edition of his work – the technique involved a preliminary sketch which was then transferred (often by a form of tracing) onto the copperplate by incising it with a sharp engraving tool. Unlike in woodcutting, the illustration is cut into the plate, rather than standing up from it, so the ink goes into the hollows in the engraved plate and is then transferred onto the

paper by the pressure of the printing press. The process permits much finer lines to be etched into the copperplate than can be cut out from the wood and so allows for a much greater detail of geographical accuracy. As copperplates could last through 4,000 or more impressions and even then could be re-engraved by simply working over parts of the plate which had become worn down, they were often used for decades, meaning that sometimes, as in the era of competition between Dutch map-makers in the 17th century, old information kept being recycled as the same plates were reused long after the information on them had become obsolete.

Versions of copperplate engraving continued to be the norm for map production until the invention of lithography in around 1796. The brainchild of Alois Senefelder (1771–1834), a Bavarian actor, it was originally intended as a cheap and rapid means to produce playscripts and music authored by his friends. The process relies on the water-repellent qualities of grease. The image to be printed was drawn

Within the GIS window, the layer panel reads:

- ✓ Metella_circo.shp
- ✓ Str_antiche_area_2liv.shp
  - Probabile tracciato antico
  - Sepolcri r tratto basolato
  - tracciato stradale antico
  - tracciato stradale antico
  - Tracciato stradale antico
  - tracciato stradale antico
  - tracciato stradale antico
  - tracciato stradale antico
  - tratto basolato
- Tin_2liv
  - Breaklines
    - Hard
    - Soft
  - Elevation Range
    - 95.389 - 101
    - 89.778 - 95.389
    - 84.167 - 89.778
    - 78.556 - 84.167
    - 72.944 - 78.556
    - 67.333 - 72.944
    - 61.722 - 67.333
    - 56.111 - 61.722
    - 50.5 - 56.111
- Punti_m ancanti.shp
- ✓ Curve_caff_tv.shp
- Gps14ott03_dew.shp
- Gps13_ar ag03.shp
- Gps12_ar ag03.shp
- Gps11_ar ag03.shp
- Gps_lugl03.shp
- Edifici_polig_2liv.shp
- ✓ Edifici_area_2liv.shp
- ✓ Area_scena_2liv.shp
- ✓ flu_tot_geod.tif
- ✓ Dew_2liv
  - 51.517 - 57.015
  - 57.015 - 62.513

onto a stone surface (stone being *lithos* in Greek, and hence the term lithography, or stone-writing) using a grease-based crayon or paint. The rest of the stone was then treated with gum arabic and diluted nitric acid, which made it water attractive. When an oil-based ink was then applied to the stone it would only stick to the part coated in the greased crayon (i.e. the lines of the map or other illustration). This could then be pressed down on paper in a printing press to produce the final image, and multiple stones drawn with different colours used to create a multicolour image.

Variations on these processes appeared, such as etching, introduced in the 16th century in which the metal plate is coated with acid-resistant wax, and then the image carved into the wax and acid poured over it, which then 'bit' the image into the plate. New technological advances such as photography enabled greater automation such as photolithography, invented in the 1870s, by which a photographic negative could be imposed on a zinc plate which had a special sensitized coating, creating an impression that could then be incised. Nowadays most printers use a computer-to-plate technology in which the map (or other image) is transferred directly from digital files

by using lasers programmed to cut the image onto a heat-sensitive metal plate. What took master cartographers like Fra Mauro the best part of a decade to produce in the 1440s can now be transferred onto a plate in a matter of seconds and thousands of copies printed in an hour. Or in what would have seemed to medieval or even Renaissance cartographers a miracle, the map no longer even has to be printed, being viewable or transferable by millions of users simultaneously from a smartphone. The physical production of our map, then, will no longer be a problem, but, just as in the golden age of cartography, someone has to decide what information to include, how to present it and then actually draw the map.

ABOVE

Geographical information system (GIS) display of the topography, landscape and archaeological features of Caffarella Park in Rome, Italy, 21st century

CHAPTER 3

WHYS AND WHEREFORES

THE PURPOSE OF MAPS

The cartographer has gathered all the information necessary to create the map. Depending on the era, plumb lines, *gromas*, quadrants, sextants or GPS stations have been deployed and the base material collected, collated and transmitted back home. But before actually beginning to draw the map there are several crucial decisions which must be made. The first of these, and perhaps the most important, is what the map is actually for.

This has been touched on to some extent already: some of the very earliest maps have a ritual purpose, others arose from the needs of growing bureaucracies in early city-states; yet others represented statements of power by rulers, or stores of geographical knowledge. To modern eyes, their now-general use to 'find the way' only becomes predominant quite late in mapping history. All maps have a 'view', a purpose towards which they are directed, even if it's not quite the use to which we put them today, and these have fallen into several broad categories throughout history.

The first of these is the use of maps to state or promote an ideology or, more broadly, to express a particular understanding of the way the world (or the cosmos) works. Early states imposed order on what before had seemed chaos, their rulers establishing hierarchies that provided greater certainty in terms of the supply of food, albeit at the cost of a level of subservience for the vast majority of the population which they had not experienced in more egalitarian small-scale farming communities. Maps, too, created a sense of order. The earliest world map we possess, known as the *Babylonian Map of the World*, comes relatively late in the history of the Ancient Near East, dating from around 600 BC, a millennium after the city of Babylon had reached its first apogee under Hammurabi. His law-code, drafted around 1760 BC, contained terms later perceived as so harsh that they gave us the expression 'an eye for an eye, a tooth for a tooth', imposing order of a rather different kind. By the time the clay tablet some 12.5 cm x 8 cm (5 x 3¼ in) was incised with a stylized portrayal of the world, Babylon was ruled by Nebuchadnezzar II (605–562 BC). He recreated Babylon's glory days out of the shattered remnants of the Assyrian Empire, projecting Babylonian power as far as Egypt, the Phoenician city-states of modern Lebanon and Jerusalem, which he sacked in 587 BC, deporting most of its population back to Babylon. He was a great builder king, reconstructing the royal palace and the vast ziggurat of Etemenanki (whose sky-piercing bulk probably gave rise to the legend of the Tower of Babel). For such a man, and for his people, Babylon must truly have seemed the centre of the world, which is precisely how the *Babylonian Map of the World* depicts it. A circle representing the city sits firmly in the middle, with parallel lines running through it indicating the course of the Euphrates. Arrayed around it are a series of names, and some circles representing regions and cities within the Babylonian orbit, such as Habban, capital of the Kassites, Urartu (the successor-state to the Hittites) and Assyria. Bounding the central area is the circular course of the 'Bitter River' beyond which lie eight outlying areas, regions which fade into fable, such as one 'Where Shamash (the Sun) is not seen' (since it is in the north, and the Babylonians believed that having traversed from east to west during the day, it returned back to its starting point through the Underworld, never passing into the north). Topographic precision this was not, but it expressed the centrality of Babylon as the keystone of the world in terms that would have satisfied Nebuchadnezzar II, the conqueror of much of it.

He, too, was the keystone of his empire, which collapsed just 23 years after his death, when Cyrus II of Persia overran it. By then, far to the West, the

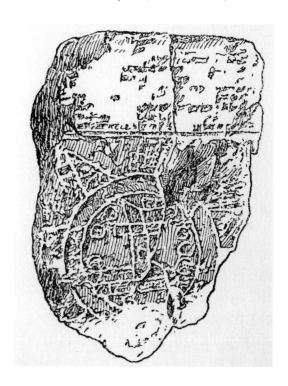

82
7-14
509

92687

LEFT

*Babylonian Map
of the World*, 6th
century BC; and
modern diagram
to help parse it
(opposite)

RIGHT

Map of Roman
roads through
Britain, based
on the *Antonine
Itinerary*, William
Stukeley, 1723

forerunners of another great empire were establishing a tenuous hold on a peninsula jutting out into the Mediterranean. The Romans, who would create the largest state the world had yet known, were inveterate builders: each major town within the empire became a 'mini-Rome' with a central forum, a basilica (or law court), temples to the major gods, such as Jupiter and Minerva and, in many cases, an amphitheatre, where gladiators fought each other and wild beasts to the delight of crowds who accepted the bloodthirsty spectacle in part-payment for their political subjugation. The empire was bound together, too, by

an ideology of empire, an almost accidental evolution after the Republic, ruled by two annually elected consuls and a quarrelsome Senate of the city's elite, which collapsed into civil war and re-emerged in 27 BC as an actual empire, with an actual emperor (of whom Augustus, Julius Caesar's adoptive son, was the first).

The Romans mapped. They did so at a practical level and on a small scale to determine the parcelling out of land in new settlements established for retired military veterans, a process known as cadastration, which yielded maps such as one from Arausio (Orange) in southern France (see p.29). The very first reference we have to a Roman map, though, comes in 174 BC, when Tiberius Sempronius Gracchus is said to have set up a table containing a map of Sardinia after commanding a victorious Roman army there. As Rome's territory expanded, the demands of imperial administration meant that such occasional flourishes were insufficient and that more ambitious mapping was needed. The *Cosmographia Iulii Caesaris*, which is probably the work of Julius Honorius, a rhetoric teacher of the 4th or 5th century AD, claims that Julius Caesar appointed four geographers to survey the four quarters of the world. They were somewhat dilatory in carrying out their task, allegedly taking over 30 years to bring it to completion. The whole thing, though, is probably apocryphal, but Augustus's chief lieutenant Marcus Vipsanius Agrippa (*c.* 63–12 BC) did commission a world map shortly after his imperial master's accession. Presumably inscribed on marble, it was set up on the Porticus Vipsania, a colonnade in the centre of Rome.

From the mother-city, the Romans built a network of roads that radiated out through the empire, stretching as far as Britain in the far north-west and what is now northern Iraq in the east. Generally built with stone and crushed gravel bound together with cement – a Roman innovation – they were topped off with a surface of larger paving blocks. These were state-of-the-art thoroughfares, ancient superhighways which facilitated the movement of goods and official messengers. Most importantly, they allowed the rapid movement of Rome's legions, as these were redeployed to make new conquests, stem barbarian intrusions or – as happened all too often after the empire's first century – to stifle or support pretenders to the imperial throne. The roads formed spokes which linked the cities, the nodes of empire, to each other, and a tradition grew up of itineraries, lists of the principal routes which connected them, together with the distance (in Roman miles or in days) the journey should take. One of the most substantial of these is the *Antonine Itinerary*, which was probably compiled in its existing form in the late 3rd century AD, but has become attached by its name to the Antonine dynasty of emperors which ended with the murder of Severus Alexander by mutinous troops along the Rhine frontier in 235. It contains details of 17 such principal routes through the empire, and a number of sub-routes in each, totalling 225 in all. The British section is divided into 15 such shorter itinerary segments, seven of which radiate out from London, showing that the London-centric nature of Britain's transport system is almost two millennia

old (though the three originating in Calleva, now the small village of Silchester near Basingstoke in Hampshire, equally emphasize that alternatives are possible!).

The most striking cartographic statement of Rome's imperial might – and one of the very few to survive in anything like a complete form – is not in fact a Roman original. It was found in a monastic library in 1494 by the German humanist Konrad Celtes. He in turn bequeathed it in his will to his friend Konrad Peutinger (1465–1547), after whom the map became known as the *Peutinger Table* (or *Tabula Peuteringiana*). In its original state it was an elongated piece of parchment 6.75 m long x 34 cm wide (22 ft x 13¼ in) bearing a graphic representation of a series of itineraries, similar to those of the *Antonine Itinerary*, which show the main routes between the 555 towns portrayed. Originally, there were almost certainly more towns, as the section which contains Britain has lost all but a portion of the south of the province. Over 400 of the towns are shown with towers and a few with more lavish illustrations, such as Constantinople and Rome, which both have depictions of Tyche (the goddess personifying the Fortune of the city). In the case of Rome she is seated on a throne, bearing an orb and spear, and for Constantinople she is orb-less but wearing a helmet. Alexandria is shown with one of the most famous landmarks of the ancient world, the Pharos lighthouse, whose beacon had guided mariners into its harbour since its construction in the early 3rd century BC.

The map is probably a medieval copyist's version of what might have been a 4th-century original. It is, though, an eloquent statement in the mapping of a world view which was diminished (though not entirely extinguished) as the western Roman provinces fell one by one into the hands of barbarian invaders, with Italy itself succumbing in 476 to Odoacer, a Germanic general in Roman service who simply swept away the last western emperor and ruled it instead as a king. The empire clung on in the East, but then much of it in turn fell to a new set of invasions, as the armies of the Islamic caliphate overran its holdings in Syria, Palestine and North Africa from the 630s. The new rulers inherited cultures of scholarship that were centuries old, melding existing practices with their own traditions to create hybrids and innovations that burst into a cultural golden age under the Umayyads and Abbasids from the 7th to 10th centuries. Geographers such as Muhammad ibn Musa al-Khwarizmi (*c.* 780–850) built on Ptolemy of Alexandria's lists of

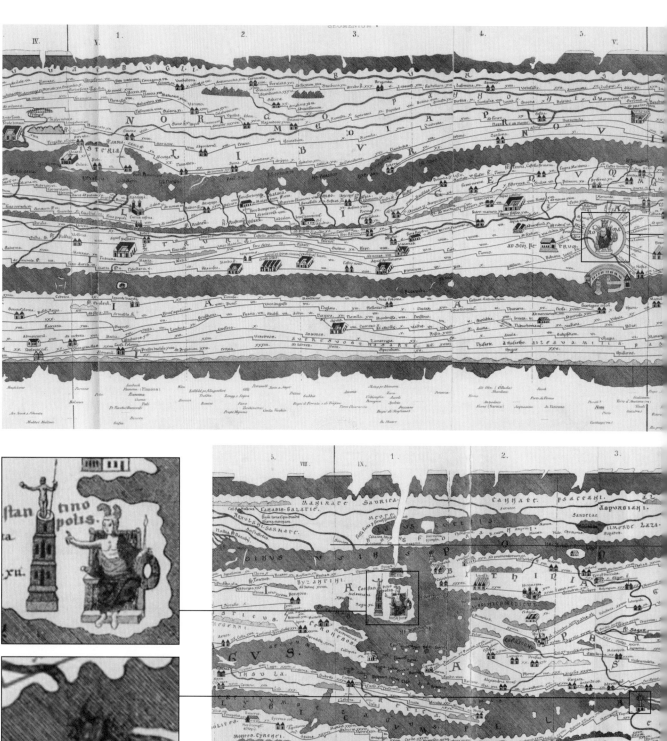

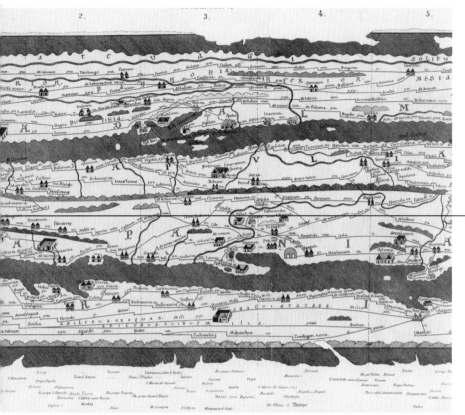

MAIN

Details from the
Peutinger Table,
4th century AD
(1888 copy, based
on 12th–13th-
century version).

INSET ABOVE

Rome

INSET LEFT TOP

Constantinople

**INSET LEFT
BOTTOM**

Pharos Lighthouse
at Alexandria

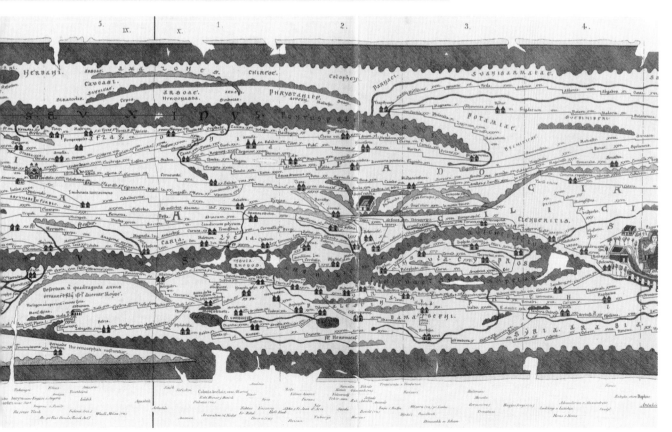

latitude and longitude to construct maps of the Islamic world – around 830 he drew for his *Kitab Surat al-Ard* ('Book of the Image of the World') featured over 4,000 place names. Among the most striking is one showing the course of the Nile from the umbrella-like source in the Mountains of the Moon to the green square that represents the Mediterranean, all cut through with a series of red lines, which represent the 'climes' or climatic bands into which late Greek geographers divided the world.

A more specifically Islamic world view was expressed in the work of the most renowned Islamic cartographer of all, Abu Ishaq al-Istakhri (or al-Farisi) who lived in Istakhr in southern Iran in the early 10th century. Little is known of his life, but his *Kitab al-masalik wa-al-mamalik* (Book of Routes and Kingdoms) is a striking attempt to map the whole of the *umma*, or the world of the Islamic community. The book contains 20 regional maps showing itineraries within the Islamic world – perhaps in a nod to the itinerary maps of the Greeks and Romans. Discarding any attempt to depict distance geographically or the topography of the land, his is an elegant composition of lines, and circles or squares for the towns, colour coded to show the main routes in red and even distinguishing between salt water (green) and fresh water (blue). Regions outside the Islamic world are excluded entirely, appearing only in the overall world map.

An even more overtly ideological view of the world appears in the Christian topographies which emerged in Europe in the centuries following the collapse of the Roman Empire, when learning became the preserve of a small minority, mainly centred on the Church (and particularly on monasteries). Such world maps are generally referred to as *mappae mundi* ('maps of the world'). Among the most widely reproduced were those compiled by Isidore, who became Bishop of Seville around 600, as part of his *Etymologiae* ('Etymologies') an encyclopedic compilation of the entirety of classical knowledge and literature – or at least those parts that Isidore saw fit to preserve. The map is extremely simple, showing the three continents into which the world was supposed to be divided (Asia at the top and Africa and Europe at the bottom), separated by great dividing rivers, including the Mediterranean, all set within a circular encompassing ocean, giving the map the shape of a 'T' set within an 'O' (from which this and its many imitators became known simply as T-O maps).

Medieval Christian cartography was not especially concerned with showing the physical reality of the world or

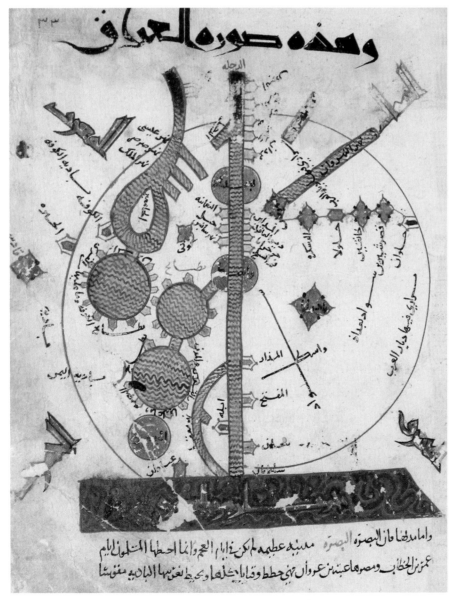

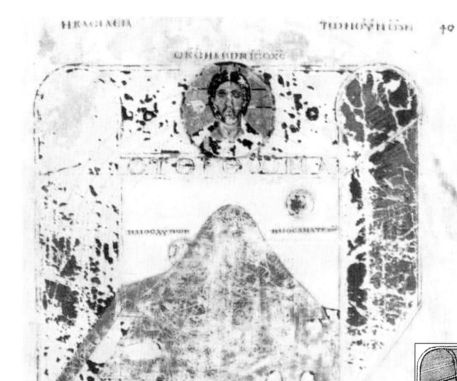

LEFT

Topographia Christiana, Cosmas Indicopleustes, mid-6th century (top); and modern diagram (bottom)

providing a means by which to navigate around it. Its space was spiritual, and its focus was on depicting the centrality of the biblical narrative and in particular the life of Christ. This was given a physical reality by, in general, showing Jerusalem, and the area around it in which most of the events narrated in the Old and New Testament took place, at its centre. Figures from the Christian past were co-opted to serve as inspiration, even if they had no direct map-making role themselves. One very idiosyncratic image of the world came from the *Topographia Christiana* ('Christian Topography') of Cosmas Indicopleustes, written in the mid-6th century by a Greek speaker whose nickname indicates he was probably a merchant who had travelled to India. He took it as his task to disprove what he saw as the erroneous view that the Earth was spherical. He instead showed its landmass as flat, but with the Heavens forming the curved shape

of a box (intended to be modelled on the tabernacle within which the tablets of the Ten Commandments given by God to Moses had been transported by the early Israelites).

For some reason, Cosmas's heavenly box did not catch on. Instead, slightly more conventional religious maps became the norm, such as the *mappa mundi* compiled by Beatus of Liébana, an 8th-century monk who lived in Asturias, one of the small Christian kingdoms which had clung on in the north of Spain following the conquest of much of the Iberian Peninsula by an Islamic army that crossed the Straits of Gibraltar in 711. Much like Isidore's map, the world is still divided into three continents, with Asia at the top and Jerusalem at the very centre, but it contains a far greater level of detail, sprinkled with stylized walled towns (of which only

Rome approaches Jerusalem in size) and four great rivers – the Tigris, Euphrates, Geon (Nile) and Phison (possibly the Indus or Ganges) – which run dramatically across the canvas. At the top of the map (and so to the very east of Asia) Beatus includes a feature which was to become a perennial in the early Middle Ages, the Earthly Paradise (from which Adam and Eve were expelled after eating the apple from the Tree of the Knowledge of Good and Evil). Beatus depicts the tree still standing there, with the entrance to the paradise guarded by a cherub wielding a fiery sword (in case any of Adam and Eve's descendants felt tempted to try to sneak back in).

By the 14th century, Christian mapping had reached its peak in vast compositions such as the *Hereford Mappa Mundi*, which teem with creatures such as manticores (legendary creatures with the head of a man, the body of a lion and the tail of a dragon or scorpion) or the mythical giants Gog and Magog. By then, though, European mapping, at least, had once more begun to take a more practical turn. On a small scale, this had always been the case – a schematic plan of the Abbey of St Gall in Switzerland dating from c. 820 shows that the skills inculcated by Roman surveyors had never been wholly lost in the enthusiasm to portray a Christian-inflected world. In addition, the gradual recovery from the political and economic doldrums of the early Middle Ages had, by the 1200s, produced a varied landscape of increasingly prosperous towns linked by trade routes along which both necessities such as grain and wool and luxury goods (such as the finished cloth produced in large quantities by the weavers of Italy and the Netherlands and more refined products, such as books, and even maps) passed.

Seaborne commerce became particularly important, as maritime republics in Italy such as Amalfi and Pisa, and then Genoa and Venice, established their dominance in the central and eastern Mediterranean, vying with Catalan merchants in the west. Their sea captains were practical men, more interested in profit than the location of the Earthly Paradise, and their most pressing concerns were to navigate around shoals and sandbanks, rather than avoiding the snares of sin. From the very end of the 13th century, their needs were answered by new forms of map known as portolans, which are almost schematic in their simplicity and were intended as guides to the coastlines these trading ships plied. Drawn on vellum parchment made from calfskin, they often have a curious protrusion, where the original shape

of the animal's neck can be made out. The epicentre of this mapping tradition was in Italy, above all Genoa, and in the possessions of the Catalan kingdom, particularly Majorca. With a focus on the ports, headlands and islands, much of the inland interior of the portolans is generally left all but blank, but they are criss-crossed by a series of rhumb lines which form a triangular mesh of waypoints across the sea to help with navigation (see p.135). Typical of them is the 1325 portolan by Angelino Dulcert (or Dalorto), originally from Italy, but who transferred, together with his cartographic skills, to Majorca around the 1330s.

The portolans were genuinely practical maps, which must have been used in many cases aboard ship (in a very few cases the boards to which they were affixed during consultation survive). This type of

BELOW
Plan of Abbey of St Gall, Switzerland, *c.* 820

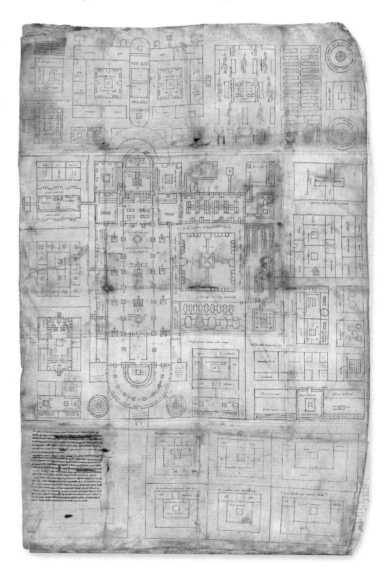

mapping would eventually wither away, but as ships undertook ever longer voyages (culminating in the first circumnavigation in 1519–22 by a flotilla under the command of the Portuguese navigator Ferdinand Magellan, and then, after his death by Juan Delcano) more sophisticated and elaborated maps proliferated. The coastal chart, or *roteiro*, of João de Castro, who served from 1547 to 1548 as viceroy of the little Portuguese empire in India (centred on Diu and Goa) shows a wealth of detail of the coasts around the Indian Ocean, including dozens of measurements of magnetic declination (the angle between magnetic north as shown by a compass and true north) which he took on his outward voyage to India. Sadly, de Castro did not live long to enjoy his chart as he died before his pleas to be recalled to Lisbon were granted by the Portuguese court, expiring in the arms of his friend, the Jesuit missionary St Francis Xavier (though some posthumous consolation came in the form of the positive reception of the three *roteiros* which emerged from his voyages and his fame as the discoverer of magnetic declination).

Coastal charts continued to be a principal driver for the improvement of cartography, particularly in

the hands of the Dutch, who after the foundation of the Verenigde Oostindische Compagnie (the VOC, or Dutch East India Company) in 1602, expanded their range from the waters off the Netherlands and the Baltic down across Africa and thence to South America and the Indian Ocean. Established to help the Dutch muscle in on the Spice Islands trade, the VOC (or as it was colloquially known 'Jan Compagnie') was one of the first successful joint-stock companies in the world (in which shareholders spread the risk between them of such hazardous voyages rather than one single captain risking ruin if things went wrong). The *Heeren XVII* (or 'seventeen gentleman') who formed its governing body achieved this and more, elbowing aside the Portuguese, until by the mid-17th century it was Amsterdam, and not Lisbon, that ruled the waves of the East Indies, presided over by the company's governor from his fortress headquarters in Batavia (now Jakarta).

All these voyages, both long- and short-distance, needed charts and a vast cartographic industry grew up in the Netherlands to provide them. In their origin, the pilot guides, or 'rutters' as they came to be known, were simple books containing directions for sailing

BELOW

Portolan chart, Gabriel de Vallseca, *c.* 1447

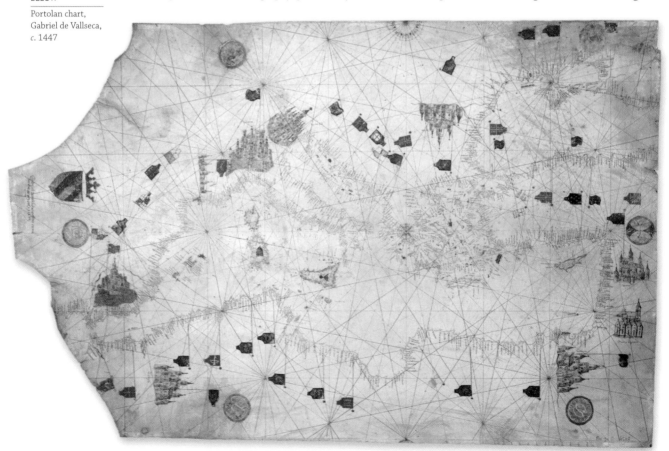

and warnings about coastal hazards. Much of the information was held in the heads of experienced local pilots, but it never hurt to have things down in black and white on paper. Originating in the late 15th century – in France, rather than the Netherlands, as it happens, with *Le routier de la mer* ('The Map of the Sea') by Pierre Garcie – by 1520 these had started to feature crude illustrations of landmarks such as dunes and church spires, although they still largely circulated in manuscript form. The Dutch began printing rutters in 1532 with *De kaert vander zee* ('The Map of the Sea') by Jan Severszoon, but this was a text-based affair, and it was only slowly that coastal profiles became more sophisticated until they culminated in the *Spiegel der zeevaerdt* ('The Mariner's Mirror') by Lucas Janszoon Waghenaer. Born around 1533 in the north Dutch town of Enkhuizen alongside the Zuider Zee, a settlement whose nickname 'the Herring City' gave a clue to the source of its prosperity, Waghenaer's early career as a pilot, both locally and on longer voyages between Cadiz in Spain and western Norway, gave him a wealth of material on which to draw for his compilation of coastal charts. He chose to bind these together into a single volume, producing for the first time something like a comprehensive pilot's guide to north-western Europe, which was published in 1584. With its handy tables of tides, instruction on how to use a cross-staff to take navigational measurements, the use of portolan charts, and its inclusion of a profusion of buoys, reefs, shoals and safe passages on its 44 pages of charts plus an overall map of western Europe, it provided everything an aspiring pilot could possibly want. So successful was it that in 1592, Waghenaer published a second, more portable edition, entitled the *Thresoor der zeevaert* ('Treasure of the Sea'), whose easier-to-handle oblong shape, smaller size and more detailed accompanying notes, as well as the extension of its range to cover the northern seas as far as Scotland and the White Sea, north of Russia, was even more popular than the original. It was no wonder that such compilations of

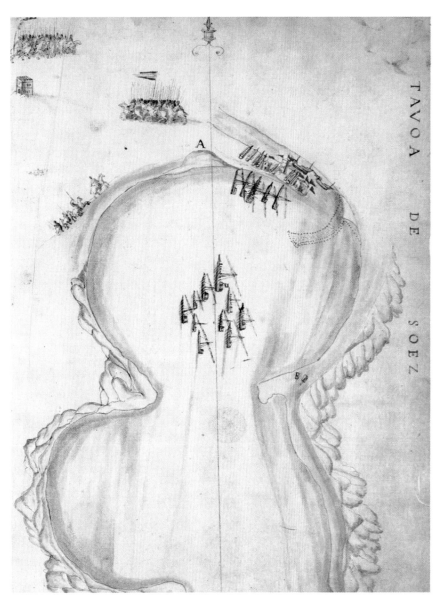

pilots' charts came to be universally known by a corruption of his name as 'Wagoneers'.

Naturally, those who ventured into what were for them new regions of the world mapped them, not least to prove to their sponsors the worth of the voyages they had undertook, and to provide information for those who followed them. Many of the most famous products of the great age of European voyage, such as Martin Waldseemüller's 1507 map (in which America is named for the first time, see p.193) come from this desire to memorialize or glorify or simply to wonder at the vastly enlarged extent of the world as seen from Lisbon, Seville, Amsterdam or London. The annals of mid-16th century cartography are filled with ever more

see p.193

ABOVE

The Gulf of Suez, *Roteiro do Mar Roxo* ('Roxo Sea Route'), João de Castro, 16th century

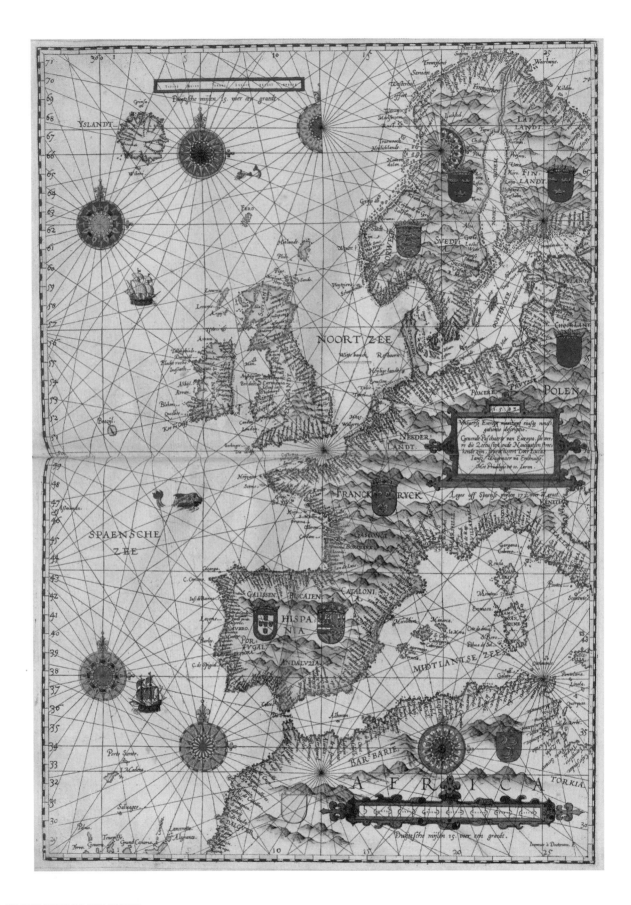

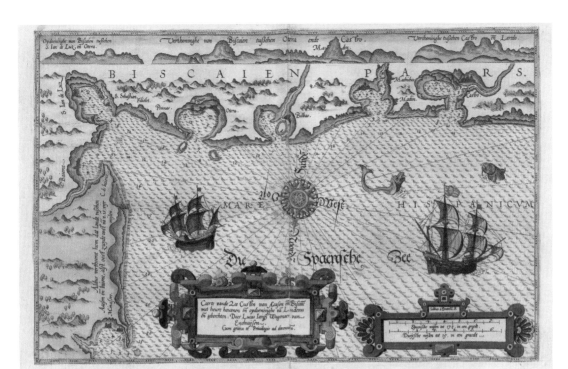

resplendent productions (of which Gerard Mercator's famous 1569 map of the world is but one, see p.128), but a more specific purpose was served by maps of the new regions which the European maritime powers were first exploring, then settling. As exploration turned to settlement and colonization, a tradition of colonial mapping emerged, which produced maps such as those of the British geographer James Rennell (1742–1830), whose work culminated in the *Map of Hindoostan* published in 1782. North America, too, became intensively mapped, first by the British colonial power, beginning with the very first map drawn on the continent – a simple affair published by John Foster, a printer from Boston, in 1677. They became gradually more sophisticated until Lewis Evans' *A Map of the Middle British Colonies*, which was

printed on a press owned by the future Founding Father Benjamin Franklin in 1755.

A still more important landmark was the Mitchell map, commissioned by the British Board of Trade and Plantations, the body which supervised the economic and political well-being of Britain's Thirteen Colonies in North America – a task to which, before long, it was to prove itself thoroughly unsuited as the colonists' opposition to rule from London exploded into violent confrontation. Drafted at a time when there was increasing concern that the French (who were ensconced not only in eastern Canada, but in a string of territories down the Mississippi as far as Louisiana and western Florida) were encroaching on what should, according to the 1713 Treaty of Utrecht, have been British land. The map's author, John Mitchell

BELOW

Map of Hindoostan, James Rennell, 1782 (1788 edition)

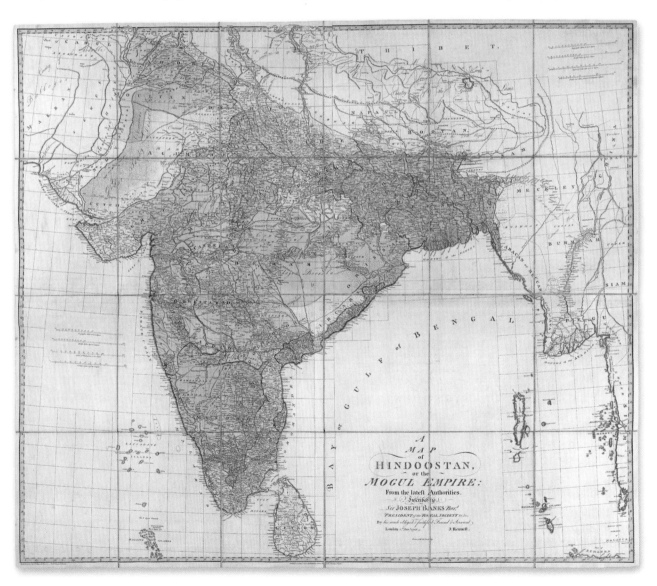

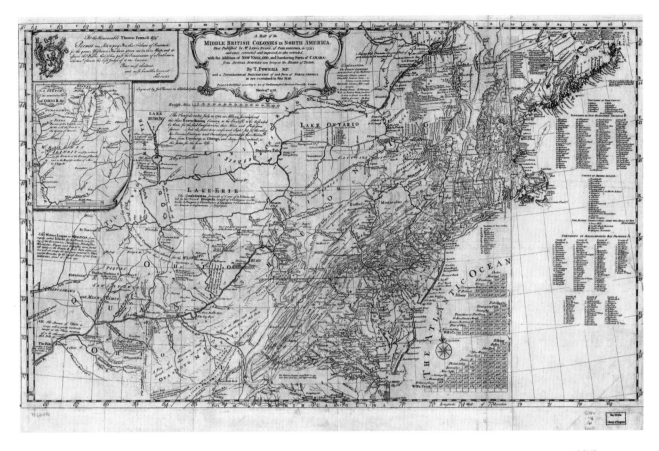

ABOVE

ABOVE

*A Map of the Middle
British Colonies
in North America,*
Lewis Evans, 1755

(1711–68), knew the colonies well, being himself from a well-to-do family of Virginia merchants. He hadn't originally intended a career in map-making, being far more inclined to medicine, which he studied at the University of Edinburgh in the late 1720s, before returning to Virginia in 1731. There he occupied himself with an increasing interest in botany and writing tracts blaming British troop ships for the waves of epidemic disease striking the colonies. It was when Mitchell fell victim to one of these in 1745, that the course of his life changed. He took ship to Britain to recover, almost perishing when the vessel was attacked by a French privateer off St Malo – by ill chance Britain was once again at war with France during the Austrian War of Succession. All of Mitchell's precious botanical collection was carried off by the privateers and so when he finally reached London, he consoled himself by turning to cartography.

Conscious of the French threat to Virginia and the other colonies – one which he felt all the more keenly given his recent misadventure – he set to producing an improved map of North America, using Henry Popple's 1733 *A Map of the British Empire in North America* as the basis. Mitchell also managed to insert

himself into the fashionable intellectual life of London, being elected to the Royal Society in 1748. His growing fame brought Mitchell's work to the attention of the Board of Trade and Plantations, which then allowed him access to its archives, crammed with local geographical records and surveys. They even allowed him to peruse reports from the colonial governors about the extent of French encroachment and where exactly the frontier lay between the two powers' territories. Finally, in 1750 the first draft of the map was ready, and then on 13 February 1755 the final version, bearing the stamp of approval of the Board for his *A Map of the British and French Dominions in North America*.

It was the last great cartographic enterprise of British North America. Though it had its flaws – Mitchell labelled the town of Worcester, Massachusetts, incorrectly as 'Leicester' – it was well respected. So much so that a copy of the fourth edition – which included additional details of the treaties which defined the frontiers of Quebec and of the Proclamation Line of 1763 which was supposed to mark the boundary between the Thirteen Colonies and the lands of Native Americans beyond – was still used by Richard Oswald the British 'Peace

Commissioner' tasked with negotiating the final peace deal in Paris which recognized the independence of the United States in 1784.

Mitchell's map, though it formed part of the tradition of colonial mapping, was born out of fear of war with the French (a consummate irony, in that its most prominent use was precisely after the humiliating defeat against the colonists which had in large part been abetted by their alliance with France in 1778). More directly, the needs of the military have been one of the principal drivers of cartography, at least since the 16th century. Although armies long before that must have made use of guides and possibly some form of sketch maps, generals had to wait until maps became sophisticated enough, and the means to produce and distribute them reliable enough, to make them of real strategic, and even tactical use.

Somewhat before that, the 16th century saw the rise of a kind of commemorative mapping, recording events on the battlefields for the information or edification of the public back home. Events such as

the siege of Malta in 1565 were recorded in dramatic, semi-pictorial maps, in which the invading Ottoman army could be seen clustered around the beleaguered Knights of St John, the walls of forts such as St Elmo pounded almost to rubble by the Turkish siege. Pitched battles, too, received the same kind of treatment, with serried ranks of opposing forces often showing a rather idealized (and occasionally inaccurate) view of the fighting. The Thirty Years' War, with its impossible tangle of shifting alliances that devastated Europe's heartlands between 1618 and 1648 as no conflict has since (around a third of Germany's population is said to have perished) also offered fertile ground for cartographers. The plan by Matthäus Merian (1593–1650) of the Battle of Lützen (notable for the death of the Swedish warrior-king Gustavus Adolphus, shot as he became separated from his troops in the literal fog of war caused by palls of gunpowder smoke) is one such image. Almost every subsequent major battle on the European continent or in North America received its battle plan, some heavily annotated, such as Jakob van der Schley's

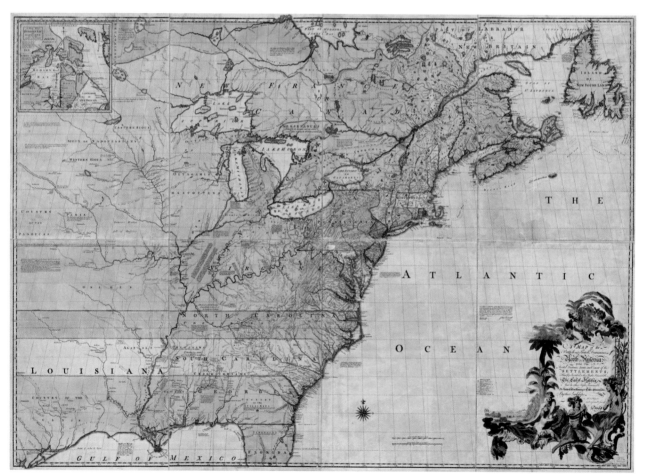

map of Frederick the Great's triumphant defeat of the Austrians at Leuthen in 1757 or Wellington and Blücher's final defeat of Napoleon in 1815, a 'damn near run thing' as the British commander remarked afterwards, which spawned a plethora of explanatory maps.

By then, though, mapping had itself become a tool of warfare, with military surveyors accompanying generals on their campaigns, such as the staff of the British Quartermaster-General (QMG), who accompanied the troops during the Peninsular War Campaign from 1808 to 1814. The pre-war maps of the Iberian Peninsula on which the Duke of Wellington (1769–1852) – or Viscount Wellington of Talavera as he was for most of the campaign – relied were woefully inadequate: another British general acidly remarked of Thomas Faden's maps of Gibraltar and Minorca (both at the time British possessions) that they were 'only fit for burning'. The Quartermaster-General's Office had been thoroughly reorganized in 1803 to make it fit for more than occasional bridge-building and keeping the odd amphibious sally onto the continent supplied. Its representative in the Peninsular Campaign, Sir George Murray (1772–1846), proved himself an incredibly adept military cartographer, deploying his initial staff of two permanent QMG members and around 20 officers seconded from various other units to produce a stream of high-quality reconnaissance maps which smoothed Wellington's way through what otherwise would have been unknown terrain. Those of the Lines of Torres Vedras on the outskirts of Lisbon, where the British and their Portuguese allies held off a French counter-offensive under General Masséna for nearly 10 months between November 1809 and September 1810, show a delicacy and fine detail in the delineation of the surrounding hills that belies the utilitarian military purpose of the cartography. Ironically, at the very end of the campaign, when Wellington pushed across the Pyrenees and into France itself in October 1813, he no longer had to rely on fresh mapping produced by his own staff,

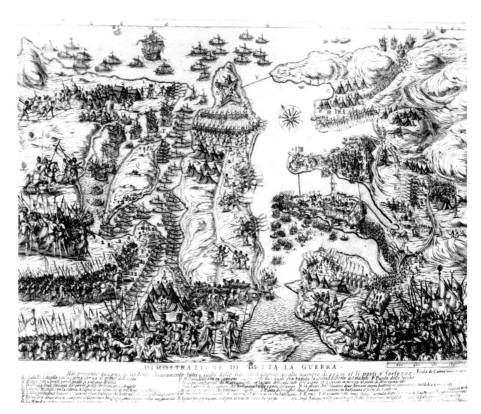

ABOVE

Pictorial map of the Siege of Malta in 1565, 16th century

as he could now use sheets from the Cassini map of France which had just, finally, been completed (see p.34).

The tradition of military cartography was continued in most major armies, including those of the contending sides in the US Civil War, where Union map-makers such as Robert Knox Sneden (1832–1918), who had begun his career as an architect, and so knew a thing or two about draftsmanship, and William H. Willcox (1832–1929), who used his military experience to go on to design skyscrapers in Seattle, created memorable maps of battles such as First Bull Run (1861) and Gettysburg (1863). The two World Wars spawned veritable cartographic industries, either in the official histories which chronicled them after their end (in the case of the First World War amounting to 109 volumes for the British version, illustrated with thousands of maps) or near the front lines, chronicling the achingly slow shift in the 800 km (500 miles) of trenches which snaked across France and Belgium, each yard's advance from which was won only at the cost of hundreds of lives. By the Second World War, the effort was even greater, with the German forces employing over 1,500 officers in its map production unit, which is calculated to have produced a staggering 1.3 billion printed maps by 1945.

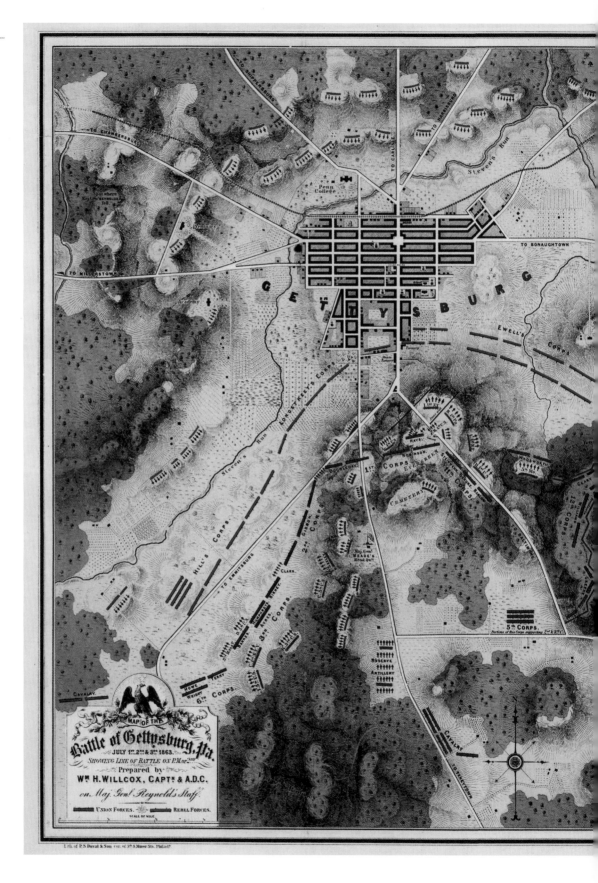

Victory in war often brought new frontiers. Louis XIV's Wars of Devolution (1667–68) won France new territories to the north-east as its armies bit off pieces of the Spanish Netherlands and gnawed away at the previous borders in a series of sapping sieges. In the 18th and 19th centuries Tsarist Russia expanded its border through a mixture of warfare, aggressive diplomacy and the planting of towns in thinly settled regions of Siberia's vast taiga, while the exigencies of war found even long-established states such as the Austro-Hungarian Empire finding themselves in need of mapping. Other states, such as Denmark and Switzerland, threatened by acquisitive neighbours, felt the imperative to define their frontiers as a pre-emptive gesture. All these countries saw maps of their national borders as a power statement, a kind of cartographic secret weapon in the struggle to assert themselves against rivals. The map of France, though, took over a century to complete, with the measurement of the first meridian (to be used as a baseline for the rest of the survey) being laid out under the supervision of Giovanni

Domenico Cassini in 1669. The project then consumed the lives of four generations of Cassinis, until it was eventually completed 146 years later in 1815, a quarter of a century after the French Revolutionary state had dispensed with the services of his great-grandson Jean-Dominique. Far less prolonged was the birth of the national map produced by Britain's Ordnance Survey, an organization set up in 1791, which in 1801 produced its first map of Kent. It was interrupted for 15 years from 1825 by the need to complete a survey of Ireland and bedevilled by problems with the standard measure being used to lay out the survey's meridian lines, which led to the moulding of a special bar rod made of brass and iron which did not shrink or expand appreciably when the temperature changed. That bar perished in the fire in October 1834 which destroyed the Houses of Parliament – where it had been lodged for safekeeping – but another was rapidly recast and the survey continued, to be finally completed in 1842. If there were bragging rights to be had, France's map had taken 146 years, and Britain's 41.

Not all maps were made for the use of politicians, generals, navigators, explorers or even for those simply trying to find their way. Many, and especially from the 18th century onwards, were produced as educational tools for use in schools. The very first was

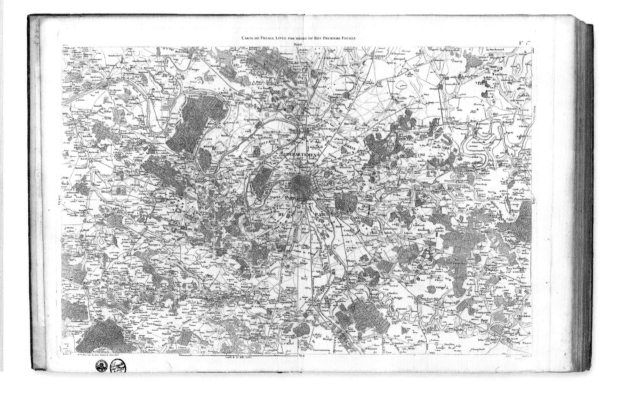

the brainchild of the German schoolmaster Johann Strube, whose *Orbis terrarum veteribus cogniti typus in binis tabulis* ('An Arrangement of Knowledge of the Old World in Two Tables') was published in the 1660s, and was an atlas specifically designed for schoolchildren which had two versions of each map, one without the place names, so that the pupils could fill them in as a form of test. By 1710, the market had grown, particularly in Germany with the publication of the *Kleiner Schulatlas* ('Little School Atlas') by Johann Hübner (1668–1731), a German geographer and polymath, who used his position as rector of the high school in Merseburg to engage in a series of educational experiments – many of them centring on a 'question and answer' pedagogic style.

This, the first atlas specifically marketed at the educational sector, was soon imitated in other European countries, with works such as the 1779 *Atlas Nouveau* by Edme Mentelle (1730–1816). A playwright turned schoolmaster, Mentelle's pupils at the École Militaire where he was a professor included Napoleon Bonaparte, who fortunately did not hold it against his former teacher that he had also acted as tutor to the future Louis XVI, designing him a beautiful terrestrial globe complete with undulating submarine mountain ranges.

Most modern school atlases – and indeed many of the earliest educational maps – are to some extent thematic, showing subjects such as the geology of a country, population density or the distribution of

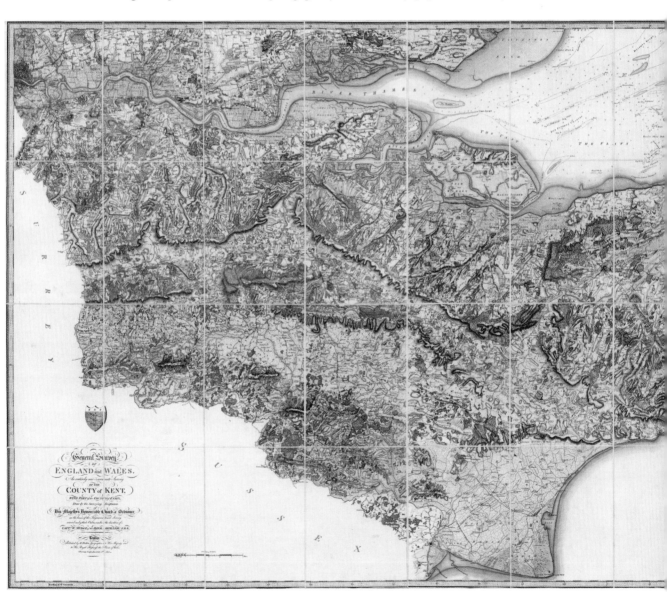

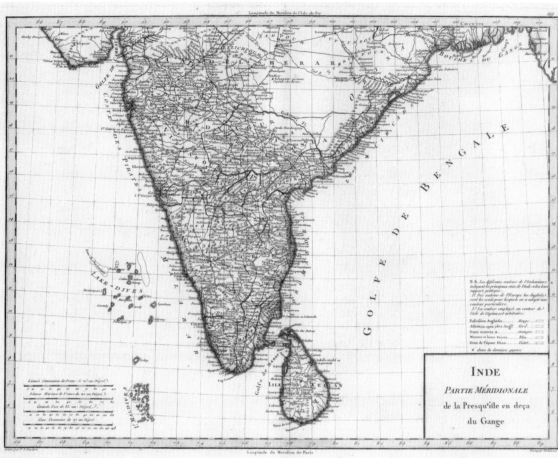

INDE

PARTIE MÉRIDIONALE

de la Presqu'île en deça

du Gange

ABOVE

India, *Atlas Nouveau*, Edme Mentelle, 1779

local languages or ethnic groups. Such thematic mapping can be turned by today's cartographers to almost any subject – bird migrations, the results of elections, the spread of a pandemic or, in a significant subset of the field, to the mapping of history, by showing the development of national borders, vicissitudes of war, flows of peoples, locations of archaeological sites or any one of a multitude of subjects that make up the historical landscape. Thematic mapping began early – arguably the *Turin Papyrus*'s shading for various different types of rock is the first example and the St Albans monk Matthew Paris's map of the Anglo-Saxon heptarchy (the seven states which dominated England from the 7th to 9th centuries) drawn around 1250 may represent the first attempt at historical mapping – but it was the advent of printing in the mid-15th century that provided the impetus for the production of a wider spectrum of mapping types. The Reformation, with its concern for the literal nature of religious truth embedded in the Bible (as opposed to in pronouncements of the Papacy), led Protestant scholars to focus on sources, and so to produce maps which accompanied their new translations or commentaries on the Bible. By the 1590s individual maps had burgeoned into whole historical atlases, with the compilation by Christiaan van Adrichem (1533–85), a priest from Delft in the Netherlands, of the *Theatrum terrae sanctae* ('Theatre of the Holy Land'), published in Cologne in 1590, which included plans of Jerusalem and the areas settled by the 12 tribes of Israel. The Renaissance fascination with the classical world began to make itself felt in historical atlases, too, with the publication from 1579 in gradually enlarged editions of the *Parergon* by Abraham Ortelius (1527–98), as a side enterprise to his monumental *Theatrum orbis terrarum* ('Theatre of the Globe of the World') world atlas, whose range of subjects included ancient Gaul, the Roman expansion in Italy and the

RIGHT

Jerusalem,
*Theatrum terrae
sanctae*, Christiaan
van Adrichem,
1590

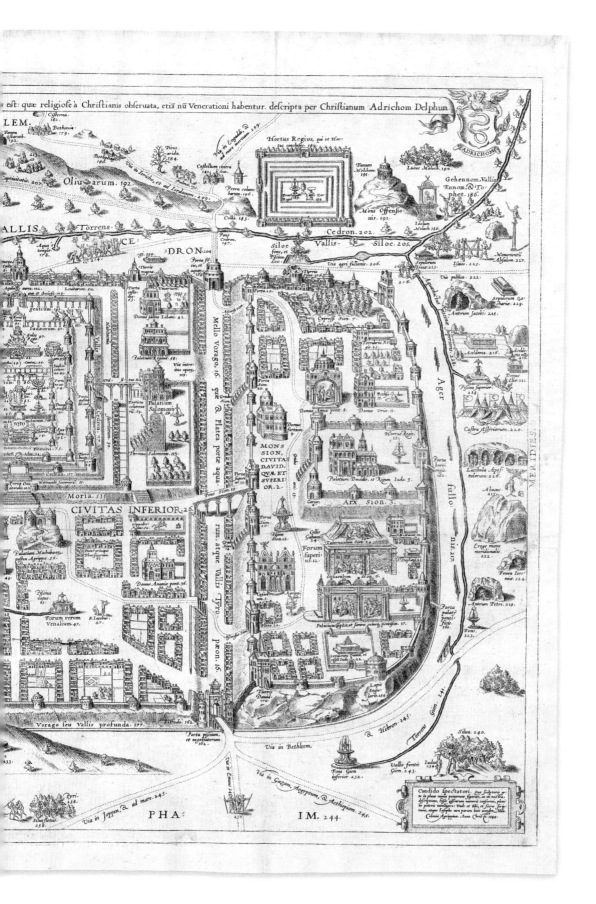

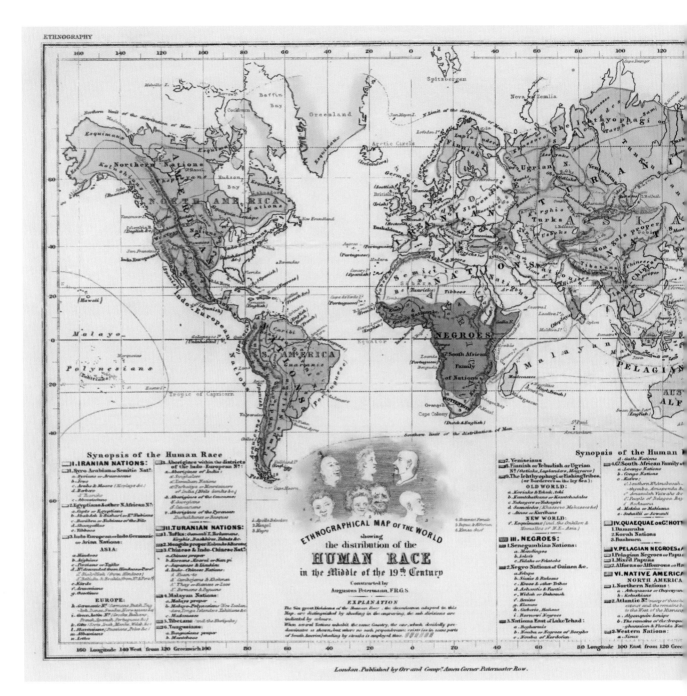

ABOVE

Ethnographical
Map of the World,
*Atlas of Physical
Geography*,
August Heinrich
Petermann, 1850

conquests of Alexander the Great. Ever since then no self-respecting cartographic shelf has been complete without its share of historical atlases, whose highlights have included the *Genealogical, Chronological, Historical and Geographical Atlas* compiled by the French emigré Emmanuel de las Cases (1766–1842) in London in 1801 and the *Times Atlas of World History*, first published in 1978, whose beautiful hill-shading (initially hand-drawn) and innovative integration of text and maps set the standard for the next four decades.

A wider range of subjects was treated in the 1829 *Atlas physique, politique et historique de l'Europe* ('Physical, Political and Historical Atlas of Europe') by Maxime-Auguste Denaix (1777–1844), who had learnt the map-maker's art as head of the French army cartographic office. As well as its headline coverage of the political and historical development of the continent, it also included maps of linguistic distribution and of European flora and fauna. The widespread adoption of lithography, a printing process invented by the Bavarian playwright Alois Senefelder around 1796 (initially as a cheap method to reproduce playscripts, see p.40) allowed a finer gradation of tints to be shown and enabled a huge leap in the sophistication of thematic mapping. It needed also the genius of August Heinrich Petermann (1822–78), a German cartographer who moved to Scotland in 1845 to help out with an English edition of Heinrich Berghaus's *Physikalischer Atlas* ('Physical Atlas'), and then to London, where he managed to secure himself a position as Physical Geographer-Royal to Queen Victoria in 1868. He published a series of innovative atlases including the *Atlas of Physical Geography* in 1850, among whose maps was one of the pattern of waves caused by the Lisbon Earthquake of 1755. Petermann's successors as thematic map-makers have been legion, from those treating more conventional subjects such as the distribution of crops, or population density, for example, Charles Oscar Paullin's

exemplary *Atlas of the Historical Geography of the United States* (1932), to entire atlases dealing with thematic subjects such as the *Atlas of Breeding Birds of Britain and Ireland*, first published in 1976, and even entirely imaginary worlds, such as the splendid maps of Middle-earth accompanying J.R.R. Tolkien's *The Lord of the Rings* (1973). With the capacity in the digital age to create digital and thematic overlays to maps with relative ease, it now seems that the only limit to which subjects can be mapped, and how, is the cartographer's imagination.

A display of ideology, an assertion of power, a military tool, a delineation of the nation's borders, an educational device, an illustration of avian migrations or a simple means of finding the way: the purpose of the map has been chosen. Who, though, is to draw it?

BELOW

An example of a thematic atlas – a map showing the spread of the 1918 Spanish flu, *The Atlas of Disease*, 2018

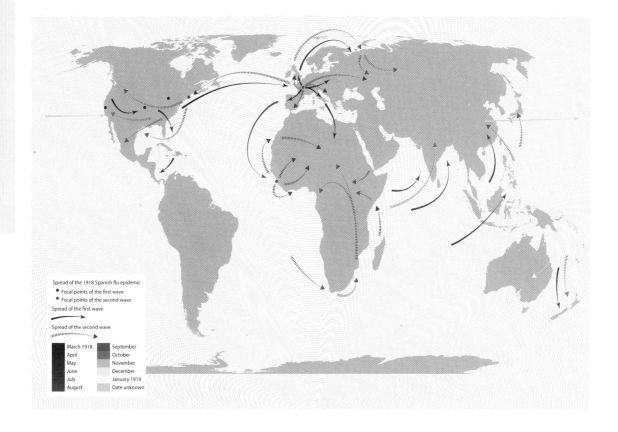

Spread of the 1918 Spanish flu epidemic
- Focal points of the first wave
- Focal points of the second wave

Spread of the first wave

Spread of the second wave

March 1918	September
April	October
May	November
June	December
July	January 1919
August	Date unknown

CHAPTER 4

OLD TIMERS

THE FIRST MAP-MAKERS

I t's all very well meticulously gathering the information for the map, *gromas* and sextants in hand, mountain ranges and oceans traversed, and then determining its purpose, shaped by ideology or simple wayfinding, but someone must actually create that map.

We don't know the identity of those who crafted the very first maps, such as the town plan at Çatal Höyük or even the *Babylonian Map of the World*, but as time goes on the cartographers emerge from the shadows and become identifiable people with stories that can be told. At first isolated names, by the classical era we know the identity of dozens, and then hundreds of map-makers in the golden age of cartography in the 16th and 17th century. It would take a volume 20 times the size of this one to chronicle the lives and

achievements of them all, but the following is a selection of some of the most notable up to the end of the medieval period, from whom the selection of our hypothetical map-maker might be made.

The philosophical school which emerged in the Greek colonies of Ionia, what is now western Turkey, in the 6th century BC was the first to speculate on the nature of the world (other than attributing it to divine whim) and so, understandably, some of its members were also the first to try to map it. The earliest to have

RIGHT

Roman mosaic of
Anaximander, with
a sundial,
3rd century AD

72 TO THE ENDS OF THE EARTH

attempted this feat is said to have been Anaximander (*c.* 610–546 BC) about whom vexingly little is known: only a bare six lines of his work has survived, but he is said to have believed the universe was made up of a nebulous substance known as 'the boundless'. He was apparently well travelled and introduced the *gnomon* or sundial to Sparta and, according to the later Roman geographer Strabo (*c.* 64 BC–AD 24), published the first geographical map.

Perhaps a little less elusive might be Hecataeus (*c.* 560–480 BC), another Milesian, who wrote the *Periodos ges* ('Circuit of the Earth'), the first Greek treatise on geography. He, too, seems to have travelled widely, including to Egypt, then under the control of Cambyses II of Persia (*r.* 530–522 BC), where he gained first-hand an appreciation of the might of the Persian Empire. He tried his hand at statesmanship, seeking in vain to dissuade his fellow citizens in Miletus from joining a revolt of the Ionian Greek cities against Persia which erupted in 499 BC. The Milesian leader Aristagoras is said to have taken a *pinax* or bronze tablet showing a map of the entire world as part of his campaign, though presumably not the world map which Hecataeus, who vigorously opposed the war, had himself composed. That one is said to have shown the world as circular, with a bounding ocean surrounding it, a feature of most early Greek world maps, which the historian Herodotus mocked, noting how unlikely it was the Earth was an exact circle as though drawn 'with a pair of compasses'.

Two centuries later, Greek cartographers had made significant strides. Dicaearchus of Messana (*c.* 360–296 BC), who as a pupil of Aristotle (384–322 BC) had access to an intellectual milieu that embraced all the latest developments in politics, history and philosophy, also wrote a geographical treatise (confusingly also entitled *Periodos ges*), which included a world map. Only tantalizing fragments of his work survive, including a history of Greece, a work on the soul (which he believed was not immortal) and a treatise on measuring the height of mountains which, oddly, he wanted to prove were not as high as they seemed in order to confirm his theories about the Earth's spherical nature (mountainous bumps on

whose surface would have upset his sense of symmetry). On his world map Dicaearchus was the first cartographer to insert a parallel, in his case a line of latitude, dividing the world in two at a line which ran eastwards from the Straits of Gibraltar through Sardinia, Sicily, Asia Minor and as far as the western edge of the Himalayas, where his geographical information petered out.

Dicaearchus's *Periodos*, and with it his world map, are long lost and so there is no way of assessing whether the criticism levelled at it by the Greek historian Polybius (*c.* 200–118 BC) and Strabo – that he got his measurements wrong and portrayed the inhabited portion of the world as far narrower than it really was – was justified. Almost a thousand years later, Ambrosius Theodosius Macrobius (*c.* AD 370–430) was still carrying the flame for classical cartography. As proconsul of Africa in 410 and praetorian prefect of Italy in 430, he was a witness to the buckling of Rome's frontiers under the growing weight of barbarian incursions. His former area of operations in North Africa suffered invasion by the Vandals, a Germanic group who crossed the Strait of Gibraltar in

ABOVE

The World According to Hecataeus of Miletus, 19th century reconstruction

RIGHT
Macrobius's map
of the World,
Abbo of Fleury,
10th century

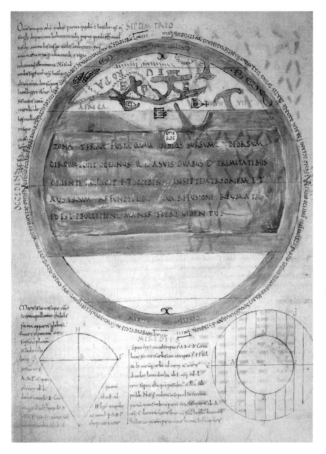

Although Macrobius's map, like those of so many of his predecessors, vanished over the ages, it did influence a series of medieval imitators who incorporated his zonal division on their much-simplified maps of the world. Despite a flirtation with a non-spherical view of the Earth (as championed by Cosmas Indicopleustes in the 6th century, who, despite his apparent extensive travels as a merchant, became convinced, once ensconced in a monastery in Egypt's Sinai Desert, that it was shaped like the Old Testament Ark of the Covenant, see p.51), an alternative tradition persisted, of maps which showed the world as round. These maps divided it into two (or sometimes three) landmasses, riven by great rivers (usually the Nile, Tigris and Euphrates) which rendered it into the shape of the letter 'T', within the 'O' of the circle, and seem to have originated with the 7th-century Spanish bishop, Isidore of Seville (see p.50). Among its masters was the Benedictine abbot Beatus of Liébana (c. 730–800) who wrote a *Commentary on the Apocalypse of St John* around 776. From his eyrie in the Picos de Europa mountains in the north of Spain, it must have seemed like his world really was in the midst of an apocalypse. The Kingdom of Asturias, in which his monastic house lay, was in the last Christian region to survive the conquest of the Visigothic Kingdom by Islamic Arab-Berber armies in the decades after 711. The vibrant illustrations of his manuscript are masterpieces of medieval art, their shockingly bright hues and assemblage of strange beasts such as fire-breathing horses with lions' heads a warning to sinners that judgement is at hand. His T-O map that accompanies the work is equally bright, drawn in a style known as Mozarabic, which incorporates the influence of the Arabic culture that was just beginning to flower in the lands to the south. Oriented with east at the top (where paradise is shown with four rivers issuing from it), it shows a fourth continent in addition to the traditional three (a reference to the fact that each of the four evangelists, the authors of the New Testament Gospels, was said to have been despatched to one of them), the fourth of which is 'farthest from the world, beyond the ocean, in a region unknown to us because of the heat'.

For sheer colour, yet simplicity, Beatus might be the cartographer of choice, but the net can be cast a little wider. One of the most renowned of early

429 and steadily advanced eastwards, swallowing up town after town until they finally took Carthage, the greatest prize, 10 years later. His main contribution to map-making came in a curious work, a commentary on Cicero's *Somnium Scipionis* ('Dream of Scipio'), in which the earlier author describes a sleep-vision by the general Scipio Aemilianus shortly before his final conquest of Carthage at the end of the Third Punic War in 146 BC. He is granted vision of the universe by his dead grandfather Scipio Africanus – renowned for his defeat of Rome's almost-nemesis Hannibal – which demonstrates to him how, despite its apparent might, Rome is just a small part of a greater whole. The commentary explains how he is shown the celestial spheres in which the planets are said to circulate, and, most importantly for Macrobius, the climatic belts into which the Earth was considered to be divided. The northern hemisphere, the one in which all the regions known to classical geographers were situated, was divided into a cold zone in the far north, then a temperate one and to the south a hot zone, with the assumption that beyond the burning and impassable heat of the equator there was a balancing southern set of climatic zones.

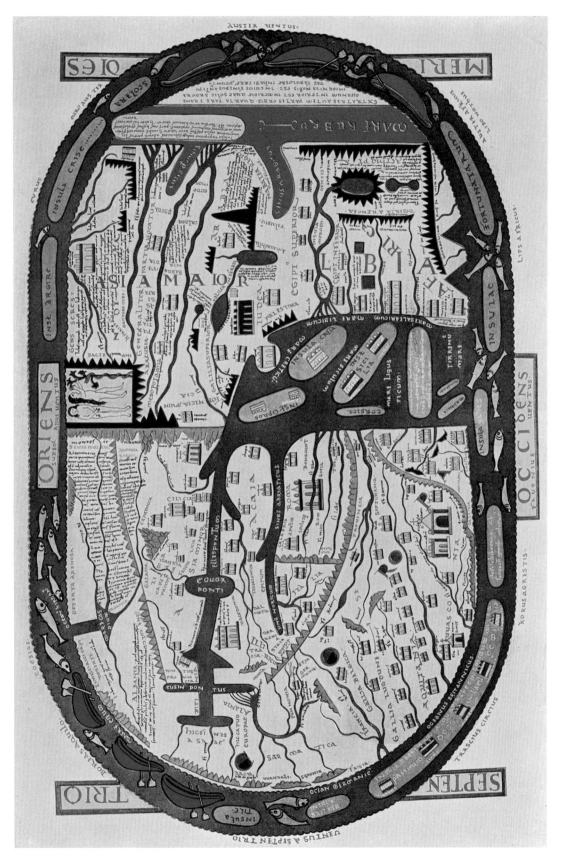

LEFT

T-O map,
*Commentary on
the Apocalypse
of St John*,
Beatus of Liébana,
c. AD 776
(11th-century
copy)

Chinese cartographers, Pei Xiu (224–271) became a minister in the newly established state of Western Jin. He was selected not for his map-making ability, but for his reputation for virtue and knowledge of the Confucian Classics – a talent that came in handy in his initial posting as Prefect of the Masters of Writing (in effect the imperial secretary). He was then promoted to Minister of Works and immediately set about commissioning a survey to replace the existing Han-era maps which he criticized for their sloppiness, stating 'one cannot rely on them' as they, in an unforgivable cartographic sin, showed things which were simply not there. In his *Yu gong diyu tu* ('Regional Maps for the Tribute of Yu'), a work on cartography which included maps, he set down six basic principles to guide future map-makers, including those that distances should be in proportion to each other, and consistent means be used to measure road lengths and the height of hills and mountains.

Pei Xiu's reputation in China endured for many centuries. In Japan, one of the first known cartographers became equally famous. Gyōki (668–749) was a Buddhist monk who entered the monastery of Asuka-Dera in the imperial capital of Nara at the age of 15, but later adopted an itinerant life, preaching Buddhism, offering succour to the poor and building temples (almost 50 are attributed to him). He and his followers also carried out public works, building dams, canals and bridges to improve the life of the people. His travels seem to have inspired him to reflect on the shape of Japan, and he is said to have compiled a series of maps (which may have been associated with an imperial order issued in 738 for the creation of provincial

mapping). Although nothing survives directly to prove that Gyōki really did make maps, a genre of slightly stylized maps of Japan, with sparse topographical information included and a rather flattened shape to the Japanese islands, came to have his name attached to them (one of the oldest, created in 1306, is held in the Ninna-ji Temple of Kyoto and bears an inscription warning that it should not be shown to outsiders).

There is something strangely comforting in the idea that just as European monks were huddled in their scriptoria laboriously copying lavish manuscripts, including splendid maps of the world such as the Beatus *Apocalypse*, their Buddhist counterparts in Japan were doing the same. By the time Beatus and Gyōki were working, map-making had become established in another part of the world, too. The culture of scholarship which flourished under the Muslim Abbasid dynasty from its new capital in Baghdad, founded in 762, made it the centre both for the transmission of knowledge from the classical world and a vibrant centre of innovation in learning in its own right. The *Bayt al-Hikmah* or House of Wisdom, established around 830 in Baghdad, became the epicentre of it and among its greatest stars was Muhammad ibn Musa al-Khwarizmi (*c*. 780–850), a polymath with a huge range of interests which included astronomy, geometry and algebra. In the latter his contribution, solving six standard forms of equation, was so great that a corruption of his name gave us the modern term 'algorithm' (in Latin he was known as Algorismus). He also produced the *Kitab Surat al-Ard* ('Book of the Image of the World'), which included a list of over 4,000 locations, with their latitude and longitude. It was all rather like Ptolemy of Alexandria (see p.92), and indeed al-Khwarizmi claimed to have extracted the information from the Greek geographer, adding Macrobius to his list of influences by including a division into seven climatic zones in the world map he included in his book.

Only one copy survives with just four maps, including a famous map of the Nile, showing the fictional 'Mountains of the Moon' believed by Ptolemy to be the river's source (see p.149).

While Arab and Persian cartographers were reaching ever greater heights of excellence, their European equivalents were floundering somewhat, the scholarship of Rome crystallized into conformist collections acceptable to the Christian Church, map-making caught in a limbo between the lost technical knowledge of the Romans – though a few

isolated maps may have survived – and before a new burst of map-making in the 14th century. In this relatively dark period Gerald of Wales or Giraldus Cambrensis (*c*. 1146–1223) would probably not recommend himself for topographic accuracy, but for novelty – his is among the very first cartographic representations of Ireland – and for the vividness of his writing, he would make an entertaining choice. Born in Pembrokeshire, he overcame the disappointment of being rejected as candidate for the bishopric of St Davids (by no less a figure than

ABOVE

Map of the Nile, *Kitab Surat al-Ard*, Muhammad ibn Musa al-Khwarizmi, *c*. AD 820 (11th-century copy)

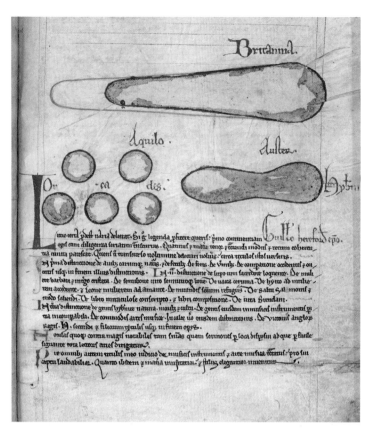

Henry II of England, who may have held Gerald's distant relationship to the Welsh royal family of Deheubarth against him) and went to study canon law and theology at Paris, one of Europe's principal centres of ecclesiastical learning. Despite earlier royal disfavour, in 1184 Gerald entered the service of Henry II as a chaplain and was selected to accompany the king's brother John on an expedition to Ireland the following year. Out of that trip came the *Topographia Hibernica*, which he completed in 1188 and which is illustrated by his rather schematic map and enlivened by a narrative of Irish history and customs, spiced with some rather unlikely tales of chimerical half-lions, half-female creatures and a fish which had three golden teeth. He can hardly have endeared himself to his Irish hosts as he described their countrymen as completely savage and given to 'abominable treachery'. He followed this up with a similar work on Wales, the *Descriptio Cambriae*, in which he is rather more sympathetic to his countrymen and – at a time when much of Wales was yet to be conquered by the English – he advises that 'while the English fight for power, the Welsh fight for freedom'. The latter part of his career was again embittered by being once more blackballed as a candidate for the bishopric of St Davids in 1199 and, after a pilgrimage to Rome in 1207, he fades into obscurity.

Not all medieval cartographers were as well travelled as Gerald, but some managed to achieve even greater fame for their geographical erudition. Ranulf Higden (*c.* 1280–1364) was a Benedictine monk at the Abbey of St Werburgh in Chester, a retreat which he seems scarcely to have left in his adult life. Yet it did not stop him composing the *Polychronicon* (1342), a universal history of the world up to Higden's own times, which became one of the publishing sensations of the 14th century and was one of the first books printed (now in English translation) after William Caxton introduced the printing press to England in 1475. The maps which accompanied it included a fine world map with personifications of the wind arrayed around the outside border and elements Higden considered of especial importance picked out in red (including the Pillars of Hercules, looking alarmingly as though they are going to sink off the coast of Spain). Versions of his maps, which have their roots in early Christian *mappae mundi* are circular, almond-shaped or oval – the latter because it was supposedly the shape of Noah's Ark. So famous did Higden become that he was even summoned to the court of Edward III in

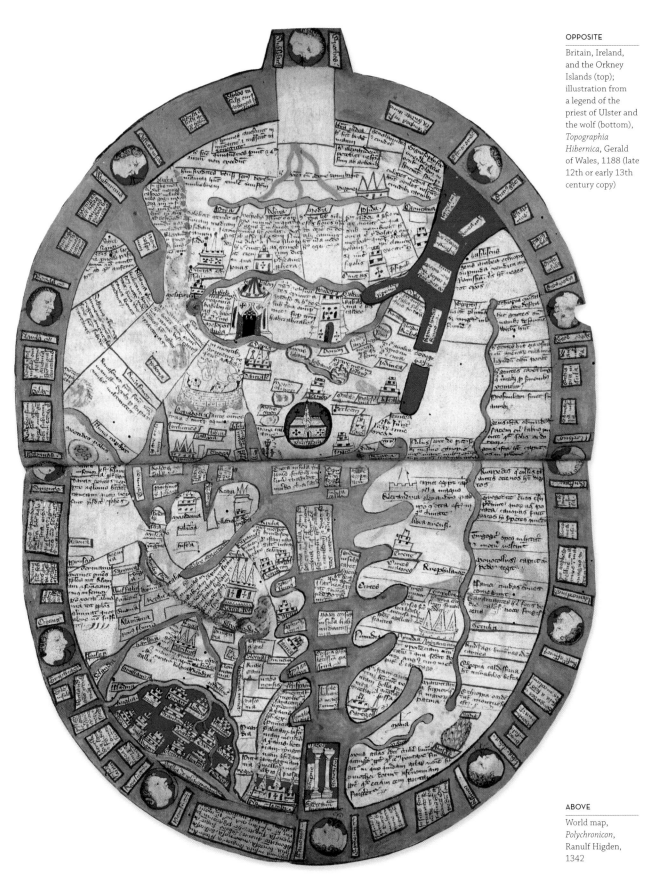

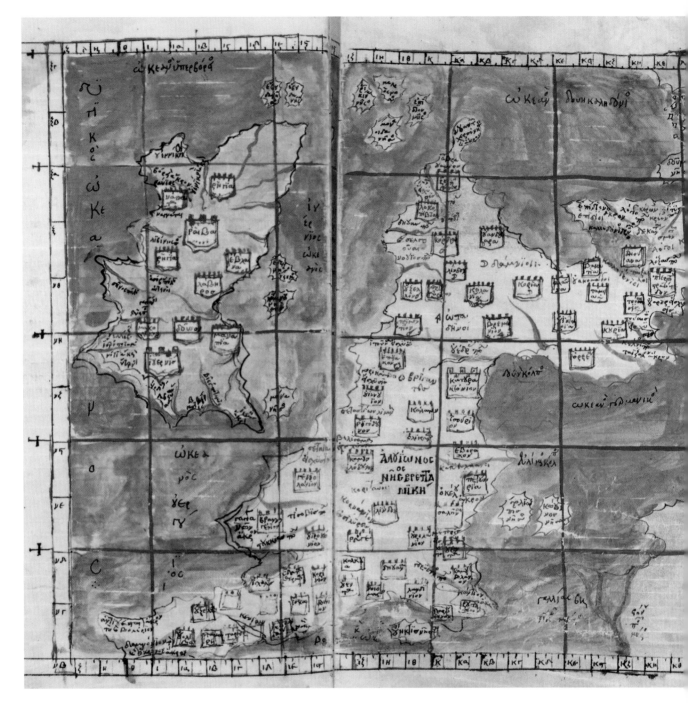

1352 'with all your chronicles, and those which are in your charge to speak and take advice with our council on certain matters which will be explained to you on our behalf'.

If a cartographer with royal connections is insufficient a catch, then one who (though relatively little known) arguably had the greatest influence of any map-maker during the 14th century might pass muster. Although the Byzantine Empire, the modern name for the eastern Roman provinces which survived the collapse of the empire in the West in the 5th century, was not known for its intellectual vibrancy, it did transmit, or at least preserve, a great deal of ancient learning and manuscripts which would otherwise have been lost. In its twilight, as much of it had been lost to invading Ottoman Turks, Christian kings in the Balkans, misdirected crusaders and other sundry adventurers, it underwent something of a

miniature intellectual renaissance of its own. One of those responsible for the revival in scientific studies was Maximus Planudes (1260–*c*. 1310), a scholar and theologian who established a monastery for laymen in Constantinople (more a gentlemen's club for the retired than a hothouse of prayer), where he gathered manuscripts from throughout the rather diminished empire. In between a new edition of the *Greek Anthology*, writing a treatise on Arabic numerals (the cumbersome Roman version were still in use at the time), a definitive collection of Greek prose from classical times to the 11th century AD and acting as an ambassador to Venice, he decided to research Ptolemy's long-neglected *Geography*. It took a concerted search, but in 1295 he came across a copy. Although the text referred to 26 maps, there were none with the manuscript that he had unearthed and so Planudes had new ones

drawn, using the instructions contained in the manuscript. These were so striking that the emperor Andronicus II (*r*. 1282–1328) had a copy made for himself and others followed suit. It was one such manuscript that Manuel Chrysoloras, leading light of a later generation of Byzantine scholars, brought with him when he came to Florence in 1397, sparking interest in the West in Ptolemy (once humanists in Italy had learnt enough Greek to appreciate it!). Planudes had unwittingly ignited a cartographic revolution.

Of course, when western European cartographers began their intense engagement with Ptolemy's maps – ironically just a century before the Ptolemaic world view was radically upended by the voyages of Christopher Columbus – they had the benefit of over a century of experience of map-makers working within the portolan tradition. Many of these are little more than names; the earliest of whom with any clue to his identity is Pietro Vesconte (*fl*. 1310–30), who, from inscriptions on his maps, claimed to be Genoese, but appears to have spent his active career in Venice. His earliest chart of 1311 was followed by several others of the Mediterranean, and then in 1320 by a larger atlas. This was appended to the *Liber secretorum fidelium crucis* ('Book of the Secrets of the Faithful of the Cross') by Marino Sanudo (*c*. 1270–1343), an

BELOW

Engraving of Ptolemy of Alexandria in his observatory, 19th century

aristocratic Venetian, whose forebear Marco had acquired his own mini-state based in Naxos in the Aegean as 'Duke of the Archipelago' when the Byzantine Empire was dismembered by the armies of the Fourth Crusade in 1204. Despite this rather dubious heritage – the Fourth Crusaders had been supposed to travel to the Holy Land to recover control of Jerusalem but had been diverted by the Venetians in payment of the funds to transport them across the Aegean – Marino Sanudo lobbied vigorously for the launching of a new crusade to revive the Crusader States in Palestine and Syria (the last significant stronghold of which had been lost when Acre fell to the Mamluk Sultan al-Ashraf Khalil in 1291). Despite his liberal use of Vesconte's mapping, Sanudo never acknowledged the authorship of a cartographer whose work shows an increasing sophistication of knowledge even outside his home domain (the Isle of Man starts to appear on his work from 1321, whereas before it was largely absent).

Perhaps the most stunning piece of mapping surviving from the 14th century is the Catalan Atlas, a kind of hybrid of a Christian *mappa mundi* and a portolan, drawn on four leaves, which together would make a huge map some 3 m wide x 65 cm tall (6½ x 2 ft). It is packed with figures from myth (such as the giants Gog and Magog somewhere in Siberia) and from history, most notably Mansa Musa, the ruler of Mali, rumours of whose wealth were based on his very real pilgrimage to Mecca, during which his lavish spending of gold in Cairo caused a crash in the value of the metal, and who is shown on the atlas's

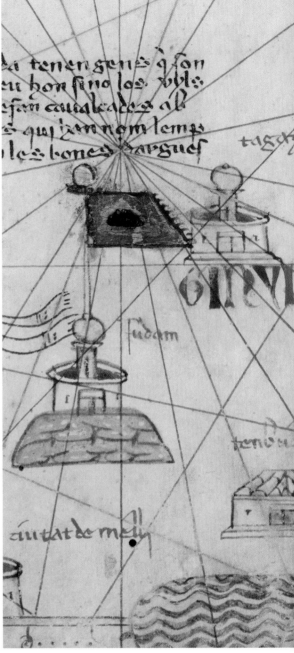

first map leaf contemplating a large gold nugget he holds in his hand. The atlas was the work of Abraham Cresques (1325–87) and his son, whose cartographic workshop in Palma, Majorca, produced maps for Pedro IV of Aragon (who had conquered Majorca from his cousin Jaime III in 1343) and his son John. So valuable did Pedro find Cresques' services that in 1381 he awarded him the title *Magister mapamundorum et buxolarum* ('Master of World Maps and Compasses'), and exemption from having to wear the identifying

aqueſt ſenyor negre es .
muſſe melly ſenyor dels n
de gineua/aqueſt rey es
rich/el pius noble ſenyor
eſta p̃ nda p̃ labandagia.
qual ſeꝛzaill en la ſuna

buda

gougeu

LEFT

Mansa Musa,
Catalan Atlas, 1375

badge which other members of the Catalan Jewish community were forced to display.

The main reason for these accolades must have been the *Catalan Atlas*, a piece of lavish cartographic diplomacy which was commissioned from Abraham as a gift to Charles, the future King Charles VI of France, but then the dauphin. The map-making tradition was carried on by Abraham's son Jafudà (or Yehuda), but the magic of the royal protection afforded by the *Catalan Atlas* had clearly run out, as in 1391 he was forced to convert to Christianity and adopted the name Jaime Riba. It was long believed that Jafudà had taken refuge in Portugal, where he entered the service of Prince Henry the Navigator, whose school of navigation at Sagres became the driving force behind many of the early Portuguese voyages down the west coast of Africa. Although the identity of the 'Jacome de Mallorca' who became Henry's favoured cartographer is now disputed, whoever he was certainly came from Majorca and was succeeded before 1439 by Gabriel de Valseca (c. 1408–67), another Jewish Catalan convert, who compiled one of the first really accurate maps of the Azores (though also including a scattering of imaginary mainstays of 15th-century Atlantic mapping, such as Antillia and Brasil, see Chapter 8).

The Portuguese voyages had already opened a maritime window on the world to Europeans who had for centuries been confined in their horizons to the Mediterranean in the south, the uncertain borderlands with the Islamic world to the east and the Baltic to the north, with little practical knowledge and much speculation and wishful thinking about what might lie to the west. That window grew larger by the mid-15th century and coincided with a significant increase in the number of maps produced which relied on Ptolemy as their model rather than medieval *mappae mundi* or portolan charts. At least two of the most notable cartographers of the era were monks, such as Fra Mauro (c. 1400–64), who created a stunningly beautiful world map from the refuge of the Camaldolese monastery of St Michael on the Venetian island of Murano around 1450.

More prolific was Nicolaus Germanus (c. 1420–90), a monk at the Benedictine Abbey

of Reichenbach in south-western Germany from 1442. By 1464 he had made his way to Italy and, armed with a knowledge of mathematics, cartography and a passion for Ptolemaic mapping which he had somehow acquired, he began producing revised versions of Ptolemy's *Geography*. In all he created about 15 versions over the next 20 years, most notable for the *tabulae modernae* ('modern tables') which included parts of the world that were unknown to Ptolemy (such as Scandinavia and West Africa). He also displayed his cartographic skill by introducing dots to show the location of places on the map (rather than just putting the place name in the rough locality) and employing a new trapezoidal projection, in which the lines of latitude were equidistant from each other but those of longitude converged on the Poles. One of the earliest of these, in 1466, was produced for Duke Borso d'Este of Ferrara, who was so taken with it that he wrote a personal letter of thanks praising Nicolaus 'for his excellent

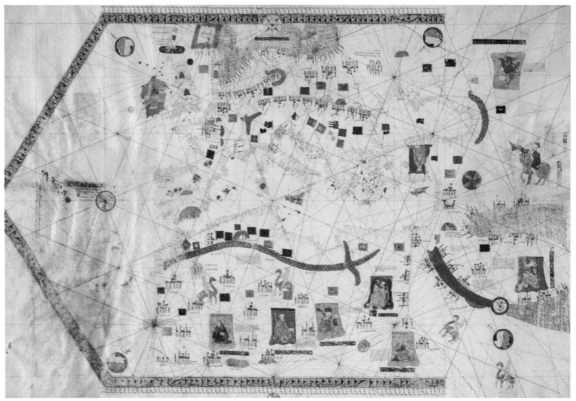

book' together with 100 gold florins, and then, a
month later, sent a further 30 gold florins. Nicolaus
continued drawing maps in the early 1480s, and in
1488 he was visited by the humanist Conrad Celtis
in Florence who heard him complain that others had
made use of his work and derived all the glory and
profit from it (clearly, the stream of donations from
rich patrons had dried up).

An even more illustrious cleric cartographer was
another Nicolaus, Nicolaus Cusanus (1401–64), also
known as Nicholas of Cusa, who was born at Kues
between Koblenz and Trier on the River Mosel. He
came from a well-to-do merchant family and was
educated at the University of Heidelberg, where he
studied philosophy, but then transferred to Italy, where
he gained his doctorate in canon law in 1423. There he
associated with a humanist circle which included the
mathematician Paolo dal Pozzo Toscanelli (1397–1482),

also a talented cartographer, who produced a world
map that may have influenced Columbus's decision
to voyage across the Atlantic in 1492 (see p.154). By
1427 he had entered the service of the Archbishop
of Cologne, cultivating on the side a huge variety of
intellectual interests, which ranged from unearthing
a new manuscript of the comedies of the Roman
playwright Terence, to proving that the Donation of
Constantine (the allegedly 4th-century document on
which the Papacy based its claim to secular power over
much of central Italy) was a forgery. By the 1430s he
had been ordained a priest and attended the Council
of Basel in 1432 called to re-establish papal supremacy
after a period of rifts, schisms and anti-popes, but
which ended in acrimony and the transfer of most
of the delegates to Ferrara, more safely in the papal
orbit. Nicolaus was then sent to Constantinople in
1437 as part of a mission to attempt to reunite the

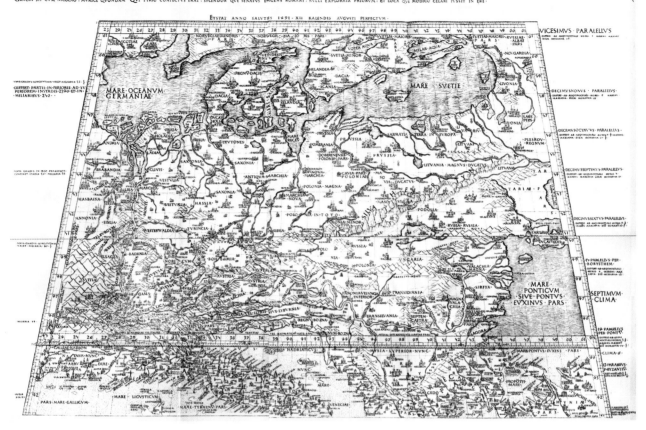

QVOD PICTA EST PARVA GERMANIA TOTA TABELLA: ET LATVS ITALIE GELIDAS QVOD PROSPICIT ALPES: SAVROMATVM QVI TRVCES POPVLI: GENTES QVI PROFVNDO VIGNE ADRIACO: PELOPIS REGNVM QVE VETVSTI:
PANNONIOS ET FINDIT AGROS QVA FRIGIDVS HISTER: ATQVE LICAONIOS TERRARVM QVICQVID IN AXES VERGIT: ET EQVOREAS RHODANVS QVA VERBERAT VNDAS: ET MVLTE PVNCTIS VRBES VILLE QVE NOTATE:
GRACIA SIT CVSE NICOLAO: MVRICE QVONDAM QVI TYRIO CONTECTVS ERAT: SPLENDOR QVE SENATVS INGENS ROMANI: NVLLI EXPLORATA PRIORVM: ET LOCA QVI MODICO CELARI IVSSIT IN ERE·

EYSTAT ANNO SALVTIS 1491·XII·KALENDIS·AVGVSTI·PERFECTVM·

Orthodox and Catholic Churches, and achieved the apex of his career in 1448 when he was elevated to become a cardinal.

Nicolaus wrote widely on astronomy, philology and political science. By a rather convoluted path he prefigured Copernicus by asserting that the Earth could not be the centre of the universe (but only because he reasoned that only God could be the centre of the universe, and as he was a non-corporeal being, then if the universe had a physical centre, it could not be God). During his travels, this intellectual magpie picked up much about mapping and manuscripts both of Ptolemy's *Geography* and the *Antonine Itinerary* (see p.47) He wrote a cartographical treatise *De figura mundi* ('On the Figure of the World') in 1463 which has, unfortunately, since been lost. His cartographic legacy instead relies on the map he made of central Europe, showing the area between Flanders and the Danube Delta and between Jutland in Denmark and northern Italy. Because there were few sources to go on, he probably obtained a great deal of his information during a trip he made as a papal envoy to Germany in 1450–52. The final version, now known as the Eichstätt

map was probably completed in the early 1470s, and represents the first map of the region which shows it with any degree of accuracy. By this time, though, Nicolaus had been dead for almost 10 years.

By then the age of scholar monks had only a few decades left to run before the Reformation shaped a radically different intellectual landscape in Europe. The world as Ptolemy knew it (albeit with a few judicious additions by cartographers such as Nicolaus Germanus) was also in its last years. Almost the final map created before Christopher Columbus's voyage revolutionized Europeans' understanding of the world was produced, by chance, in 1492, the very year that the Genoese navigator landed in the Americas: a globe by Martin Behaim (1459–1507), which is the oldest world globe to survive. It was not the very earliest, as terrestrial globes are referred to in the 1430s and Duke Philip the Good of Burgundy had one in 1467, according to an inventory of his library, which referred to it as having 'the form of an apple'. Made in 1444 by his court astronomer Guillaume Hobit, it took three-and-a-half years to construct. Referring to such globes as 'apples' clearly already had a track record by

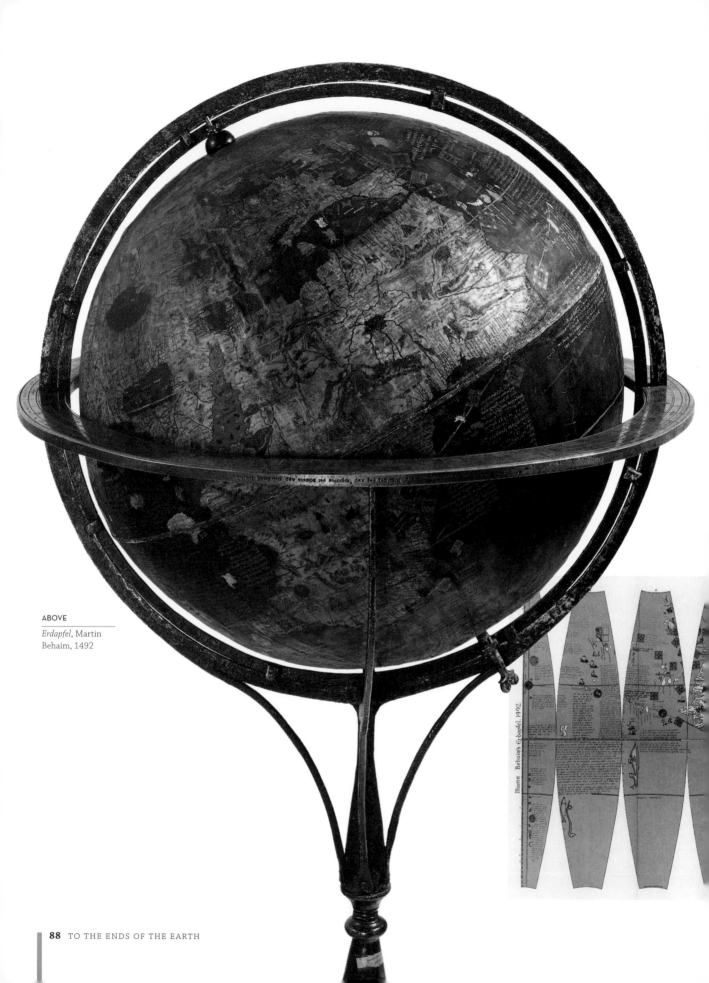

ABOVE

Erdapfel, Martin Behaim, 1492

Martin Behaim's Erdapfel, 1492

the time Behaim created his *Erdapfel* ('Earth Apple'). Behaim wasn't himself a prominent cartographer, but by trade a cloth merchant from Nuremberg, who spent several decades in the service of the Portuguese, participating in voyages down the west coast of Africa sponsored by King Joaõ II. He certainly seems to have visited the Azores and may have sailed down as far as Guinea. When he returned to his hometown in 1490, his reputation as a man versed in the new geography preceded him and he was commissioned by the council of magistrates to produce a world globe. It took a team of artists and craftsmen to translate the knowledge Behaim had gleaned into the globe. The spherical clay ball which formed its core was fashioned by the local artisan Hans Glockengiesser, while another craftsman, Ruprecht Kolberger, made the structure into which the *Erdapfel* was slotted. The artist Georg Glockendon painted the map itself onto strips of linen which had been fixed to the clay sphere during firing.

The most striking thing to modern eyes about the *Erdapfel* is what it does not show. Where the Americas should be there is a simply a foreshortened stretch of ocean between western Europe and Cipango (or Japan), a deceptively short distance made even more enticing by the placing of the legendary island of Antillia as a convenient, but fictitious, resting point along the way. It was notions such as this – but not Behaim's globe itself, which was not complete in time for Columbus to see it – that inspired the first

European voyages across the Atlantic. Shortly after the first of them set off, Behaim returned to Portugal – he had only been in Nuremberg to sort out his late mother's estate – where he died in 1507. By then, doubtless word had reached him about the new lands which his globe had entirely omitted, an occupational hazard for cartographers in an age when every year brought new coastlines and interiors in need of mapping and the redundancy of what had seemed the most up-to-date images of the world.

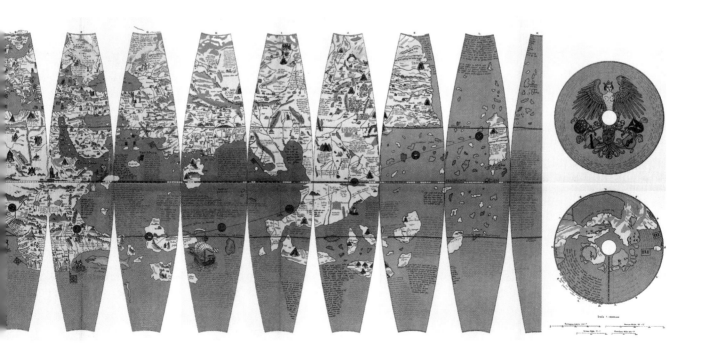

CHAPTER 5

IN THE ROUND

GLOBES AND SPHERES

It seems intuitive that a map should be flat, on a surface that can be spread out and easily consulted (or equally as two-dimensional images viewed on a computer or smartphone screen). Yet we all know that the world itself is not flat, and no mapping projection can ever accurately represent the areas, angles or distances on the ground in two dimensions. The answer? A globe.

The assertion of the 17th-century Dutch mathematician and surveyor Gemma Frisius (1508–55) that 'The mounted globe … is the only one of all instruments whose frequent usage delights astronomers, leads geographers, confirms historians … is admired by grammarians, guides pilots, in short, aside from its beauty, its form is indescribably useful and necessary for everyone' probably goes further than most cartographers today would allow in their praise of the globe, but it has a certain appealing truth about it.

The manufacture of globes is a very ancient practice, divided into two complementary but related areas. The observation of the heavens by ancient astronomers, with the sky appearing roughly in the shape of a hemisphere, suggested the idea of a spherical model of the sky marked with the planets and constellations, with the very first mention of such a creation being by the Greek poet Aratus of Soli (*c.* 315–240 BC) who described one which had been built by the renowned astronomer Eudoxus of Cnidus (*c.* 408–355 BC). The other, and to us more familiar, form of globe is a terrestrial sphere depicting the geography of the Earth, and these seem to have come a little later, with the first reference being to one built by the Greek philosopher Crates of Mallos around 150 BC.

The oldest globe that still survives is part of a sculpture – the *Farnese Atlas*, a marble statue of Atlas, though he is shown holding up a model of the heavens, rather than the Earth. Dating from around AD 150, it shows 17 constellations in the northern sky, one of the oldest star maps in existence. It forms part of a tradition of models of the heavens which later resulted in the construction of armillary spheres (three-dimensional models representing the paths of celestial bodies) and astrolabes, which show the same phenomena, but on a flat plane. While other forms of cartography languished, these were produced in some numbers in the Middle Ages, particularly in the Islamic world, such as the magnificent celestial globe built by the Mosul astronomer Muhammad ibn Hilal around 1275.

Well before then, the idea of constructing globes (and maps) had been given an intellectual coherence by the Greek geographer Ptolemy of Alexandria (*c.* AD 90–168) whose *Geography* provided co-ordinates for the location of places, which could then be mapped. As far as we know, however, no one in Europe actually constructed a globe again until 1325, the date at which the celestial globe acquired

by the German cardinal and astronomer Nicolaus Cusanus (or Nicholas of Cusa, see p.86) was built. An intricate construction with a celestial sphere mounted in an outer sphere made of three brass rings which could be manipulated to show the precession of the equinoxes (the gradual shift of the stars in the night sky over the years), Nicolaus bought it for a bargain 38 guilders in a job lot with other astronomical instruments and manuscripts in 1444.

A terrestrial globe is mentioned in a manuscript from Vienna, the *Regionum sive civitatum distantiae* ('The Distances of Regions and Cities'), dating from 1430–35, but the first terrestrial globe to survive was the *Erdapfel* (or 'Earth Apple') made by the Nuremberg cartographer Martin Behaim in 1492 (see p.89). A collaboration with the artist Georg Glockendon, it set the model for globe construction for centuries, created from a clay spherical core (later papier-maché or paperboard was used) on which a layer of vellum or paper was then laid, before the sphere was split in two, and the vellum sheet cut into 12 elliptical

tooth-shaped sections on which the map was then drawn (or, as time went on, printed). The two halves of the sphere were then reattached and the map sheets (or 'gores' as they were termed) were pasted onto it and varnished. Ornate brass or other metal rings fixed the globe onto a metal or wooden frame which then allowed the globe to be rotated.

Globes captured the spirit of the age in the 16th century, when it seemed discoveries of new lands (or at least new to Europeans) were being made almost every year and a globe seemed a striking and apt way to capture them. It is no accident that the first printed map gores to survive were made by Martin Waldseemüller (1470–1520), whose 1507 world map fixed the New World's name as 'America'. He was a man who understood that the geography, as it had been transmitted ever since Ptolemy, had changed for ever.

Among the greatest map-makers of the era was Johann Schöner (1477–1547), born in Karlstadt in Germany, whose career as a Catholic priest was cut short by his superiors on account of his worrying

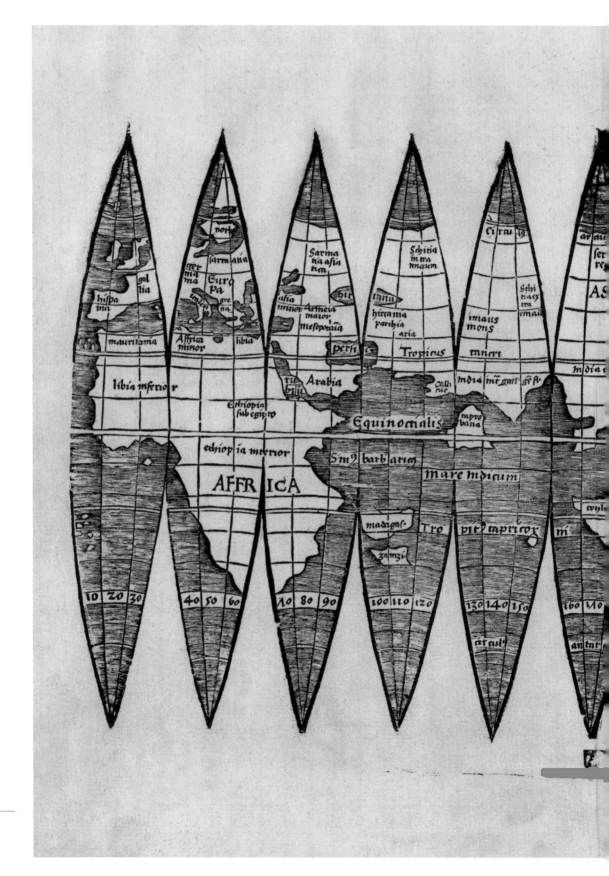

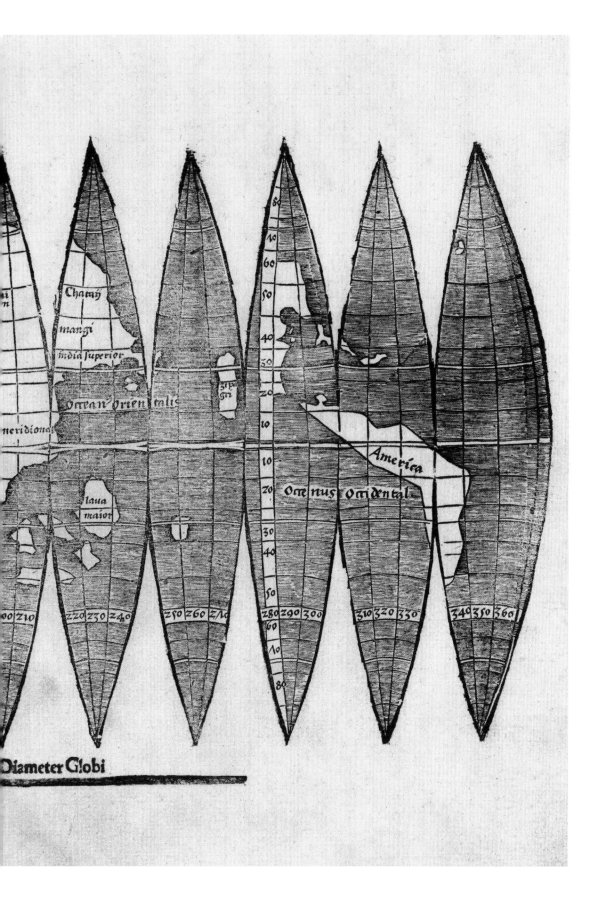

Chatay

mangi

India Superior

Occan Orientalis

meridional

Iaua
maior

31 fri
gri

80
70
60
50
40
30
20
10
10
20
30
40
50
60
70
80

00 210   220 230 240   250 260 2/0   280 290 300   310 320 330   340 350 360

America

Ocea nus Occidental

Diameter Globi

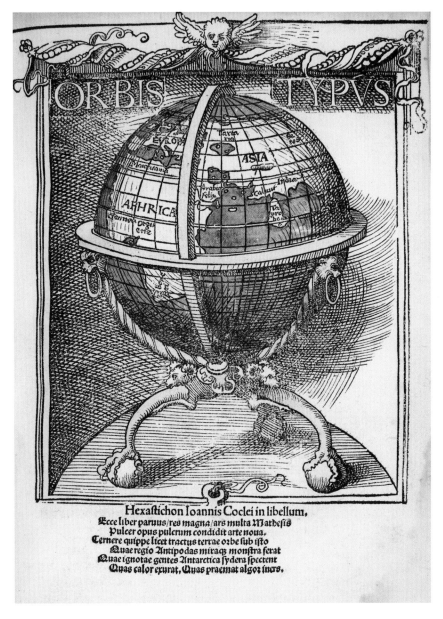

Hexaſtichon Ioannis Coclei in libellum.
Ecce liber paruus/res magna/ars multa Mathefis
Pulcer opus pulcrum condidit arte noua.
Cernere quippe licet tractus terrae orbe fub ifto
Quae regio Antipodas miraq; monftra ferat
Quae ignotae gentes Antarctica ſydera ſpectent
Quas calor exurat, Quas praemat algor iners.

ABOVE

Title page of
*Luculentissima
quaedam terrae
totius descriptio*
('A Most Lucid
Description of All
Lands'), Johann
Schöner, 1515

interests in astronomy and the three children he had with his concubine. On one, made in 1515, he shows a strait of water between 'Basilie Regio' (or Tierra del Fuego) and South America, a full five years before Ferdinand Magellan (1480–1521) actually discovered it. He was the also the first to make a pair of matching terrestrial and celestial globes, the second of which may well have formed the model for that shown in Hans Holbein's celebrated painting of *The Ambassadors* (1533).

By 1530 Gemma Frisius had produced his *De principiis astronomiae & cosmographiae decque vsu globi* ('On the principles of astronomy and cosmography through the use of the globe'), a manual for aspiring terrestrial globe-makers (which may explain his excessive enthusiasm for their production). The rest of the 16th century saw no let-up in their production, with masterpieces such as the diminutive 11-cm (4¼-in) diameter celestial globe by Caspar Vopel, which is encased in a cradle of 11 metal rings to form a complex armillary sphere. Gerard Mercator (1512–94), too, turned his hand to constructing terrestrial globes, some of which are marked with stars to guide the confused terrestrial traveller at night. The masters of later 16th-century globe-making, however, were the Van Langren family, one of whom made the first map of the Moon. Arnold Floris van Langren (*c.* 1525–1610) had been a pupil of the astronomer Tycho Brahe, who created a massive celestial sphere, some 2.7 m (9 ft) in diameter at his Uraniborg observatory in Denmark, and it was perhaps there that he developed his taste for globes. Van Langren's earliest masterpiece, a 33-cm (13-in) diameter terrestrial globe built around 1586, took advantage of the increasing skill of conventional Dutch cartographers such as Lucas Janszoon Waghenaer (see p.55), and began a period of about a century in which Dutch globe-makers such as Willem Janszoon Blaeu (1571–1638) became dominant.

Blaeu's 1617 globes, which had a diameter of 68 cm (27 in), were the largest produced until that date in a market which had become focused more on luxury tastes than the practicalities of navigation at sea (where such leviathans would have been impractical). Just as the middle of the century saw the scales of global maritime supremacy begin to tilt towards the British, so London became the centre of a new, thriving trade in globe-making, beginning with Joseph Moxon (1627–91) who spent much of his youth in the Netherlands where his Puritan father had fled to avoid religious persecution. On his return to London about 1650 he used what he had learnt there to print maps and build globes, two of which the diarist Samuel Pepys acquired. He also produced globes at the opposite end of the size scale from

LEFT

Pair of globes
(terrestrial and
celestial) for Sultan
Murad III, Gerard
Mercator, 1579

OPPOSITE

Terrestrial table
globe, Jacob Floris
van Langren, 1589

Blaeu, his business catalogue described his 1670 globe as 'Concave hemispheres of the starry orb, which serves for a case to a terrestrial globe of 3″ diameter made portable for the pocket', making him arguably the inventor of the pocket globe.

In patriotic fashion, Moxon's diminutive globe showed the course of Sir Francis Drake's circumnavigation of the world, but he, and other British globe-makers such as Robert Morden (*c*. 1650–1703) who created a larger 76-cm (30-in) globe in 1675, faced stiff competition in the international market. Vincenzo Coronelli (1650–1718) like many cartographers a cleric (in his case a Franciscan monk), created a huge pair of globes for Louis XIV of France in the early 1680s, with a diameter of over 3.85 m (12½ ft). The fee he received from the king was a handy addition to his already comfortable stipend of 400 florins a month as Official Cosmographer of the Venetian Republic. It was also part of a gigantism in globe-production that would culminate in such monsters as that presented by Duke Frederick of Holstein-Gottorp to Tsar Peter the Great of Russia in 1714, which was over 3.1 m (10 ft) in diameter and had a door through which a dozen people could cram into the interior to experience a planetarium-like effect on a celestial sphere inscribed on the inside, or the even more gargantuan 9.7-m (31¾-ft) *Pancosmos* created by the German globe-maker Erhard Weigel (1625–99), into which an even larger crowd could squeeze, to be treated to displays of meteorological phenomena such as fog and lightning.

Globe-makers such as John Senex (1678–1740), best known for his conventional *English Atlas* of 1714, carried on the tradition in London, which was inherited by George Adams (1709–72) who achieved the cartographic heights of mathematical instrument-maker to the Board of Ordnance in 1748 and provided maps, instruments and globes to James Cook's expedition to the South Seas to observe the Transit of Venus in 1769.

As the expedition of Cook and other European explorers, particularly in Africa, filled in the blanks in European maps, globe production spread to all corners of the world they portrayed, with the first successful

manufacturer in the United States being James Wilson (1763–1855), who made his first globes in his Vermont farmhouse and never travelled outside New England to see the world portrayed on his work. By then globes had become a fixture in the libraries of educated households and in school classrooms. What had once been a novel and almost mystical way of comprehending the universe, was now commonplace.

CHAPTER 6

SURFACE MATTERS

MATERIALS FOR DRAWING MAPS

On what surface is the map to be drawn? For a long time the answer to this question would have appeared obvious: on paper, on course. Yet in the 21st century doubt is creeping in. Most of the maps we summon on our phones or computer screens exist in a kind of electronic limbo, as intangible data in an innumerable collection of computer servers that make up 'the cloud'. It's a return to an era more than 2,000 years ago, when paper was not yet even invented and maps were drawn, inscribed, engraved and, in some cases, chiselled on a surprising variety of surfaces.

The very first maps may have been ephemeral affairs scratched in the dirt with sticks, which soon washed away. Something of this tradition, but with a philosophical bent, survived in the sand mandalas created by Tibetan Buddhists.

Mandalas are a representation of the Buddhist universe (and are yet another form of ideological or religious mapping) and appear as early as the 1st century AD on carvings and in manuscripts. A physical representation of a mental or sacred space, they act as a guide to meditation as the observer works his way

through the labyrinth of representations and meanings portrayed on them. In the 15th century, Tibetan Buddhists took this one stage further by creating mandalas made of brightly coloured sand. First mentioned by the Buddhist scholar Gos lo tsa ba Ghzon ndu dpal in 1476–78, their value lies partly in their very impermanence: they are created to be contemplated and then destroyed in a gesture symbolic of the transience of all physical things and as a lesson in not becoming too attached to material objects.

RIGHT

Marshall Islands
'stick map',
c. 1920s

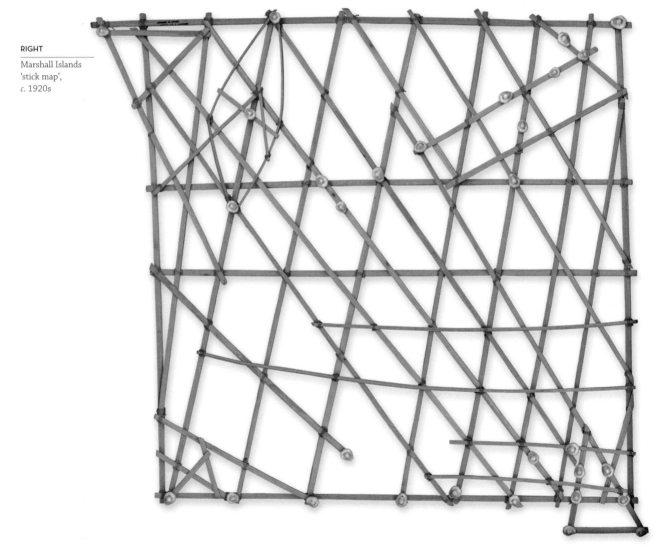

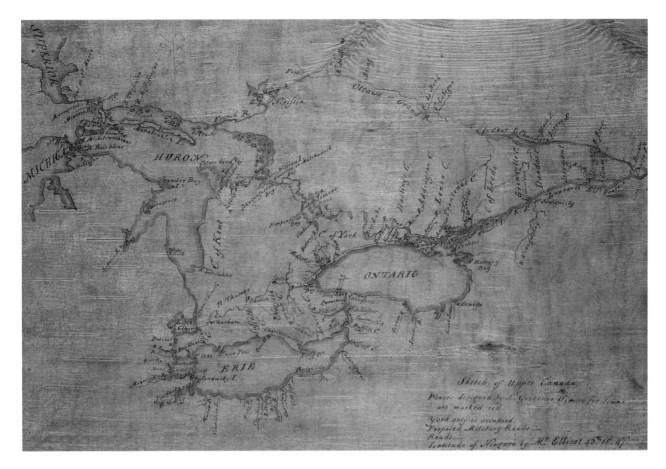

ABOVE

Sketch of
Upper Canada
on birchbark,
Elizabeth Simcoe,
c. 1795

Slightly more permanent than sand (although likely to decay unless carefully preserved) are maps made of wood. A tradition arose in the Pacific, in particular in the Marshall Islands, of 'stick maps' which showed the routes between islands. Their uniqueness lies in the laying of the network of sticks to show ocean swells and currents. These were of vital importance to the early Polynesian navigators who ventured out from around AD 500 on outrigger canoes to conduct voyages of exploration and settlement, which were arguably more impressive than those of European navigators such as Columbus or Magellan a thousand years later. Although the tradition is probably of great antiquity, the techniques were passed in secret within the islands' ruling families and they only came to the notice of outsiders in the 1860s when European missionaries came across them, and a detailed description was only made in the 1890s by a certain Captain Winkler of the Imperial German Navy. He described the main swells, such as the *rilib* or 'backbone', which the Marshallese chronicled on their stick maps, and even the *okar* or interference pattern in currents caused by the presence of a nearby island. Although now superseded by modern navigational devices, the craft of making them

was still alive in the 1960s, giving a sense of the very first attempts that humans must have made to give physical representation to the space around them.

The Marshallese stick maps are not the only maps to have been created from wood, although most have been drawn on its surface rather than using the material as the map itself. European explorers and scientists in North America and Siberia came across maps drawn on birchbark by indigenous peoples. Various species of the *Betula* or beech tree shed their bark in thin layers, providing an ideal medium for sketching maps, a practice that seems to have been particularly common among the Algonquian and Iroquoian peoples around the Great Lakes. The French explorer René-Robert de la Salle (1643–87) – a complex character who gave up his vocation to be a Jesuit missionary because of 'moral weakness' but who explored the Mississippi for France as far as its basin in Louisiana – came across one in 1687 among the Cenis people. This showed 'a map of their country, of that of their neighbours, and of the river Colbert, or Mississippi' and the memory of how to make them seems to have still been alive at least two centuries later along the east coast of the United States and Canada.

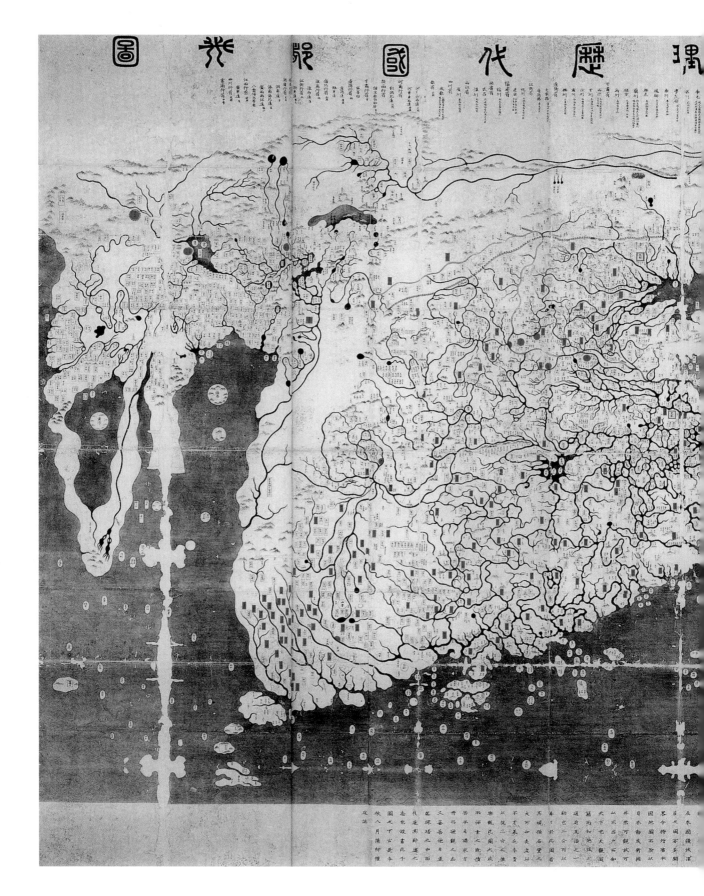

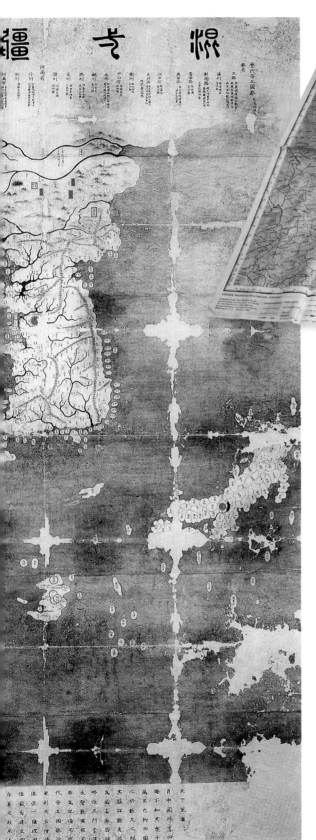

ABOVE

OSS Escape and
Evasion Map
printed on silk, US
Central Intelligence
Agency, 1944

Even more apparently perishable, but of
enduring importance in the history of cartography,
were maps drawn on silk. The earliest surviving
examples are the Mawangdui maps, found in a
Han-era tomb and dating from around 168 BC (see
p.22), at a time when the use of silk for documents
in general had become widespread. We know that
there must have been earlier examples, however, as
one of them played a central role in an assassination
attempt on Prince Zheng of the state of Qin. Not
long before the final stages of his campaign to unite
China – he became its first emperor and took the
title Qin Shih Huang Di in 231 BC – Zheng received
a message that a defector from the rival state of
Yan had gained possession of a map which bore
intelligence of vital military importance. Having a
weakness for maps in general, the prince admitted
Jing Ke, the defector, but the plot failed, as the
would-be assassin bungled his strike, and Zheng
was saved by his chief physician who bludgeoned
him into submission with his medical bag.

Textile maps had a long career in East Asia – the
Kangnido map of the world, made in Korea in 1402
is one notable example – but they were produced
independently by other cultural traditions. When the
Spanish arrived in Mexico and overthrew the Aztec
Empire in 1521, among the items of plunder which
they could not simply melt down for bullion (resulting
in the wholesale destruction of much of the Aztec
artistic production) were maps drawn on cloth created

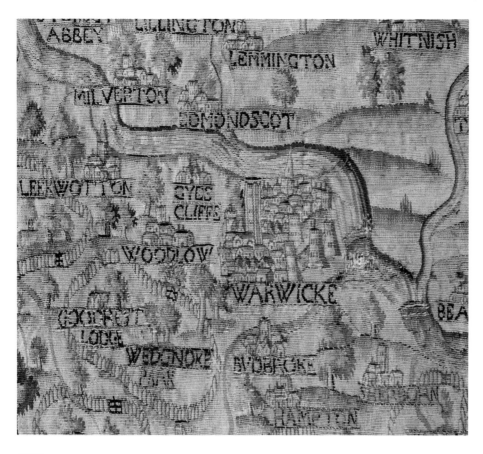

By the time Europeans encountered cloth maps in Mesoamerica, they had already adopted the practice in Europe, although woven with wool rather than agave or silk. The tradition of lavish tapestries – products of the high-end weaving houses of the Netherlands or East Anglia – which adorned the houses of the nobility and the palaces of royalty was extended to maps. One such example displayed in Greenwich Palace on the occasion of a feast attended by Henry VIII in May 1527, was designed by Nicholas Kratzer, the royal astronomer, and described as 'a connying [cunning] thing'. A particularly fine set of tapestries was created by William Sheldon, who owned a weaving business at Barcheston in Warwickshire, but who engaged in a fortuitous piece of self-promotion by producing sets of huge county maps of Gloucestershire, Oxfordshire and Worcestershire, as well as his home county. At 6 x 4 m (20 x 13 ft) in extent, they must certainly have been eye-catching and a sign of how cartographic tapestries could be used for ostentatious display. Not long after, Lord Howard of Effingham - Queen Elizabeth I's Lord High Admiral and the commander of the fleet that defeated the Spanish Armada in 1588 – commissioned the Dutch weaver François Spierincx to produce a new set of map tapestries to celebrate his triumph. He called on the best artistic talent available, with the designs made by the Dutch artist Hendrik Cornelisz Vroom (1562–1640), the greatest early Dutch

by weaving the fibres of the agave plant. Although the conquistador Hernán Cortes (1485–1547) is said to have been shown cloth maps illustrating the whole of the Aztec Empire, one of the very few to survive is the Map of Metlaltoyuca, named after the town in the state of Puebla where it was found hidden in a stone box in the 19th century. It portrays an as-yet unidentified town, with a stepped pyramid temple in the centre surrounded by a network of rivers and roads, and glyphs which denote regional boundaries (which, too, have not been deciphered).

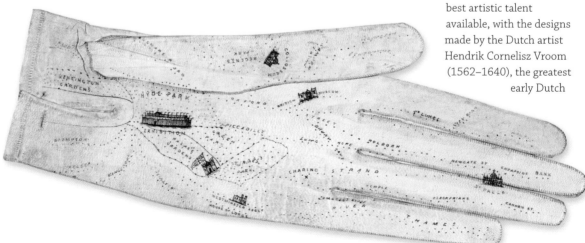

maritime painter, and the maps designed by the queen's surveyor of buildings, Robert Adams. The resulting 10 tapestries hung in the House of Lords until 16 October 1834, when they were destroyed in the fire that engulfed the Houses of Parliament, fuelled by the huge amount of combustible material stored there, including centuries of the Exchequer's records and Sheldon's maps.

On a far different scale, but still employing fabric as the medium for the map, were the 'glove maps' which came into vogue in Victorian London. One set, produced by the London corn merchant George Shove, showed a plan of the Great Exhibition of 1851 and the surrounding area, ensuring that the owner never got lost as the map was, quite literally, always on hand.

Such perishable mediums are somewhat at odds with the desire for permanence exhibited by many of the earliest maps and their creators. We have already seen how some of the very first were created on clay tablets, such as the Nuzi field map which dates from Mesopotamia around 2300 BC, or the town plan of Nippur from about 1500 BC (see p.18), which were baked after being inscribed with the maps, a process that ensured their long-term survival. Even earlier, the Tepe Gawra jar from around 4500 BC is the first example of the painting of maps onto a ceramic base,

41228

ABOVE

Pottery ostracon
of a temple plan
from Deir el-Bahri,
Egypt, *c.* 1250 BC

from the beginning, such as the Çatal Höyük fresco map from Neolithic Anatolia, which dates from *c.* 6200 BC (see p.16) and the *Bedolina Map*, from northern Italy's Val Camonica, which comprises a series of petroglyphs, which have been interpreted as a topographic map incised into a rock around just over 4 m (13½ ft) long, including what may be the huts of villages, trackways and fields.

The *Bedolina Map* was drawn sometime between 1600 and 1000 BC, by which time another set of inhabitants of the Italian peninsula had built both states of vastly greater complexity and longevity and maps of far greater sophistication. The Roman genius for engineering and determination to lay out their new settlements into intricately surveyed plots (see p.29) found its expression in stone, such as the cadastral (or survey) map from Arausio (modern Orange) in southern France produced about AD 77. Existing now only in a series of fragments, when complete it was probably affixed to a wall, a very public demonstration of who was supposed to own which plot of land. That this was a very live issue is proven by the inscription which accompanied the cadastral maps. This related that the survey had been compiled under the Emperor Vespasian (*r.* AD 69–79) to bring order to the muddle of land rights to plots originally granted to the soldiers of the II

a technique that was still going strong in 19th-century Japan when plates, bowls and sake cups showing maps of Japan and the imperial capital Kyushu were produced in large quantities (and in commemorative plates and bowls into the 21st century).

Stone, perhaps the most durable surface of all, was used as the base on which to draw maps right

RIGHT

Detail of the
Bedolina Map, Val
Camonica, Italy,
1000–1600 BC

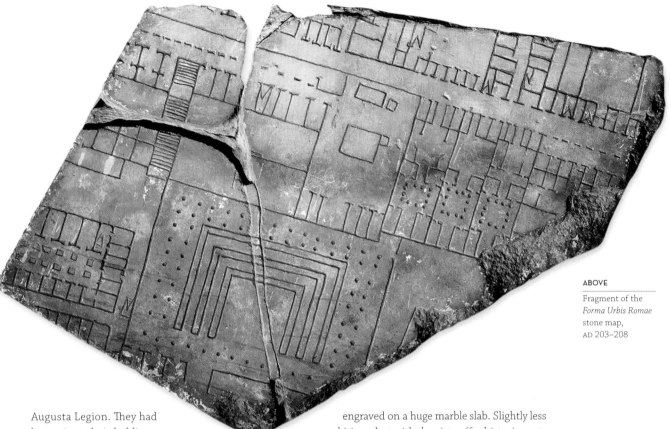

Augusta Legion. They had been given their holdings around 35 BC, by Octavian, soon to become Emperor Augustus, during his protracted campaigns against the assassins of his adoptive father Julius Caesar and other rivals for supreme power in Rome's domains. Some had sold their plot, subdivided it or otherwise alienated it, creating a confusing patchwork, where once there had a regimented pattern, divided into rectangular plots of 33½ *iugera* (this was a Roman land measure originally supposed to be the amount of land a single ox could plough without resting, but in deference to the fact that some farmer's beasts were more energetic than others, it was regularized at an area of 240 by 120 Roman feet, or around 0.25 hectares). The map as a consequence includes fine details such as annotations for *rei publicae*, land retained by the state; *reliqua coloniae*, land owned in common by the community; and *subsecivae*, the tiny slivers of land at the edge of the whole survey, in between surveyed plots or for which the owners could not be identified.

A map of the entire world (or at least the Roman-controlled part, which amounted to a substantial portion of that known) was erected by Augustus's lieutenant Marcus Vipsanius Agrippa (see p.47),

engraved on a huge marble slab. Slightly less ambitious, but with the virtue (for historians at least) of having survived in part is the *Forma Urbis Romae* (known as the Severan Marble Plan), a monumental 13 x 18 m (43 x 60 ft) map of the city of Rome itself which, from the evidence of the latest buildings included in it (an ornamental gateway called the Septizonium), was made shortly after AD 203 during the reign of the Emperor Septimius Severus. Extraordinarily, the holes showing where the map was fixed for public display are still visible on a wall just outside of the Church of Saints Cosmas and Damian in central Rome.

A slight variant on maps in stone or marble are mosaic maps, constructed with thousands of tiny glass tesserae intricately fitted together to form an overall pattern. The most spectacular of these is a map of the Holy Land on the floor of the church of St George in Madaba, Jordan. Originally created in the 550s or 560s (it shows the Church of the Theotokos, dedicated in Jerusalem in 542, but not buildings erected there after 570), its depiction of the area from Lebanon to the Nile Delta originally contained over 2 million tesserae. Unsurprisingly, for such a magnificent object designed for display in a church, it focuses mainly on sites of biblical importance, and in particular those of significance

RIGHT

Jerusalem, Madaba
mosaic map,
c. AD 550

BELOW RIGHT

Celestial globe,
Ibn as-Said as-
Sahli, 1085

for the life of Christ (Jerusalem is shown with a
particularly high level of detail), although
embellished with rather more secular decorative
flourishes such as a lion hunting a gazelle in
the Moab desert and fish swimming in the
River Jordan.

Stone maps were by no means confined
to Europe and the Middle East. After a long
cartographic hiatus in China following the Han silk
maps (see p.107), maps of the Chinese Empire begin
to appear in the 12th century during the Song
dynasty in the form of a series of stone maps. The
earliest of these, the *Jiu yu shouling tu* ('Map of the
Prefectures of the Nine Districts') was engraved in
1121 in Rongzhou (now in Sichuan) and includes the
names of more than 1,400 administrative districts,
while a single stele engraved with two separate maps
was set up there around 1136. The more detailed of
these, the *Yu ji tu* ('Map of the Tracks of Yu'), shows a
remarkably accurate coastline of eastern China and
also includes the first appearance of a reference grid
in cartographic history – a finely engraved lattice of
squares, the sides of each of which were 100 *li* (a unit
which has varied in extent throughout Chinese
history, and now represents 500 m/1,460 ft, but
which under the Song was just over 400 m/1,310 ft).

Almost as durable a surface for cartography as
stone are various metals on which maps have been
engraved through the ages. As metal can be smelted
and shaped in moulds, it is generally a more flexible
medium (and mistakes are easier to repair than they

are on stone), although the ability to melt down a metal object (particularly if it is of a precious metal, such as gold or silver) means that the chances of maps in metal surviving are correspondingly slighter. The Frankish ruler Charlemagne (*r.* 768–814) is said to have possessed three silver tablets, which bore maps of the imperial cities of Rome and Constantinople, with the third showing the entire world (presumably, if the subject matter of the first two is an indication, based on a long-lost Roman model). These, however, have long since disappeared. So, too, has the 2-m (6½-ft) diameter disc containing a map of the world created by the Arab cartographer Muhammad al-Sharif al-Idrisi (*c.* 1100–66) for his patron Roger II of Sicily in 1153. Created using over 180 kg (400 lb) of pure silver, the value of its raw materials alone meant that it was probably melted down not long after Roger's death the following year. More fortunate was the fate of the celestial globe, or astrolabe, created by the Arab astronomer Ibn as-Said as-Sahli in 1085 in Valencia. Some 20 cm (8 in) in diameter and made of brass, it is the earliest Islamic globe charting the heavens to escape destruction and includes the positions of 1,042 stars in the night sky.

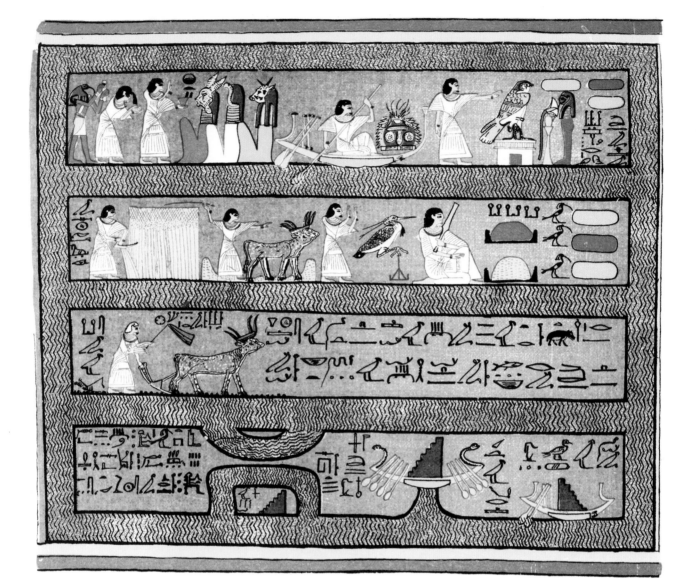

ABOVE

Occupations of Ani
in Elysian Fields,
Papyrus of Ani,
c. 1250 BC

Smaller-scale (and less precious) metal maps, however, have survived, notably the Borgia world map, made around 1430 and engraved on two copperplates riveted together, filled with black ink to pick out the details. The rather intriguing object, which has 37 holes drilled into it, possibly for attaching flags or emblems of important cities or countries (which have long since disappeared), is of unknown provenance, having been found by chance by Cardinal Stefano Borgia in an antiques shop in Portugal in 1794. Oriented to the south (as are a number of 15th-century world maps, such as that of Fra Mauro, see p.84), the most obvious signs of the era in which it was composed are the lack of the Americas (still six decades away from their encounter with Europeans) and the non-inclusion of the fruits

of the Portuguese voyaging around the coast of West Africa, which got under way in the 1430s. Adding to the almost medieval cast of the map is the cartographer's populating of practically every otherwise empty space with a variety of flora and fauna. These include a polar bear emerging from an igloo in Norway, a veritable flotilla of ships from coastal barges to galleys and ocean-going vessels, and a variety of annotations warning of 'huge men with horns four feet long' in India, of serpents that could swallow an ox whole and of the debatable lands between China and the Earthly Paradise, which are hazardous to cross on account of their being infested by cannibals.

Rather later, in the age of printing, many maps while not appearing in their final form in metal, were originally engraved on metal plates, which were then used to create the image (alongside the main text) in a printed book. One of the most intriguing of these is known as the *Copperplate Map of London*. Originally on 15 plates, of which just three have survived, it was most probably created in 1558 (as it shows a cross in the churchyard of St Botolph-without-Bishopsgate, which was destroyed in an anti-Catholic riot that year) and shows a dense labyrinth of medieval streets in the City of London, a sign of how such a city had grown organically without any sense of town planning.

The most common medium on which maps are produced today is of course paper, a flat and relatively smooth surface which is ideally suited to the printing press. It was preceded by papyrus, made from reeds that grew prolifically along the banks of the River Nile and which was used for a huge number of

documents, many of which have survived because they were interred in tombs or discarded in rubbish dumps, where the dry conditions in Egypt's deserts impeded their decay. Among them are relatively few actual maps, although the 12th-century BC *Turin Papyrus* showing a mineral-rich section of the Eastern Desert indicate that these must have existed (see p.19). There are, though, a larger number of map-like objects, such as those associated with the magic required by the deceased to survive in the afterlife, which show such exotic locations as the Fields of the Dead, providing a guide for the soul in its post-mortem journey.

For much of the ancient and medieval world, where papyrus reeds were not available, animal skins were used instead. Cut from calves, cows or sheep (and occasionally goats), these were cleaned with lime

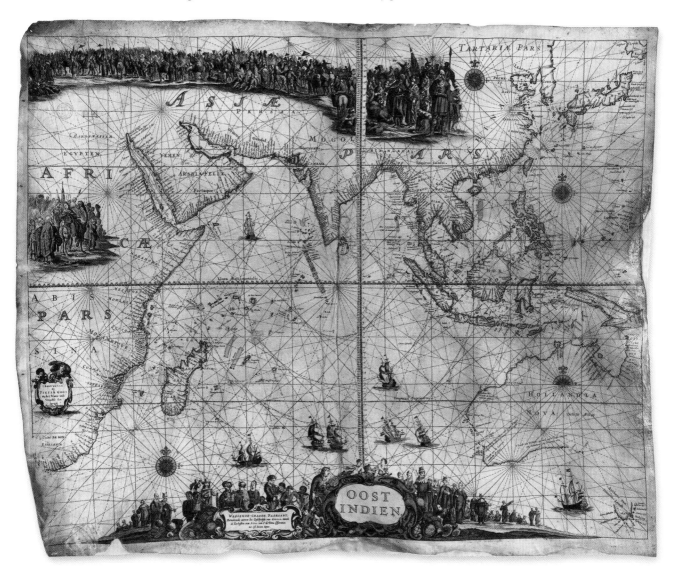

and then stretched on frames to produce vellum or parchment. Such day-to-day maps as the Romans produced for administrative purposes must have been drawn on such a surface, but it is only from the later Middle Ages that we have surviving maps, including the *Anglo-Saxon Mappa Mundi* (dating from *c*. 1000, see p.120) and the whole gamut of *mappae mundi*. Most of the portolans, which navigators used to find their way around the Mediterranean, were also produced on vellum and even after the advent of the printing press in the 1450s, its durability in the unavoidably damp conditions at sea (with the animal skin being able to absorb more moisture without

perishing) meant that it was in use as late as the 1680s, when the Dutch cartographer Pieter Goos's chart of *Oost Indien* ('the East Indies') was published.

In mapping terms, though, it was paper that became king, even though it took a long time for it to establish its global dominance. It was allegedly devised by the Chinese imperial official Cai Lun around AD 105, who after his appointment as chief of the palace workshop dedicated to producing instruments, resolved to find some more economical way of producing manuscripts other than the very expensive silk or the rather inconvenient bamboo. His use of what would otherwise have been waste material, such as rag, bark and even fishing nets, took a while to catch on and even longer to travel westwards out of China, reaching Baghdad around 793, and from there being transmitted to Europe, where paper mills are recorded in Italy in the 13th century. In Japan, maps were produced on paper as early as the 8th century, but in Europe, paper's heyday, for books in general as well as maps, only came from the later 15th century, after the invention of printing, with the first printed map appearing in a 1472 edition of Isidore of Seville's venerable *Etymologiae* (a work originally dating from the 7th century).

Since then, many thousands of maps have appeared on paper, in atlases, single-sheet maps or embedded in other works, dwarfing the entire production of maps in all other media through history. Its seemingly unchallengeable position was only threatened in the age of computing, with the first Global Information Systems (GIS) on mainframe computers in the 1950s. Now, though, in the 21st century, billions of smartphone users

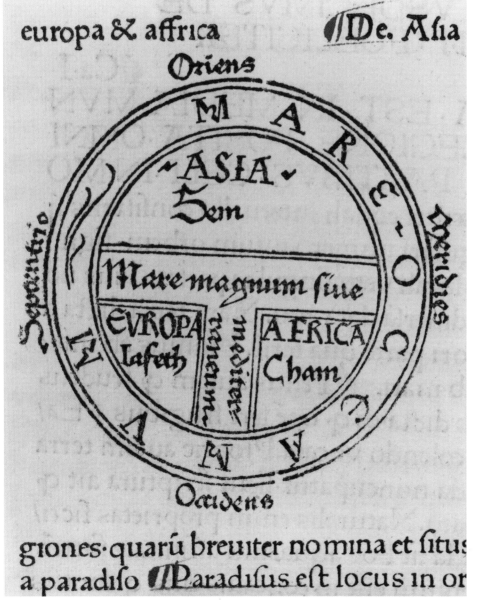

can summon up a map of their location (or almost any other on the planet) in a few clicks, touches or swipes. From their very first appearance on stone, and through all the permutations of durable, more perishable and even ephemeral media, maps now exist in numberless quantities in the flickering of liquid crystal displays or light-emitting diodes, or the even more intangible medium of data stored electronically on myriad computer servers.

ABOVE AND LEFT

Now everyone can easily summon a map wherever they go

CHAPTER 7

A MAP OF MANY PARTS

THE COMPONENTS OF A MAP

Having resolved to draw a map, established what the map's purpose (overt or implicit) should be, and having gathered the information – whether through surveys, travellers' accounts or simply modifying those to compile it – the would-be cartographer now must decide on the best way to translate all this onto the surface of the map or globe.

Even the simple matter of which way should be 'up' is not as straightforward as it seems, and there is no compelling reason why north should be at the 'top', as it is in most modern maps. The very word 'orient', in the sense of alignment, is a clue to this, as in Latin *oriens* means east, and many medieval maps were oriented with east at the top, as this was the direction of Jerusalem and the Holy Land, considered the most important element in medieval Christian maps. Typical of these *mappae mundi* (or maps of the world), is the *Anglo-Saxon Mappa Mundi* created around 1025.

The earliest surviving map drawn in England, it reflects the state of geographical knowledge at the time, showing only Asia, Africa and Europe, the three continents known to the ancients. The outline of each, even the Mediterranean, is very schematic, with a bloated starfish-shaped Sicily in the west and a blood-red gash marking the Nile Delta in the east wavering into fable as it proceeds further into the continent (where an 'ever-burning mountain', *mons semper ardens*, is marked). The curiously angular nature of the map means that many of the landmasses are compressed into odd shapes,

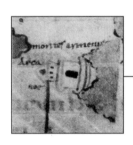

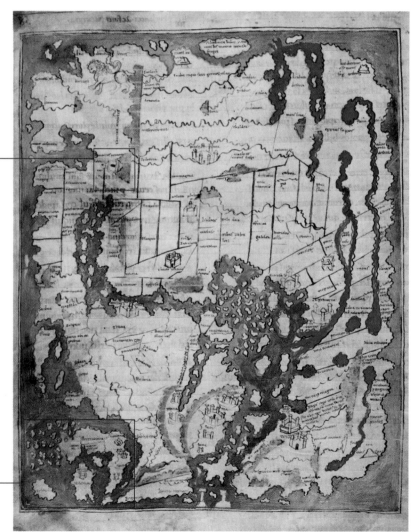

and in Asia its coverage peters out at the Red Sea, beyond which the cartographer only had myths to portray, such as those of the giant Gog and Magog, rather than geographical realities. In deference to its place of composition, somewhere in England, the map's outline of Britain and Ireland is more secure, though Cornwall – over which two knights fight for an unknown prize – is dramatically enlarged. Amid all its 150 or so place names and annotations – among which Armagh in Ireland makes its cartographic debut – it is clear that the accent is on the biblical, with Noah's Ark perched atop Mount Ararat somewhere in Armenia, and to retain the focus on Jerusalem and the lands of the Bible, the orientation has east at the top (which explains Britain's rather uneasily squashed position at the bottom left of the map).

If east was the direction of choice for medieval Christian cartography, for Arab geographers it was instead the south, the direction of the holy city of Mecca. Typical of this is the world map of Muhammad al-Sharif al-Idrisi (c. 1100–66), who, though a Muslim, around 1138 took service at the court of the Christian Roger II of Sicily – a haven of comparative, if short-lived, tolerance, where a syncretic culture flourished. The surviving world map comes from a collection of 70, which illustrated all parts of the known world, though not in a precious a form as the enormous silver disc, described as '400 Roman *ratls* in weight' on which was inscribed 'a map of the seven climates', which had formed its model. As the centrepiece of the *Nuzhat al-mushtaq fi'khtiraq al-afaq* ('The Entertainment for He who Longs to Travel the World'), more laconically known as the *Book of Roger*, al-Idrisi's map has south at the top. Its bounding ocean a striking ribbon of blue, it does suffer the inconvenience that the lands south of the Nile are largely a blank, though still focusing the mind somewhat on the Arabian Peninsula (and Mecca)

ABOVE

World map showing south at the top, Muhammad al-Sharif al-Idrisi, 1154.

in the centre and, somewhat conveniently in view of his royal patron, contriving to have Sicily somewhere near centre stage.

Other orientations are of course possible – the *Forma Urbis Romae*, the fragmentary 3rd-century AD map of the city of Rome points towards the south-east – but west, apart from a handful of ancient Chinese maps, never seems to have been a popular option. Instead, north became the predominant choice, at first in China, most probably because the north emerged as the centre of imperial power: at Chang'an (now Xi'an), the capital under the Han (221 BC– AD 220) and Tang (AD 618–907) dynasties; at Kaifeng, under the early Song (939 –1127); and at sites in and around Beijing from the Jin dynasty (1153 onwards), through the Mongol rule over China in the 13th and 14th century and then into modern times. In Europe, north probably first gained a foothold because the series of co-ordinates left by

Model of an early
magnetic Chinese
compass

map. As already remarked,
most Christian topography,
as well as having the maps
oriented east, had Jerusalem
in the central position. Often,
like the *Hereford Mappa Mundi*,
such maps are crowded with
towns and other locations
from the life of Christ, acting
more as spiritual than practical
geographical guides. Given a
choice, however, most cultures
have tended to place their own
state or country at the centre.
The striking 18th-century
circular *Cheonhado* world
maps produced in Korea
have a stylized appearance,
with China and the Korean
peninsula firmly at the centre,
surrounded by a set of
concentric circles of lands and
seas, all enfolded by trees to
the east and west showing the
directions of the rising and
setting of the sun. Produced
over a period of nearly 200
years, they conformed to quite
rigid parameters. Despite
adopting different visual styles

the 2nd-century AD Greco-Roman geographer and
astronomer Ptolemy which could be – and in the later
Middle Ages and Renaissance were – used to create a
series of regional and world maps, implied that north
was at the top. Added to this, the magnetic compass
– forms of which were first invented in China around
the 2nd century BC and which by the early 12th
century AD was in practical use as a maritime
navigation technique – privileged a north–south view
of the world (Chinese compasses actually pointed
south rather than north!). The device had reached
Europe by at least 1190, when the English monk
Alexander Neckam makes reference in his *De naturis
rerum* ('On the Nature of Things') to a magnetized
needle to help mariners navigate. Gerard Mercator's
world map of 1569, which acted as the blueprint for
subsequent generations of cartographers, cemented
north's position as being firmly at the top, and from
then habit and convention took over to leave most
subsequent printed maps as north-facing.

Allied to the question of orientation is that of the
meridian, or the choice of central position for the

(from rather plain drab grey to the outright gaudy),
they almost all have the same number of place names
(around 144), with some of them entirely fictitious,
such as the 'Land of the Hairy People' and the
intriguingly named 'Land of the One-Armed'. World
maps produced in Europe after the discovery of the
Americas tended to have Europe at the centre, and
hence the newly encountered lands of North and
South America to the left of the sheet and Asia to
the right.

Similarly, maps produced in Russia placed Moscow
in the privileged centre position. In the United States,
a number of cities competed for the prize of the prime
meridian, including Philadelphia (where a meridian is
recorded as early as 1749), New York (which has a
zero meridian drawn through it on the map compiled
by Claude Joseph Sauthier in 1776), and Washington,
whose claims grew more compelling after its selection
as the national capital in 1790. Even then, a number
of different lines were surveyed, each purporting to
be the true meridian. The 1791 plan by Major Pierre
Charles L'Enfant (1754–1825) – a French-born

military engineer who served in the Continental Army during the American Revolution and, after a post-war career designing furniture for the well-heeled among the new elite, was appointed by George Washington to design the new federal capital – shows a meridian passing through the 'Congress House'. By 1804, maps were showing a meridian passing through the 'President's House', the origin of the Zero Milestone monument just south of the White House from which distances from Washington to other points in the country were supposed to be measured. By 1850, Congress had adopted a measure ordering 'that hereafter the meridian of the observatory at Washington shall be adopted and used as the American meridian for all astronomic purposes and ... Greenwich for all nautical purposes' (with the observatory in question being the Old Naval Observatory, a site whose astronomical operations stretched from 1844 to 1893, and at which two new moons of Mars, Phobos and Deimos, were discovered in 1877).

In short, the matter of the meridian had become an almighty muddle, a problem aggravated by the advent of long-distance train travel, which meant that each town set its own clock according to local observations of sunrise, sunset and noon. Once the transcontinental railroad across the United States was completed (with the ceremonial driving in on 10 May 1869 of a 'golden

BELOW

Tae Choson Chido, Korean world map, 1874.

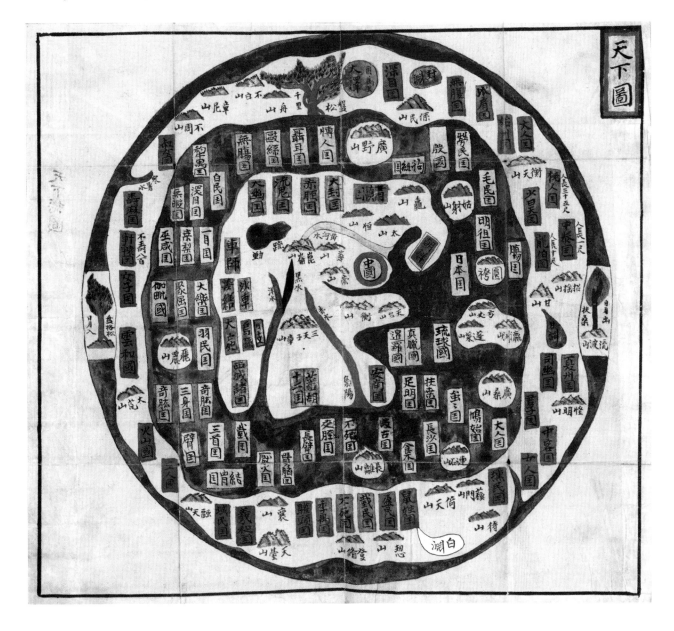

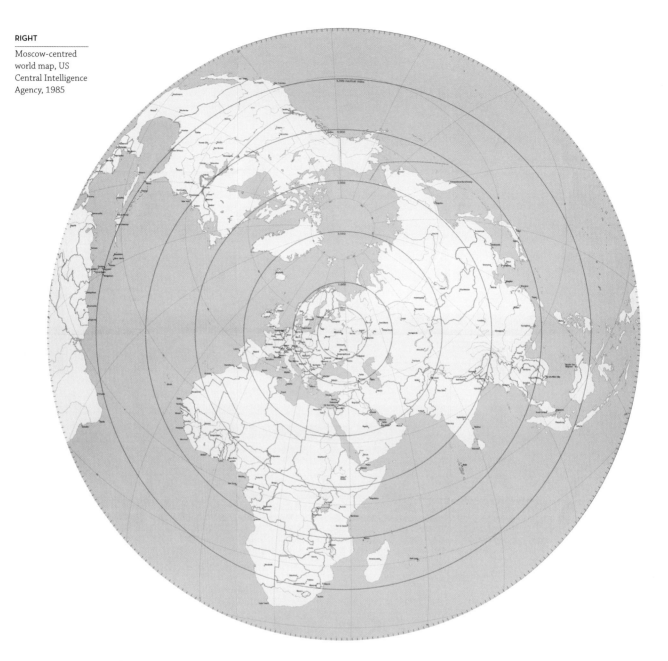

spike' at Promontory Summit, Utah, where the lines of the Central Pacific Railroad, which had been built eastwards, and that of the Union Pacific Railroad, which had been driven westwards from Missouri, met), the problem became even worse. Train timetables had to have dozens of different departure times to take account of the differing stations from which passengers might have departed. The United Kingdom had pioneered a solution when a single 'Greenwich Mean Time' was adopted by Britain's railways in 1848, with a meridian passing through the Royal Observatory in Greenwich. The railway companies in the United States pushed through

a similar measure, all agreeing that from noon on 18 November 1883 there would be four time zones covering the continental landmass (with an additional one in eastern Canada), each an hour apart, anchored at points 75, 90, 105 and 120 degrees of longitude west of Greenwich.

Although Britain and the United States were now provided with the rudiments of a time zone system, and their railway passengers no doubt mightily relieved of the need to resynchronize their pocket watches at every single station along the route, this represented nothing like a universally accepted system. There was a vigorous lobby to resolve this, not least on economic grounds (as having the world's merchant fleet unclear on the exact time was inefficient and occasionally dangerous). The railway engineer Sandford Fleming penned a paper entitled 'Time-Reckoning and the selection of a prime meridian to be common to all nations' in 1879, revealing that eleven principal meridians were in use, including El Hierro in the Canaries, and Cadiz in Spain, but that almost two-thirds of the tonnage of the world's cargo ships used Greenwich.

The logical choice seemed obvious, but political sensibilities were involved (who, after all wanted their national capital to end up as a footnote so many degrees west or east of the prime meridian?). In October 1884, 41 delegates from 25 countries gathered at the International Meridian Conference in Washington, summoned by President Chester Arthur – no doubt pleased at the order so recently created out of his country's previous temporal chaos – to determine once and for all which would be the international prime meridian. It did not take long for the delegates to come to the only viable conclusion, that the meridian would pass through the Greenwich Observatory (and that travelling east from there would count as 'plus' longitude, and westwards as minus). As a sop to those resentful that their own local time had in some way been subordinated, the conference decreed that the new 'universal day ... shall not interfere with the use of local or other standard time where desirable'.

The geographers and astronomers had agreed, but national governments were much slower in coming on board (and the conference itself had not actually mandated a system of time zones, which only slowly emerged by default as various governments declared themselves as being located in one time zone or another). Japan was the first country to do so, in 1886, with France adopting Greenwich Mean Time as the reference point for its own national time in 1911. The United Kingdom itself followed a curiously muddled approach, given it had secured the meridian prize for Greenwich, and it was only in 1925 that *The Nautical Almanac*, with the blessing of the Royal Astronomical Society began to use GMT as its official time.

Deciding where to centre a map is an easy task compared to the next conundrum facing the

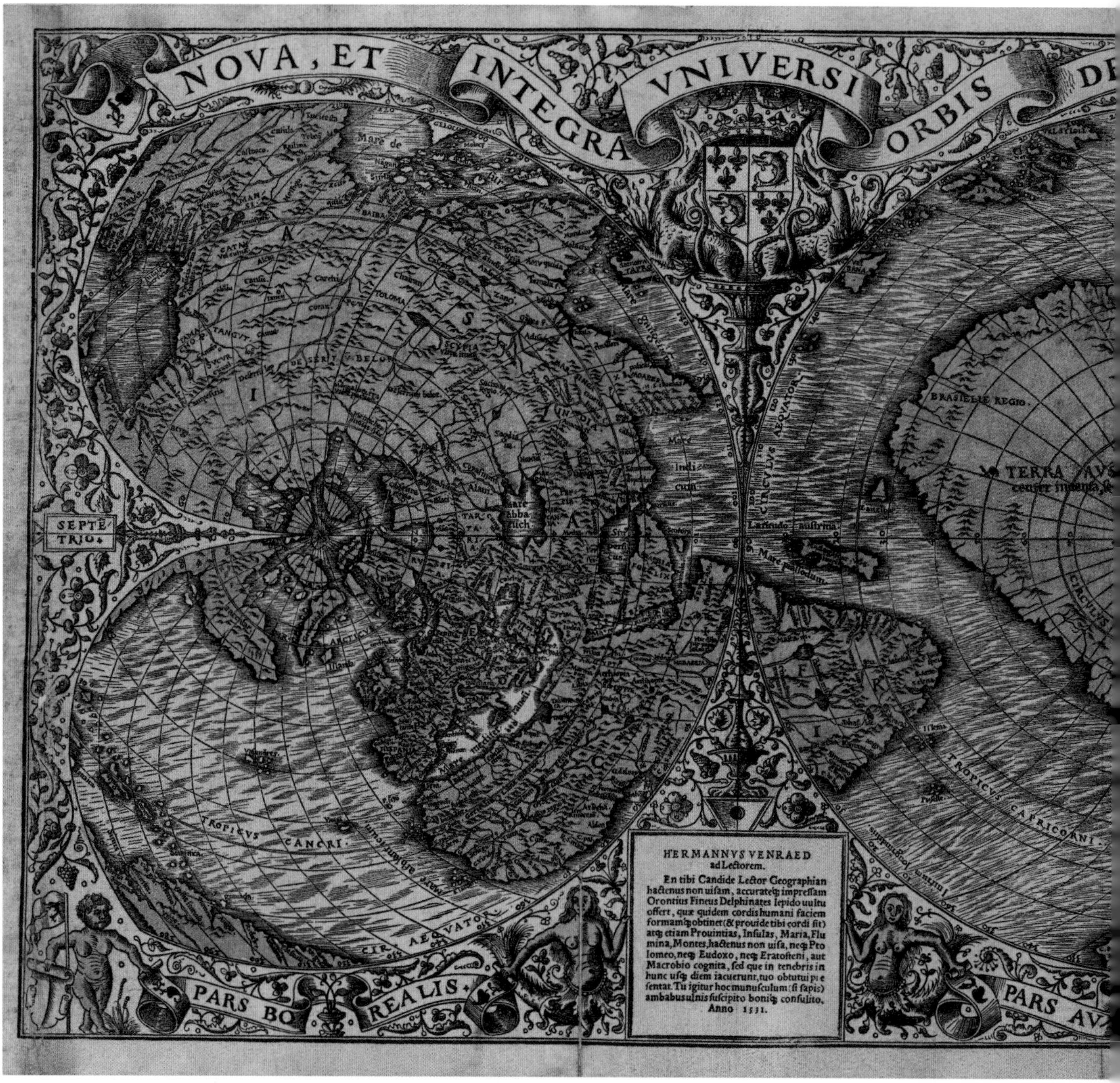
NOVA, ET INTEGRA VNIVERSI ORBIS
SEPTĒ TRIO.
TROPICVS CANCRI
TROPICVS CAPRICORNI
BRASIELIE REGIO
PARS BOREALIS
HERMANNVS VENRAED
ad Lectorem.
En tibi Candide Lector Geographian hactenus non uisam, accurateq; impressam Orontius Fineus Delphinates lepido uultu offert, quæ quidem cordis humani faciem formamq; obtinet (& prouide tibi cordi fit) atq; etiam Prouintias, Insulas, Maria, Flumina, Montes, hactenus non uisa, neq; Ptolomeo, neq; Eudoxo, neq; Eratosteni, aut Macrobio cognita, sed que in tenebris in hunc usq; diem iacuerunt, tuo obtutui presentat. Tu igitur hoc munusculum (si sapis) ambabus ulnis suscipito boniq; consulito.
Anno 1531.

ABOVE

World map with a cordiform projection, Oronce Finé, 1531

cartographer, of which projection to use. The problem arises because the Earth is – more or less – a sphere, but apart from globes on which its surface can be accurately represented, projecting an image of its seas and landmasses onto a flat surface, a map, always involves some form of compromise. It's a little like peeling an orange and trying to lay it flat – there will always be gaps or, if the peel is pushed together, bulges created. Ever since the Greek philosopher Pythagoras in the late 6th century BC, most serious astronomers and geographers had long understood that the Earth was spherical – despite a commonly held misapprehension that ancient and medieval scholars believed that it was flat (which would actually have made map-making considerably easier!). The earliest map-makers, such as Dicaearchus of Messina (*c.* 350–290 BC) and Eratosthenes (*c.* 275–194 BC), generally ignored the problem and it was only Hipparchus (*c.* 190–127 BC) who tried to devise a systematic method of assembling all the points on the map in such a way that, even if there was some distortion of the size of landmasses or the distance

between places, this was at least logical and consistent.

A wide variety of such systems, or projections, eventually emerged. To Hipparchus we owe the stereographic or azimuthal projection, in which the lines of latitude emerge from the Pole and are true there, and in which angles between places are preserved, but the distances are not, and orthographic projections, which portray the surface of the Earth like a hemisphere seen from space, but which particularly distorts shapes and areas near the edge of the map. Mathematical cartography endured a decline during the Middle Ages, during which God not geometry took centre stage in mapping, and it was not until the rediscovery of Ptolemy's mapping co-ordinates in the 15th century that cartographers began to address themselves once more to making a spherical Earth fit into a (largely) rectangular map sheet. Nicolaus Germanus's world map of 1467 used a 'pseudocylindrical' projection (as though the spherical surface had been projected onto a cylindrical piece of paper), while among the more unusual shapes chosen were 'cordiform' (heart-shaped) projections in which the surface of the Earth was divided into two conjoined flat hemispheres, rather like a two-dimensional model of the human heart.

A fine example was compiled by Oronce Finé (1494–1555), a mathematician from the Dauphiné region of France. Although he followed his doctor father in studying medicine, his first loves were mathematics, astronomy and astronomical instruments (he is said to have constructed a sundial while serving a prison sentence for having rashly made a horoscope which was unfavourable to Louise de Savoie, an influential member of the French court). He published an edition of the *Tractatus de sphaero* ('Treaty on the Sphere') by Johannes de Sacrobosco, a 13th-century English monk who gave one of the first accounts accessible to medieval Europeans of Ptolemy's celestial system and wrote no fewer than five works on the equatorium, a rather rare astronomical instrument which displayed the past or future positions of the Sun, Moon and planets according to Ptolemy's model. Finé's monumental *Protomathesis*, published in 1532, includes two volumes on astronomy and astronomical instruments, and it is no surprise that all these mathematical interests fed into his cartography. His 1531 double cordiform map is a tour de force from the point of view of its striking projection, although it includes a

number of cartographic anomalies, such as the enormous 'Terra Australis' on the right-hand (southern) section, necessary to balance the northern landmass according to Ptolemy's theories, and his joining North America firmly to Asia (as the early European explorers of the Americas presumed it was).

The most influential map projection of all, however, was that used by the Flemish cartographer Gerard Mercator in his 1569 world map. Technically a conformal cylindrical projection, it was shaped like a flattened version of a cylinder and devised so that any straight line drawn on the map would represent a constant compass bearing (hence conformal, or retaining correct angles). This also meant that the shapes of landmasses were shown correctly, but their actual sizes might be distorted, becoming proportionately larger towards the Poles and compressed towards the equator. Given that the main purpose of his maps was to facilitate navigation at

sea, this was not a particular hindrance, but has led to much subsequent criticism that his projection – which by the 20th century had become ubiquitous – unfairly magnified the importance of countries in Europe and North America at the expense of many poorer nations, especially in Africa.

All subsequent cartographic projections have been attempts to square this circle, or more accurately to circle the sphere. None of them can ever be entirely true in two dimensions to the stubbornly three-dimensional nature of the Earth's surface. They make these compromises in one of three principal ways: being conformal, retaining the correct angle between two points, and so the 'shape' of the terrain; equivalent, in keeping the areas shown on the map in correct proportion to that in the real world; or equidistant, in doing similarly with the distances between two points. Inevitably one of these will be privileged over the others and in 1973 German

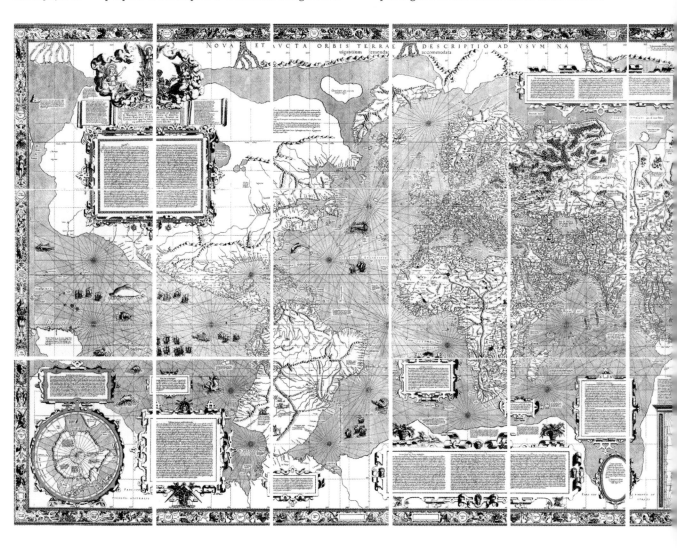

historian Arno Peters (1916–2002) came up with
what he said was a new projection, which produced
more equal areas, though to those used to the
Mercator projection it seemed to strangely elongate
the South American and African continents. In the
furious polemic which accompanied its unveiling, it
became the fashionable choice for those eschewing
old 'colonial' projections, including its adoption by
the United Nations. It was not, of course, entirely
new, being simply a fresh rebalancing of one of the
timeworn three cartographic projection choices.
Moreover, it bore a striking resemblance to the
orthographic projection devised by the Edinburgh
clergyman the Reverend James Gall (1808–95) in
1855. Before becoming a wayfinder for God in his
role as a minister at the Free Church in Canongate,
Gall had been a partner in his family publishing firm,
which specialized in maps. He took the family
speciality very seriously, and as well as the
orthographic projection devised two others, the Gall
isographic and Gall stereographic, presenting all
three at a meeting of the British Association for the
Advancement of Science in Glasgow in 1855. Even
after becoming a cleric in 1858, he continued to

pursue his mapping interests, albeit in a more
low-key fashion, producing an *Easy Guide to the
Constellations* in 1870. His focus on the heavens
is reflected, too, in his more theological works,
including *The Stars and the Angels* (1858) in which
he mused on the possible existence of life on other
planets (and supposed that the Archangel Gabriel
had flown from one of them on his way to announce
to Mary that she was to bear the Messiah).

We are all so familiar with the lines which divide
up most world or regional maps into equal square
areas, that we almost fail to notice them, until trying
(if using a paper map) to find where a particular
location is by reference to the map's index. Most early
maps used lines of latitude and longitude, the former
the angular distance of a point north or south of
the equator, the latter east or west of an arbitrary
meridian (which as we have seen was agreed in
1884 to be the meridian running through the
Royal Observatory at Greenwich). The division into
360 degrees, however, is of much greater antiquity
than this, being based on a Babylonian division of the
heavens – first recorded around 410 BC – and then
extended around 150 BC by the Greek astronomer

RIGHT

Ptolemy's world
map with longitude
and latitude
points, Nicolaus
Germanus, 1467

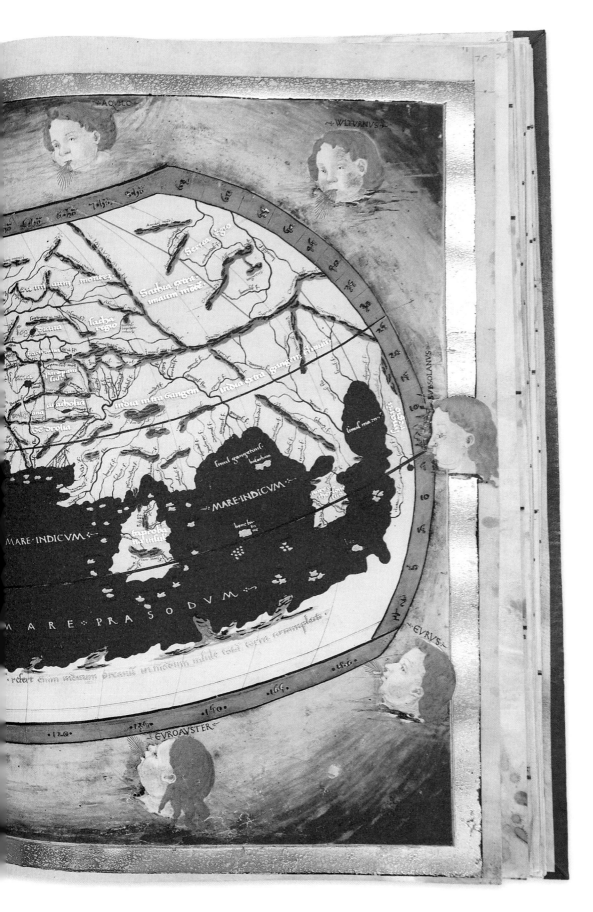

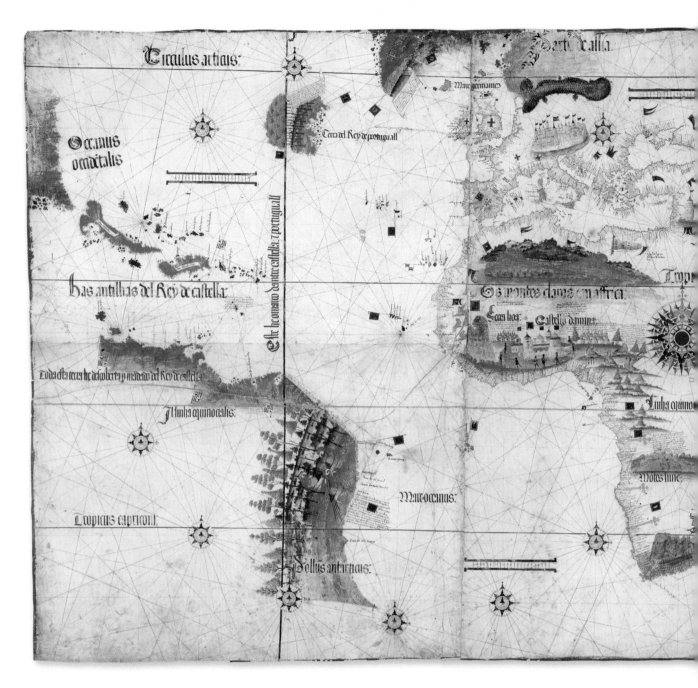

Hipparchus (see p.126) to measurements of the
Earth's surface. He also drew up lists of latitude and
longitude of important places, a system enlarged
around AD 150 by the great Greco-Roman geographer
Ptolemy, whose *Geography* contains co-ordinates for
around 8,000 locations.

Knowledge of the principles of latitude and
longitude was kept alive in the Islamic world, after
the loss of much scholarly knowledge in the West
following the collapse of the Roman Empire. Through
conduits such as Sicily (reconquered by the Normans

from its Muslim Zirid emirs by 1091) and Spain
(where by 1250, advancing Christian armies had
confined the Muslim-controlled territory to Granada),
long-lost learning percolated back into Europe. Gerard
of Cremona (*c.* 1114–87) translated the Arabic version
of Ptolemy's *Almagest* back into Latin, meaning
western European scholars had access once more to
tables of latitude and how to calculate them. The
translation of the *Geography* had to wait until 1406,
and it wasn't until 1477 that the first printed edition
of Ptolemy complete with maps was published in

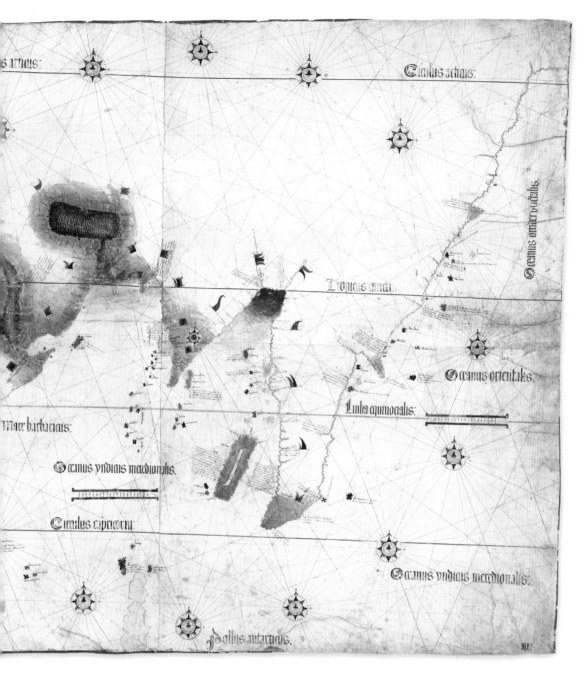

LEFT

Cantino Planisphere,
1502

Bologna. By the time Henricus Martellus Germanus produced his large world map around 1490 and Martin Behaim created the *Erdapfel* globe (see p.89), knowledge of the principles of latitude and longitude had become widely diffused. The first map that actually included some lines of latitude marked on them was the *Cantino Planisphere*, which also had the Tropics of Cancer and Capricorn indicated. The former was so called because it marks the most northerly point at which the Sun's rays strike the Earth at 90 degrees, which takes place at the summer solstice on 21 June,

when the Sun is situated alongside the Constellation of Cancer in the sky. A wobble in the tilt of the Earth's axis as it orbits around the Sun has meant that this position has now shifted, and the equinox now falls when the Sun is in Taurus, although there has been no appreciable campaign to have the latitude line rebadged as the 'Tropic of Taurus'.

Longitude lines took a little longer to catch on – some are shown on the 1477 Ptolemy map and on another published in Rome in 1478. They are, however, largely erroneous and Behaim's globe only

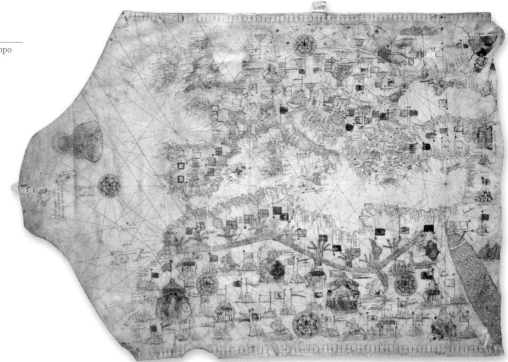

had one line of longitude indicated. The Treaty of Tordesillas, which divided Portuguese and Spanish domains in the New World along a line 270 leagues west of the Azores (see p.200), underlined the importance of being able to calculate longitude and marking it on maps (which occurs with increasing frequency during the 16th century). Determining it accurately at sea, however, proved extremely difficult as it depended on precise timekeeping between two points and no clock existed which could so without losing time, particularly in the harsh conditions aboard ship. It took the offer of a series of prizes from the British Admiralty, including one of £20,000 for anyone who could come up with a marine chronometer which could measure longitude at sea to an accuracy of half a degree, and decades of work by the Yorkshire clockmaker John Harrison to produce the H4, a diminutive chronometer only 13 cm (5 in) in diameter, which when trialled by the Admiralty's Board of Longitude in 1761 was found to lose less than three seconds per day during a voyage from Portsmouth to Kingston, Jamaica, and even that at a fairly steady rate which could be compensated for. Harrison chronometers became a regular feature of subsequent British scientific and exploratory voyages and Captain James Cook, during his second voyage from 1772 to 1775, described the H4 he had with him as 'our faithful guide through all the vicissitudes of climates'. Sadly, the Admiralty was not quite so appreciative and wriggled out of ever giving Harrison his full prize money.

Instead of lines of latitude and longitude, most sailors before the 17th century put their trust in rhumb lines (or at least their navigators and captains did). The mesh of lines which criss-cross 14th- and 15th-century portolans were so called because they 'conserved the rhumb', another name for a compass direction. The theory was that any straight line on a map indicated by a rhumb line was the shortest distance between two points along it, a very useful reassurance on long sea voyages. Also called loxodromes, the geometry works out that a ship sailing along a rhumb line or loxodrome is always not quite at a right angle to a line of latitude. The rhumb lines therefore form a kind of helix shape across the globe (and in fact if you followed one to the bitter end you'd be inexorably sucked towards the Poles). Pedro Nuñes (1502–78), the chief cartographer to the Portuguese Crown, was the first to describe the phenomenon of spiral loxodromes and it was these to which Mercator turned when devising his 1569

projection in which the in-theory spherical or helix-shaped rhumb lines are shown as straight lines.

Not all maps have grids composed of latitude and longitude lines (or rhumb lines). Many atlases and street plans have alternative forms of square grid (in modern times labelled with numbers and letters which could be referenced against a place name in an index to find its location). Such square grids, however, are of extreme antiquity, and a particular feature of Chinese mapping (which did not use latitude and longitude lines at all until Western-style cartography was imported from the 17th century). The invention of the grid is attributed to the astronomer Zhang Heng (AD 78–139), a scholar with an eclectic range of interests which included most notably – apart from the map grid – the world's first recorded seismograph, a cylindrical metal device with eight dragons' heads arranged in the cardinal directions on an upper layer and eight frogs with open mouths below them. When a tremor occurred, it shook a metal ball from

one of the dragons into the mouth of a frog which indicated the direction of the earthquake. Work attributed to the cartographer Pei Xiu (see p.76), who worked in the state of Cao Wei during the turbulent Three Kingdoms Period which followed the collapse of the Han dynasty (and with it China's unity) in AD 220, suggests that he, too, used square grids, while the now-lost *Hainei Huayi Tu* ('Map of the Chinese and Barbarians Peoples within the Seas') composed by Jian Dan (730–805) around 801 during the Tang dynasty certainly contained grids. The striking stone *Yu ji tu* (see p.112) from 1136 has a strong network of grid lines incised into it, which, against the material of which it is made, make it look like an enormous game of battleships.

Chinese square grids were also used as a means of indicating the scale of the map, with most of them including some indication of the distance which was supposed to be represented by each line of the square. The cartographer at some point must determine the scale of the map, and therefore the amount of detail which can be shown on it. One of the most ancient map representations of all, that of the temple plan held in the lap of the statue of Gudea, ruler of Lagash (*c.* 2100 BC, see p.18) has a gradated rod indicating its scale. This, and subsequent indications of scale, generally suffered from the flaw that they depended on knowing what the unit being referenced was (be it Chinese *li*, Roman *milia* or British furlongs). Only in 1806 did the French Revolutionary government's zeal

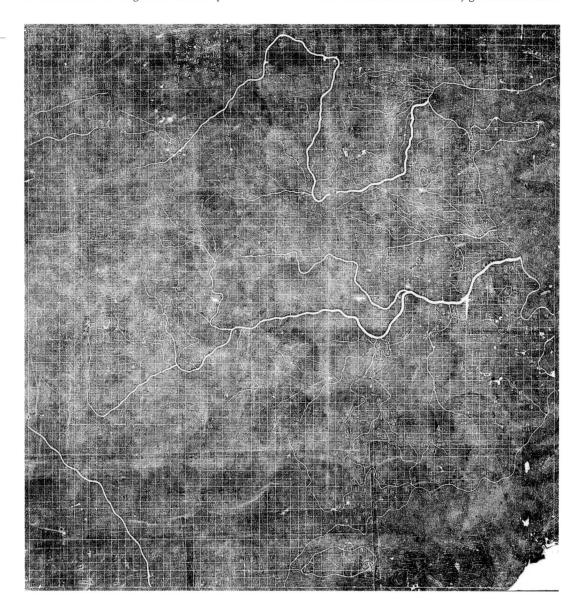

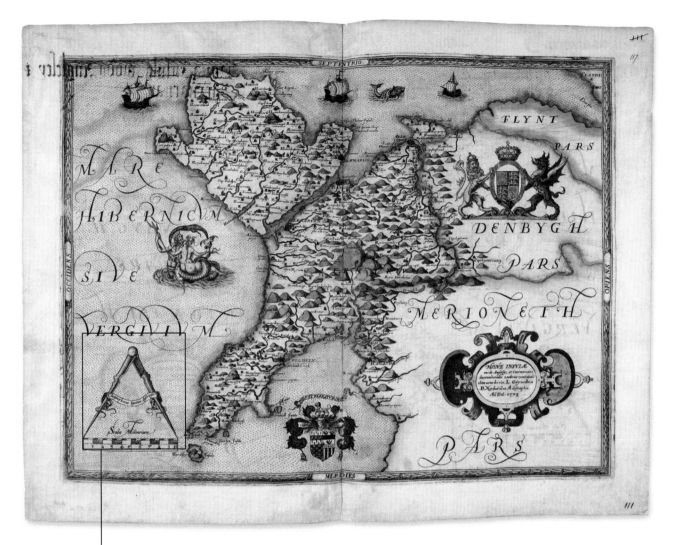

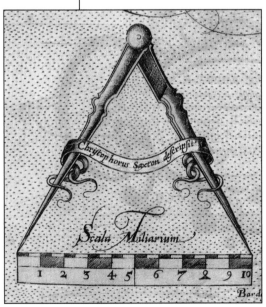

for decimal systems of measurement (and its introduction of the metre as a standard unit of measure) lead to the devising of the notion of a representative fraction, which is expressed in terms of a ratio: so, 1: 100,000 means that one unit on the map (generally a centimetre, or in those countries using imperial measurements, an inch) represents 100,000 of those units (for the metric version 1,000 metres or a kilometre). Long before the French Revolution, however, the idea of a linear scale bar, showing the map's users what a distance on the map represented in real life had become established. Some of them are beautifully elaborate, with surveyors' dividers forming a triangle against the bar, such as those accompanying Christopher Saxton's 1578 map of Caernarvonshire and Anglesey.

As we have seen, the orientation of maps was of primary importance, particularly in the eras when they were used for navigation. As well as the general

ABOVE

Map of Caernarvonshire and Anglesey, Christopher Saxton, 1578

INSET

Detail of the scale bar

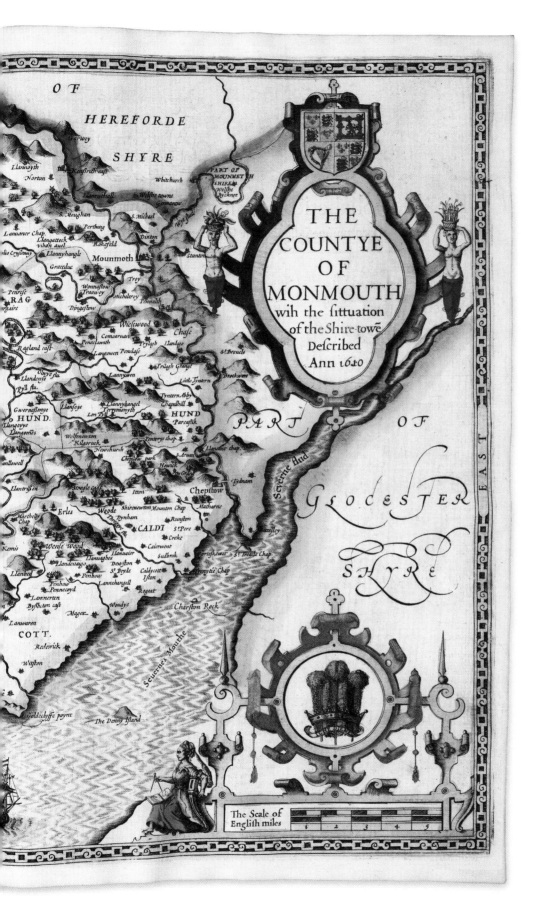

OF

HEREFORDE

SHYRE

Whitchurch

PART OF
MOUNMETH
SHIRE
Welfhe
Bycknor

THE
COUNTYE
OF
MONMOUTH
wih the fittuation
of the Shire-towē
Deſcribed
Ann 1610

Llannoyth
Norton

Kenſtritch eaſt
Llancuthall
Welfhe towne
Gornarow

S. Moughan
Perthing
S. Michael
Dixton

Lanuaner Chap.
Llangattock
vibon auel
Llannyhangle
Mounmoth

Stanton

lio Cryſſenny

Graceduc
Troy

Wonnaſton
Traowey
Micheltroy
Penn
Pennalth

Penreſt
RAG
orgaire

Dingeſtow

Wieſewood
Chaſe

Comcaruan
Penclawith
Trylgh
Llandogo

S. Breuels

Ragland caſt

Langowen Penclaſe

Obyye flu.
Llandenye flu.
Pyll. flu.

Lannyſſen

Trilegh Grange

Brockwere

Little Tyntern

Tyntern Abby

Gwerneſſenye
HUND.
Llangeuye
Llangonēs

Llanſoye
Llannyhangel
Terremonyth
Lon Pyll

Chapelhill
HUND.
Parcaſtik

Wolfenewton
Kilgaruck
Newchurch
Penwrye chap.

Llandini chap.

S. Aruan
Llantriſſen

Chepſtow park
Henrick
S. Grace.

Tydnam

Zinogle
Itton
Chepſtow

Severne and

Erles
Woode
Shirenewton
Mounton Chap
Matharne

Marthelly
Chap
Dynham
Runſton

GLOCEST

S. Perc
Teyzſey

CALDI

Creke

Kemis
Wenſe Wood
Caierwent
Sudbrok

SHYRE

Llanbed
Llancuaga
Llanuaghee
Llanuair

Penſton

Porteſkewet
S. Ireacle Chap.

Penhow
Penholw
S. Bryde
Caldycott
Iſton

Penhow
Pennecoyd
Lannerten
Lannehangell
Trynytie Chap

Byſfhton caſt
Woudye
Rogeat

Lanwaren
Magor
Charſton Rock

COTT.

Redewick

Severnes Mouthe

Witſton

Goldcclyffe poynt
The Denny Iſland

EAST

The Scale of
Engliſh miles

| 1 | 2 | 3 | 4 | 5 |

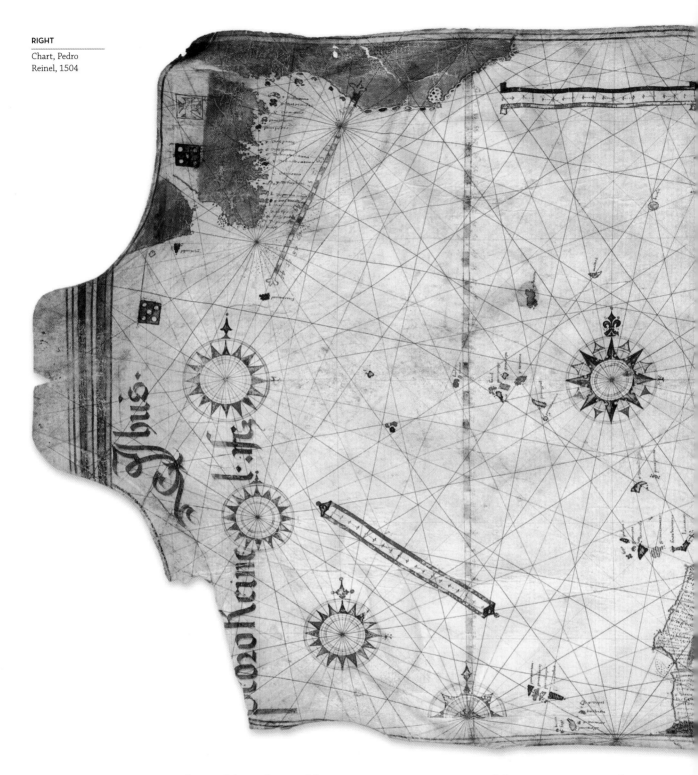

assumption that north lay at the top of the maps, cartographers also incorporated a handy device known as a wind rose, a circle with the directions of the eight main winds (each of which was believed to come from a particular direction) inscribed around it, often very ornately. The naming of winds was a very

ancient practice, and they were seen as minor deities in their own right, such as Boreas (the north wind) and Zephyrus (the west wind). After a flirtation with 12 winds, and then, in the work of the 1st-century BC architectural writer Vitruvius, with a finely gradated 24, the number had reduced by the Middle Ages to

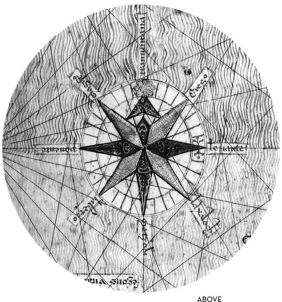

(south), *libeccio* (south-west), *ponente* (west) and *maestro* (north-west). The wind roses are thus labelled with the initials for the winds (so TGLSOLPM) with the T for the north often indicated by a spear. These gradually became even more decorative and stylized so that by the time of Pedro Reinel's chart of 1504 they have morphed into a fleur-de-lys shape with a central petal-shaped panel.

For any map to be comprehensible to its users there must be a generally understood – if not actually agreed – set of conventions regarding the symbols shown on it and the way in which the information is displayed. Early modern map-makers had something of a mania for detailed annotations imparting a wealth of information (or sometimes misinformation) about the lands shown. They took to framing this within a scroll-like panel known as a cartouche, sometimes flanked by gigantic mythological figures such as Atlas. Often the cartouche simply contained the title but sometimes, and particularly in Dutch mapping of the 17th century, the cartographer or his assistants indulged themselves with mini-works of art, showing battles, cherubs or idyllic rural scenes.

eight, which handily equates to the four cardinal points (north, east, south and west) and the points half-way in between (such as north-east). On portolans these were often labelled with the Italian versions of the names: *tramontana* (north), *greco* (north-east), *levante* (east), *sirocco* (south-east), *austro*

The information in the cartouche was easily understood, but the symbols placed on the map were the subject of more complex conventions. The tradition of doing this pictorially is an ancient one – on the *Peutinger Table* it is fairly clear which towns are fortified with walls, because the artist has drawn them around the settlement, while the Madaba mosaic map (see p.111), with its detailed images of buildings within cities such as Jerusalem is a rather extreme case. What cartographers call 'conventional signs' require a little more work to understand. The idea that a stylized wavy line should represent rivers or a pointy triangle lacking its base should be some form of hill or mountain has a certain logic about it, and is indeed very ancient, dating back to the Nuzi map from Mesopotamia 4,000 years ago (see p.7). The signs on maps generally became more abstract over time – the practice of using circles to represent towns was employed as early as the maps of the Islamic cartographer Mahmud al-Kashgari in the 11th century – and so users needed a little more help. Where the signs were numerous or the map acted as a kind of narrative device, telling the story of a battle, for example, a map legend (from the Latin *legendum*, 'that which must be read') had to be added. The first legend appeared on a map of the area around Nuremberg published in 1492 by the German astronomer and cartographer Erhard Etzlaub (*c.* 1460–1532), and by the time he produced his *Romweg* ('The Way to Rome') map, a kind of pilgrimage souvenir for those heading to the holy city, he felt the need to include a whole separate sheet explaining the symbology.

By 1585, Gerard Mercator incorporated a veritable mini-guide at the beginning of his *Galliae tabulae geographicae*, the part of his world atlas dealing with France, rather than cluttering up each individual map. Military maps in particular required legends or keys to explain which colour (often hand-shaded) indicated which side and the symbology that represented various types of unit (in general infantry versus cavalry, but shading in the latter case into fine distinctions of hussars, dragoons and lancers). By the 19th century a whole cartographic lexicon of conventional signs had grown up with crosses for rocks on sea charts, different signs for churches with towers or steeples and those without and, in the case of Britain's Ordnance Survey, for everything from pubs, police stations, cattle grids and golf courses to – where such a beast still exists – public telephone boxes. In 2015 the Survey ran a competition to design new symbols to reflect changes in society's needs. The winners included redesigns of the signs for art galleries and public toilets, but also new ones that symbolized the preoccupations and leisure activities of the 21st century: for solar farms and electric charging points. The long-ago cartographer of the Nuzi map would have found it baffling and at the same time reassuring.

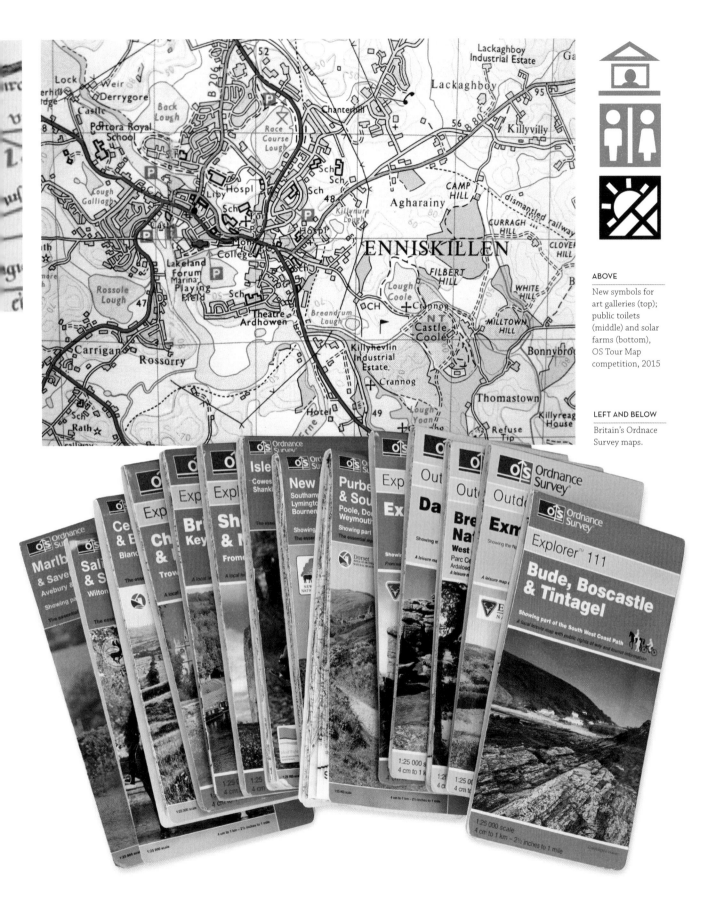

CHAPTER 8

GOING NOWHERE

PLACES WHICH WEREN'T THERE

One of the primary roles of mapping is to show us what is there, indicating the best route, landmarks along the way and insuperable obstacles on land or at sea which must be circumvented. Historical mapping is intended as a guide to the past (even if the emphases can sometimes be misleading or have an ulterior motive), and we expect thematic mapping to have basis in truth.

There are of course exceptions. Maps of imaginary places, such as Tolkien's Middle-earth, can be elaborate, replete with loving details of locations which exist only on the pages of the author's fictional creation, but the author is not pretending that the places are real, or if he or she is, then the reader is in on the game.

There is, though, another category of places which were believed to exist in the real world, and duly appeared on maps, but which are as much fantasy as the Shire or Mordor. Such cartographic phantasms are distinct from the made-up coastlines and menageries of unicorns, giants or wyverns which the map-maker used to fill in unknown regions of the globe. These were places which the compilers of the maps genuinely believed (or at least suspected) really existed. Many of them remained stubbornly portrayed in maps and atlases for centuries. Some were the object of expeditions to locate their whereabouts and a few, such as the 'Kingdom of Prester John', retained such a hold on the popular imagination that their supposed existence had significant geopolitical consequences.

The Kingdom of Prester John was one of the longest-lasting cartographic confabulations, a product of misplaced hope that somewhere, somehow, there might be a Christian kingdom which would rescue the failing Crusader States of the Levant from the local Muslim rulers who had regained their balance and unity since the First Crusade captured Jerusalem in 1099. He might even push back the waxing power of Islamic states such as the Seljuks, who dominated much of Asia Minor from the late 11th century. This hoped-for saviour, Prester (or Presbyter – 'priest') John, was believed to be a Christian ruler whose realm was situated somewhere in the East: no one was quite sure where (understandably, as he never existed in the first place). The legend seems to have first arisen in the 1140s, when Hugh, Bishop of Jabala in Syria, visited Pope Eugene III in Viterbo in central Italy, where he was residing because Rome had

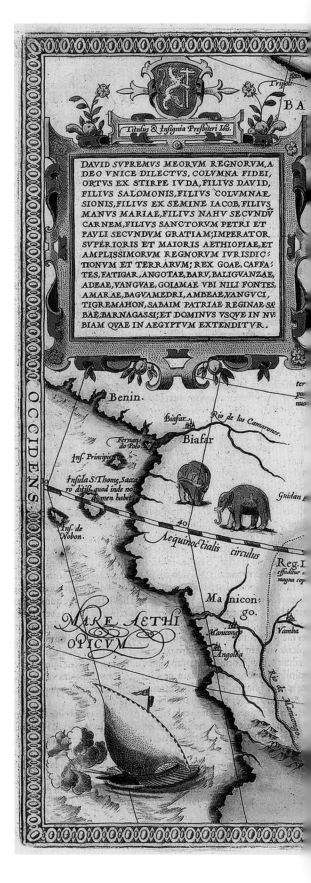

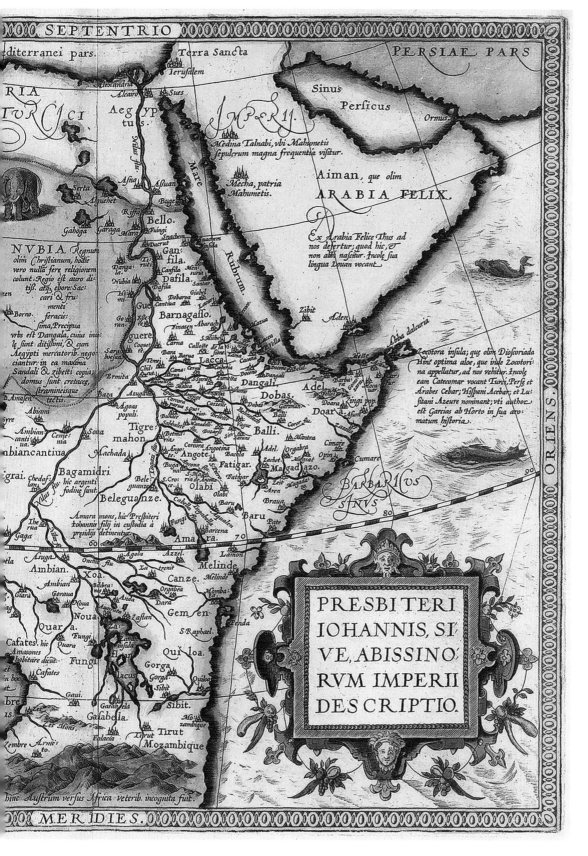

become too dangerous for the Papacy, his predecessor Lucius II having been killed by a rock hurled during an anti-papal riot incited by the Senate. Bishop Hugh delivered the exciting news that Prester John, a member of the Nestorian Church (a heterodox Christian sect which had split away from the mainstream in the 5th century over theological differences concerning the divine and human natures of Christ) was mustering his forces in defence of western Christendom. It was just as well, as the crusaders had just lost control of the county of

Edessa, one of the states they had established in the wake of the First Crusade half a century earlier, which had fallen to the forces of Zengi, the Atabeg of Mosul, in December 1144. Prester John's letter maintained that he was owed tribute by no fewer than 72 kings, that his realm extended from Babylon as far east as India, and paints an idyllic picture of a realm where 'Honey flows in our land, and milk everywhere abounds'. In this paradise on Earth, there were no poisonous snakes and even the frogs were said not to croak too loudly.

BELOW

A New World Map, showing Prester John's Kingdom in Africa, Laurent Fries, 1522

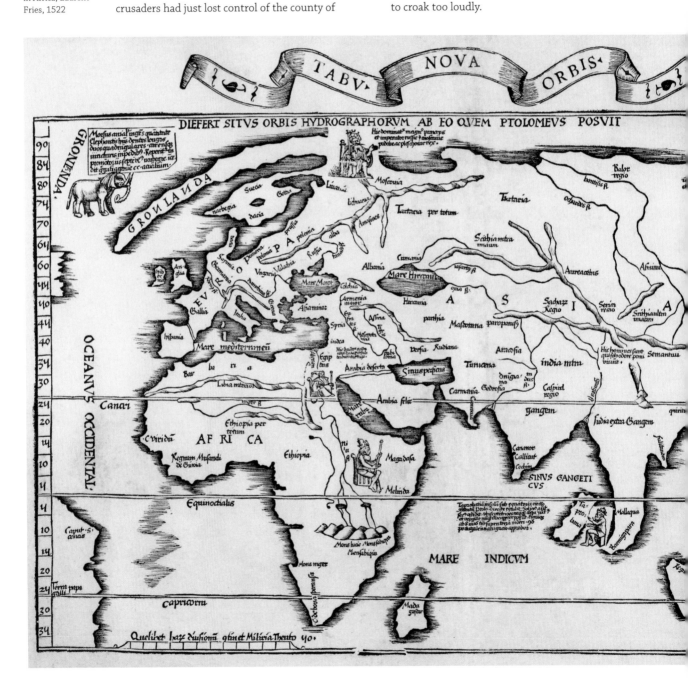

It was all of course a fantasy, possibly concocted somewhere in the surviving Crusader States to drum up support for a new crusade. Yet the hope that Prester John might swoop in from the wings and bolster the Christian cause in the Levant refused to die, even when the warrior-priest stubbornly failed to make his appearance. A century later, with the rise of the Mongol Empire, it was thought that perhaps the Great Khan might be the elusive priest-king (after all the Mongols did become known for their tolerance of Christianity, and Nestorianism, the version of the faith to which Prester John allegedly adhered, flourished in their realms). A stream of emissaries was sent, including the Franciscan friars Giovanni da Pian del Carpini in 1245 and William of Rubruck in 1253. They were met with at best polite amusement and certainly not by any substantive offer of assistance. Prester John, it seemed, must live elsewhere. Europe's hopeful gaze turned to East Africa, where the rulers of Ethiopia, rumoured to be descended from the biblical Queen of Sheba, were suitably Christian and whose contacts with the Mediterranean world were sufficiently sporadic to foster wild fantasies and rumours.

Prester John is first shown there on a portolan map by Giovanni da Carignano (c. 1250–1329) in around 1310, by which time his mooted assistance was already too late, as Acre, the last crusader stronghold in the Holy Land, had been captured by the Mamluk Sultan al-Ashraf Khalil in 1291. Nonetheless, he continued his will-o'-the-wisp existence in cartographic form, appearing on tappearing on the *Catalan World Map* of 1450, a splendidly illustrated late

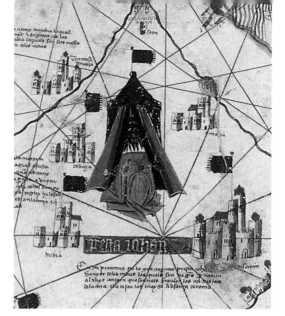

medieval *mappa mundi*, at a time Ottoman advances into the Balkans were causing deep concern in western Europe. He is still there in Abraham Ortelius's 1573 map, which is solely dedicated to showing 'A Description of the Empire of Prester John or of the Abyssinians', which includes an impressive swathe of East Africa said to be ruled by the monarch, as well as his coat of arms and details of his alleged descent from biblical kings such as Solomon and David. The first Portuguese expedition finally reached Abyssinia in 1520. The account, published 20 years later by Father Francisco Alvares, one of its members, and which was still entitled *A True Account of the Lands of Prester John of the Indies*, made it clear that the rulers of Ethiopia, powerful though they were, were unlikely to fulfil the centuries-old expectations of succour for Western states in their struggles against the Ottomans and other Islamic powers.

Ortelius's map also shows the Mountains of the Moon, deep in the interior of Africa, but still well within Prester John's alleged realm. These elusive hills had their origins in an account by the great Greek historian and geographer Herodotus in the 5th century BC. He described them as being close to Syene (modern Aswan in southern Egypt) and situated at the point at which the waters of the Nile flowed northwards into Ethiopia. They issued from fountains so deep that the Egyptian pharaoh Psammetichus had ordered ropes to be used to ascertain their depth, but after thousands of feet of twine had been lowered and the bottom had still not been reached, he gave up. The Mountains had migrated somewhat further south by the time of the account by Ptolemy in the mid-2nd century AD, who quotes the testimony of a certain merchant named Diogenes who travelled for a month into the African interior and came across snow-capped peaks which were, for the first time, described as 'mountains of the moon'. While the belief in them faded during the European Middle Ages, Arab geographers such as al-Idrisi continued to pass on the fable, and when Ptolemy's *Geography* became known again in Europe, spawning world maps such as that of Maximus Planudes around 1295, their elusive slopes reappeared in a long succession of cartographic works. The German cartographer Martin Waldseemüller's 1513 map of the southern part of Africa duly has them there, labelled the 'Mons Lune', while the *Totius Africae tabula* of Sebastian Münster (1488–1552; see p.175) from around 1550 includes two enormous (and also entirely made up) lakes which are shown draining into the Nile. A Jesuit explorer, Pedro Páez (1564–1622), who visited Ethiopia in 1618, even claimed to have seen the two fountains from which (as he believed) the Nile issued and whose depths Psammetichus had failed to plumb.

When European explorers ventured into the interior of East Africa from the 1850s, though, confidently expecting to behold the Mountains of the Moon at the source of the Nile, they of course found no such thing. Richard Francis Burton and John Hanning Speke's three-year expedition from 1856

BELOW

Totius Africae tabula, Sebastian Münster, *c.* 1550

ended with the two explorers violently quarrelling (and Speke temporarily losing his sight and hearing when a beetle became lodged in his ear), but it did locate Lake Victoria, the true source of the Nile (which was finally confirmed in 1874 when Henry Morton Stanley made a complete circuit of the lake).

Africa's Mountains of the Moon finally evaporated at about the same time as another curious inland cartographic fiction in Australia. The existence of the continent itself had long been rumoured, on no better basis than that there must – if Aristotle was to be believed – exist a southern landmass to counterbalance those known (at least partly so) in the

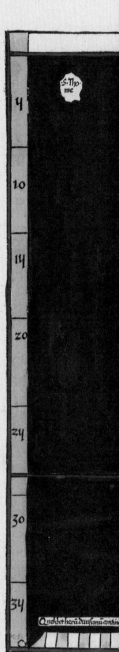

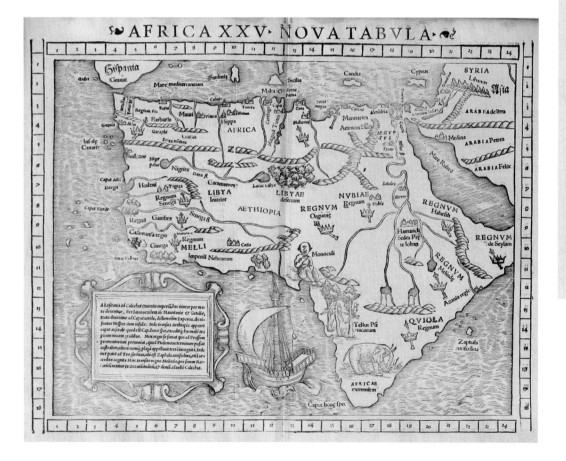

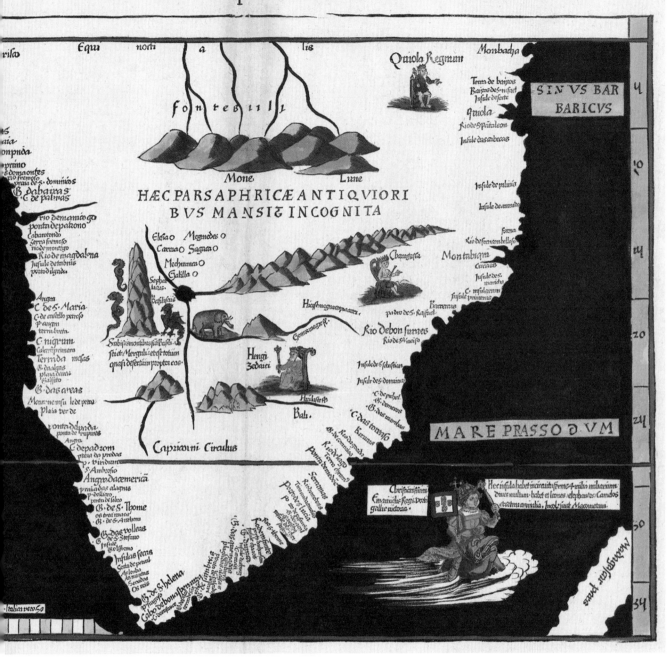

Tabula noua partis Africæ.

HÆC PARS APHRICÆ ANTIQVIORI BVS MANSIT INCOGNITA

SINVS BAR BARICVS

MARE PRASSODVM

Capricorni Circulus

north. It was a supposition carried over into Ptolemy's *Geography* and those cartographers who drew from it, and so a Terra Australis – a southern land – became a regular feature on maps. This southern continent finally achieved a kind of reality when the Dutch expedition led by Willem Janszoon (not to be confused with the globe-maker Willem Janszoon Blaeu) in the *Duyfken* happened across the Cape York

Peninsula in 1606, spending some weeks mapping the coastline and interacting with the local Wik-Mungkan people. There are tantalizing hints, however, that the Portuguese may have beaten the Dutch to it, as an island named Java la Grande begins to appear on maps from the mid-16th century. It took its name from a location mentioned by Marco Polo as being beyond 'Java Minor' (or Sumatra) and which he wrote

ABOVE

Tabula Nova Partis Africae, Martin Waldseemüller, 1541

RIGHT AND INSET

World map; and
detail of Java la
Grande, Guillaume
Brouscon, 1543

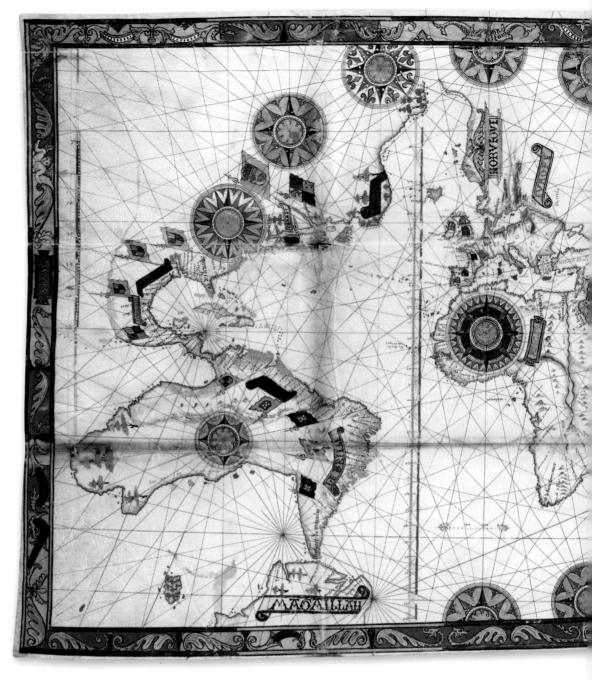

'is under the dominion of one king' and inhabited
by 'idol worshippers'. The island makes its debut
on maps in the 1540s, appearing on the Dieppe
map-maker Guillaume Brouscon's world map in
1543, and is still there in Nicolas Desliens' 1566
version at the northern edge of a positively vast
southern continent. To its east there lies a jutting
section of land which – and it may be coincidence –
rather resembles the actual outline of Cape York in
northern Australia. The occurrence on some of the
Dieppe cartographers' depictions of Java la Grande

on Portuguese flags lends credence to the suggestion
that they believed that the area was claimed or
colonized by the Portuguese, who maintained
outposts at Malacca and in a number of the Spice
Islands of what is now Indonesia before they were
pushed out by the Dutch in the 17th century.

Whichever European nation first encountered the
coastline of Australia, and whether it was the
Portuguese or the more securely attested Dutch who
made the earliest maps, it was the British expedition
led by Captain James Cook (1728–79), which landed

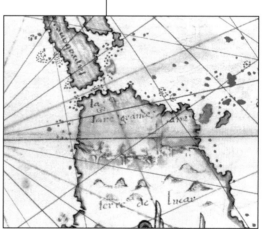

on the east coast of the continent in April 1770, that was the true precursor to European colonization. Early European settlement clustered around the coastline, where the initial landings had been made, but it was assumed that rivers such as the Darling and Murray flowed inland into fertile territories that would eventually be ripe for exploitation. A map published in 1830 by Thomas J. Maslen, a frustrated would-be emigrant to Australia, who was chafing in what he called the 'Siberian Wilds' of Yorkshire after a failed career in British India, shows a large sea in the continent's interior. Published in his book *The Friend of Australia*, an attempt by Maslen to encourage others to migrate to the new colonies, it includes the enticing-sounding 'Great River or the Desired Blessing', which offered potential expeditions a direct route into the verdant heart of Australia. For good measure, Maslen also penned a letter to the *Leeds Mercury* in 1834 claiming that there was a Dutch colony already implanted in the centre of Australia (with the strong implication that the British government had best redouble its efforts to explore and settle the region), but it was all a fiction. Despite only selling a handful of copies, *The Friend of Australia* still cast a long shadow,

feeding the confidence of explorers such as Charles Sturt (1795–1869), who headed an expedition in 1829–30, that rivers flowing west from New South Wales must inevitably lead to the fabled inland sea. They turned out instead to be tributaries of the River Murray and a second attempt in 1844 foundered in the harsh terrain of the Stony Desert and Simpson Desert. If there was an inland sea, it was not one of water, but of sand and stone.

Far more water was to be found surrounding another group of mythical locations, which were alleged to lie far out in the mist and spray of the Atlantic Ocean. Generation after generation of people on the storm-lashed shores of western Ireland, Cantabria or Portugal might have gazed westwards and supposed that somewhere amid the swells and the spray there must lie undiscovered lands. It might even be that some intrepid voyagers had reached landfall in places such as the Canaries (or even the banks of Newfoundland, where huge shoals of cod could be fished), but had kept quiet about it. But no one knew for sure.

One such fog-shrouded and utterly unreachable landfall was known as Antillia, named for the legendary refuge of seven Christian bishops who were said to have fled the Muslim invasion of Visigothic Spain in 711. Seven centuries later, rumours emerged that Antillia had been found, or at least it began to appear on portolan charts of the Atlantic, beginning with one by Zuane Pizzigano in 1424. It sits in a red box far to the west of Ireland, equipped with its own mini-archipelago of seven satellite islands,

presumably one for each of the original episcopal exiles. On Grazioso Benincasa's 1482 map of the Atlantic we get even more detail, with details of bays and inlets and the names of the subsidiary islands given as Aira, Ansodi, Con, Antinib, Anssalii and Ansolli.

Antillia even played a role in the voyage of Christopher Columbus (1451–1506) which finally did discover lands beyond the Atlantic (although not Antillia). The Florentine cartographer Paolo dal Pozzo Toscanelli (1397–1482) showed the Genoese explorer a copy of a letter he had written to a Portuguese colleague Fernão Martins in 1474, in which he advised 'From the island of Antillia, which you call the Seven Cities and of

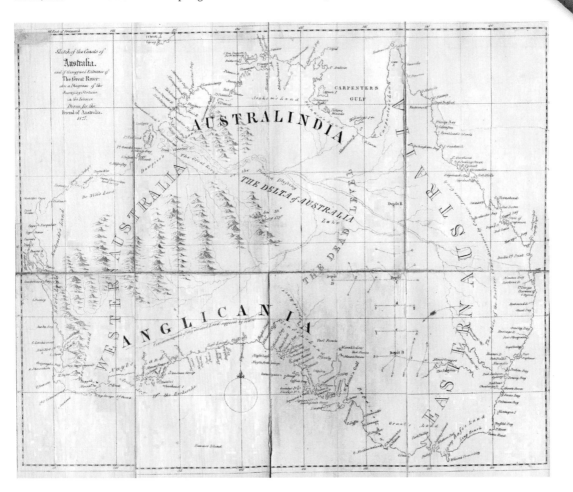

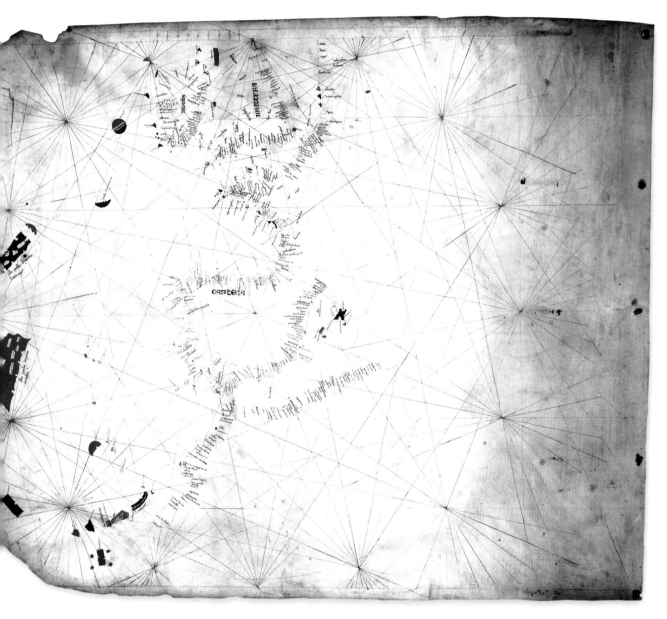

which you have knowledge, there are ten spaces [2,500 miles] on the map to the most noble island of Cipango [Japan]'. Japan was of course far further than Toscanelli's calculations made out, and Antillia did not exist at all, but it all formed part of the cocktail of miscalculation and wishful thinking that encouraged Columbus to believe that not only would the voyage across the Atlantic be short, but that it would lead him to the riches of East Asia.

Already in 1486 King João II of Portugal had sent out an expedition under Fernão Dulmo, governor of Terceira in the Azores, to locate and claim Antillia for the Portuguese Crown, but neither he, Columbus, nor subsequent searchers found anything but empty sea. The legend, though, still would not die and Martin

Behaim's *Erdapfel*, one of the last globes to be made before the Americas really were encountered by Columbus, includes the inscription:

'In the year 734 of Christ, when the whole of Spain had been won by the heathen (Moors) of Africa, the above island Antilia, called Septe citade [Seven cities], was inhabited by an archbishop from Porto in Portugal, with six other bishops, and other Christians, men and women, who had fled thither from Spain, by ship, together with their cattle, belongings, and goods. In 1414 a ship from Spain got nighest it without being endangered'.

As late as the French cartographer Pierre Desceliers' map of 1546, Antillia was still being marked, by which time it had migrated a little west and north to a site somewhere off the coast of

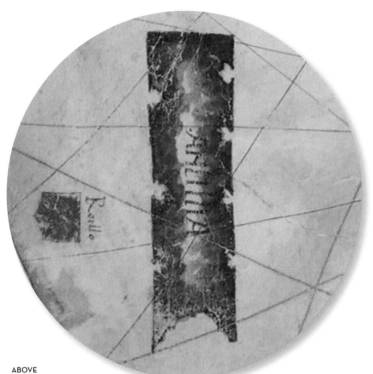

small speck to the west of Ireland. So firm was the belief in Hy Brasil's existence that even an obviously satirical account of it penned by Richard Head in 1674 could not shake it. His tale recounted a landing on Hy Brasil by Captain John Nisbet, who found cattle, sheep, large quantities of black rabbits and a tower in which a Gaelic-speaking man said he had been imprisoned by a necromancer. This encouraged otherwise perfectly sensible scholars, such as the scientist Robert Hooke – a brilliant mind of wide-ranging interests, whose discoveries included a law of elasticity, the crystalline structure of snowflakes and the science behind the diffraction of light – in their faith that somewhere on the ocean, Hy Brasil was waiting to be discovered.

Bermuda. Even Ortelius in 1570 and Mercator in 1587, otherwise scrupulous with geographical detail, felt the need to pay homage to the legend of Antillia and included it in their maps. Thereafter, the seven bishops and their descendants were left to live undisturbed in the annals of places that never were and Antillia vanishes from the map for good.

Antillia was not the only island rumoured to lie in the Atlantic. The legend of Hy Brasil, said to lie somewhere to the west of Ireland, was of equal antiquity and almost similarly stubborn persistence. It was said to be something of an earthly paradise, ruled over by a certain King Breasal, and to emerge from its underwater hiding place once every seven years. Hy Brasil was first mapped by Angelino Dalorto in 1325 when it is labelled as 'Insula de montonis' and then reappears on his 1339 portolan as Brasil. Expeditions were sent out to find it, including, if an account by Pedro de Ayala, the Spanish ambassador to England in 1498 is to be believed, a number by the English court (although he may have heard muddled reports of John Cabot's expedition to North America which really did depart in 1497 and came back with intelligence of 'new found lands'). Even in 1570, Abraham Ortelius included it on his world map as a

Still, Hy Brasil lingered on, though in diminished form, to be shown in 1753 on an Atlantic chart by the British cartographer Thomas Jefferys (c. 1719–71) as 'the imaginary Isle of O.Brazil' and then in 1769 by the French map-maker Guillaume Delisle (1675–1726) as the minuscule *Rocher de Brasil* ('Rock of Brasil') a little to the west of Ireland. Thereafter it, too disappears.

On the continent of North America other lands enjoyed an ephemeral existence and then disappeared as exploration revealed that in the spaces they had once been confidently mapped, something entirely different existed. The Seven Cities of Gold (or Cibola) believed to lie somewhere in the south-west of the modern United States proved to be mirages (though perhaps inspired by the huge cliff-face villages of the Puebloans).

BELOW AND INSET

World map, and detail of Hy Brasil, Abraham Ortelius, 1570

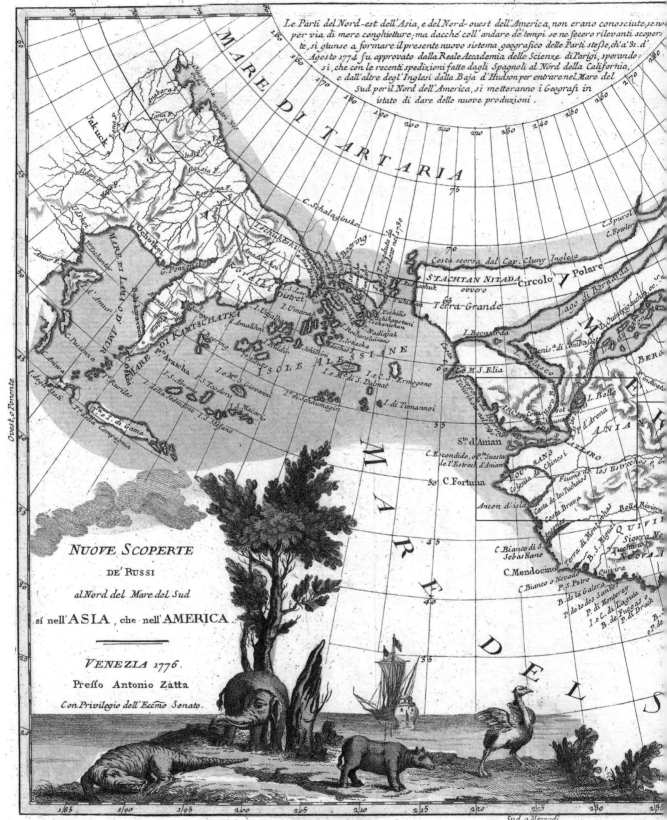

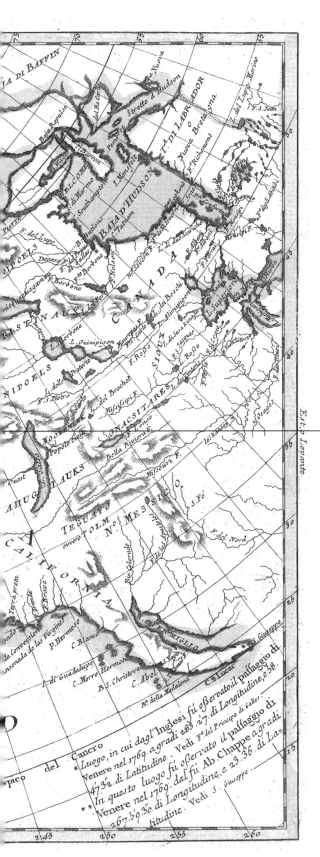

Fusang, a land first attested in Buddhist accounts
of the mid-7th century and said to lie some 20,000
li (about 11,000 km/6,835 miles) on the far side
of the 'Eastern Ocean', gave rise to the notion that
there was a Chinese colony somewhere on the
west coast of North America. It is shown on the
1776 map by the Italian cartographer Antonio
Zatta (*fl.* 1757–97) as *colonia de Chinesi* ('colony
of the Chinese'), just south of another fictional
geographical feature which was to be of far greater
long-term significance.

The dawning realization that the Atlantic was
not a short-cut to the riches of East Asia and that
the landmass which Columbus had encountered
was a continent in its own right had not shaken
the niggling feeling that there must be a way to
sail from Europe to China and Japan without
having to sail right around South America (a
dangerous route for early modern ships as
Ferdinand Magellan discovered during five
storm-lashed weeks in 1520 when his expedition
became the first to discover it). The search for this
North-West Passage (so called simply because it
was believed that there must be a navigable route
north-west across North America) sparked

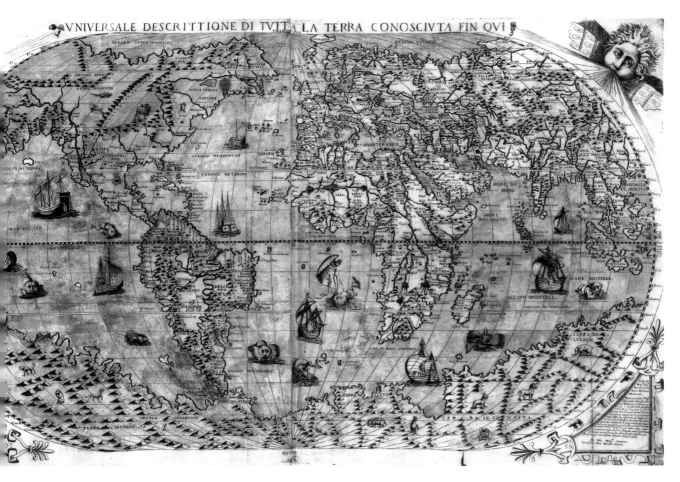

innumerable voyages, including expeditions led by Jacques Cartier in 1534 and Sir Francis Drake (c. 1540–96) in 1577–80. All of these added to knowledge of the geography of the Arctic reaches of North America – and in Drake's case ended up in the second circumnavigation of the globe – but none of them discovered the elusive passage.

Undeterred, cartographers took to showing the passage, often in the form of an invitingly wide 'Strait of Anian', or 'Estreto de Anian' as it appears in the Dutch map-maker Cornelis de Jode's 1593 map of the west coast of North America (in which he also adds, for good measure, the equally fictitious Kingdom of Quivira, fabulous rumours about which might reflect vague accounts of the Wichita people of central Kansas). The name Anian might have been borrowed from a location mentioned in the *Travels* of Marco Polo (1254–1324), a rich sourcebook liberally employed by later writers to try to confect links between what they knew of the Americas and what Polo related about Asia. That Polo's Anian probably referred to the Gulf of Tonkin in the north of Vietnam was of little account to Giacomo Gastaldi (c. 1500–66; see p.176)

who first placed it on his depiction of North America in 1561 (and to Mercator who did the same in 1567).

Some sea captains even claimed to have sailed right through the Strait of Anian, including Juan de Fuca (1536–1602) whose expedition sponsored by the viceroy of New Spain is said to have seen a huge spire of rock at the strait's entrance. The strait continued to appear in maps right until the 1720s, when Johannes van Keulen (1654–1715) placed it on the opposite side of the continent to Hudson Bay. Expeditions continued to go out in search of it, slowly exploring the network of waterways which really did create a sort of passage through and to the north of Canada. Ironically, it was the disappearance of one of them, led by Sir John Franklin in 1846–48, which finally led to the discovery of a real North-West Passage (though not in the form of the Strait of Anian). Franklin, along with the entirety of the crew of his vessels the *Erebus* and *Terror*, simply vanished, setting off a frenzy of expeditions to discover his fate – galvanized in large part by the determination of his wife Jane. Although the first indications of what had happened to Franklin came from accounts

ABOVE

World map, based on the work of Giacomo Gastaldi, Paulo Forlani, 1565

given to John Rae by local Inuits in 1853–54 (that the ships had become trapped, Franklin died and the survivors set off overland, gradually to die from exhaustion and starvation), it was another expedition, commanded by Robert McClure in 1850 that located a way through the Prince of Wales Strait. Although his ship, the *Investigator*, was trapped in the ice, he led a party by sledge to Beechey Island, so becoming the first, technically, to traverse the elusive Passage, although the route was not navigated entirely by sea until the Norwegian explorer Roald Amundsen did so in 1906.

The Strait of Anian was not the first geographical mirage to draw travellers across the North Atlantic. Centuries earlier, Viking voyagers from Iceland had extended their range westwards, and around 930, one of them, Gunnbjörn Ulfsson, is alleged to have found an archipelago of tiny islets and shoals which became named after him as Gunnbjörn's skerries. From there, apparently, in the right kind of weather, when the

freezing mists which often enwrapped the area lifted, a landmass could be made out further west. It was rumours of this that prompted Eirik the Red to go in search of it, leading to the discovery of Greenland around 982. Gunnbjörn's skerries, however, seem to have vanished, despite accounts which claim that 18 farms had been established on the island. They still appeared on maps, including one by Johannes Ruysch in 1507, on which an annotation claims that they had been destroyed during a volcanic explosion 50 years

before. Equally elusive was Hvitsark, an island said to lie between Iceland and Greenland and which was used as a navigational point by voyagers travelling between the two. The Swedish cartographer Olaus Magnus (1490–1557) shows it in his 1539 *Carta Marina* as a speck just to the south-east of Greenland, although by then all contacts between Scandinavia and the Viking colony established by Eirik the Red (which it is presumed died out some time around the mid-15th century) had lapsed, along with direct knowledge of the area. By the time the Danish King Christian IV sent out new expeditions in 1605–07, to be followed by a more sustained recolonization effort led by the Lutheran pastor Hans Egede in 1721, all trace of both Gunnbjörn's skerries and Hvitsark had vanished.

They joined a long list of lands which simply weren't there (including Atlantis which, although it began its career as an allegory of an ideal state in the writings of the Greek philosopher Plato, still did appear occasionally on 17th-century maps as a real place). The cartographers, though, could hardly be blamed. Sometimes the belief, or the simple hope, that a place existed, or the reluctance to simply leave blank spaces on the map was enough to lend them shadowy existence. If no one found them, perhaps it was because they had not searched hard enough.

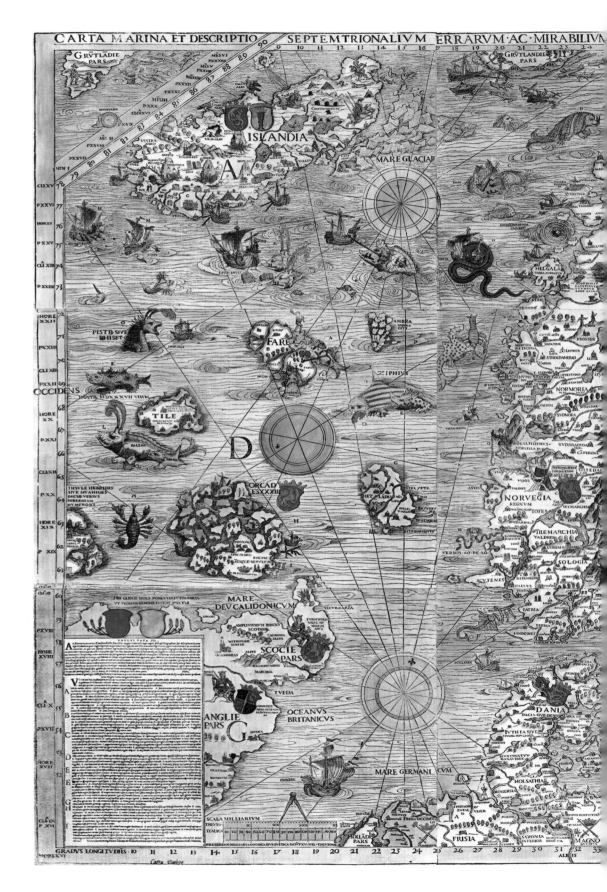

LEFT

Carta Marina,
Olaus Magnus,
1539

CHAPTER 9

THE DRAWING ROOM

KEY CARTOGRAPHERS FROM THE GOLDEN AGE TO THE MODERN AGE

A patron has been procured, engraving tools chosen, the surface on which the map is to be drawn selected and even a few illusory isles or fantastic coastlines selected or discarded from the list of places to be incorporated. Still, perhaps, a cartographer needs to be chosen (if the long 2,000-year array of them from Hecataeus to Behaim has proved inadequate). Perhaps as the 16th century approaches, new techniques are discovered and new regions of the world come into contact with each other, necessitating more and better maps, a suitable map-maker might appear. These are some of the most notable candidates, from the golden age of map-making in the 16th century and on into the 19th century.

Columbus's encounter with the Americas in 1492 not only opened up a whole new horizon for the crowns of Spain and Portugal to build themselves a colonial empire. It also revolutionized the world of cartography. Juan de la Cosa (1450–1510) literally lived this change.

A navigator, as well as a map-maker, he had met the Portuguese explorer Bartolomeu Dias when he returned from his rounding of the Cape of Good Hope in 1488, and it was perhaps in search of similar fame that de la Cosa joined Columbus's expedition as master of the *Santa Maria*, the largest vessel in the fleet. He took part in Columbus's second voyage, too, in 1493 as master of the *Mariagalante*, and sailed with

the third voyage in 1498 in a lesser role. The following year he was back in the Americas, as pilot for Alonso de Ojeda and the flamboyant self-publicist Amerigo Vespucci, becoming with them the first Europeans to set foot on the South American continent. He made three further trips to the Americas, dying when he was shot with poison arrows during a skirmish with indigenous people at Turbaco in modern Colombia. Before then he had made use of the precious intelligence he had garnered about the Americas to produce several maps, including one world map drafted in 1500, which is the first to survive that shows the new discoveries. With the half covering the Americas at a scale deliberately larger than that of the 'Old' world, de la Cosa clearly intended to emphasize the importance of the new discoveries. Including the coast of Newfoundland (only explored by John Cabot in 1497) and showing Cuba as an island (in contrast to the belief by Columbus that it was joined to the mainland), it is startlingly accurate in its depiction of a continent of which Europeans were utterly ignorant just eight years before.

De la Cosa's unfortunate end was a rare one, although this was an age in which the roles of explorer and map-maker merged, making the occupation a more than usually hazardous one. Johannes Ruysch (*c.* 1460–1533), who was probably born in Utrecht in the Netherlands,

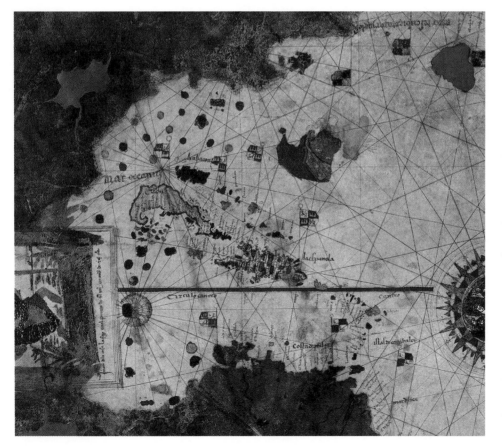

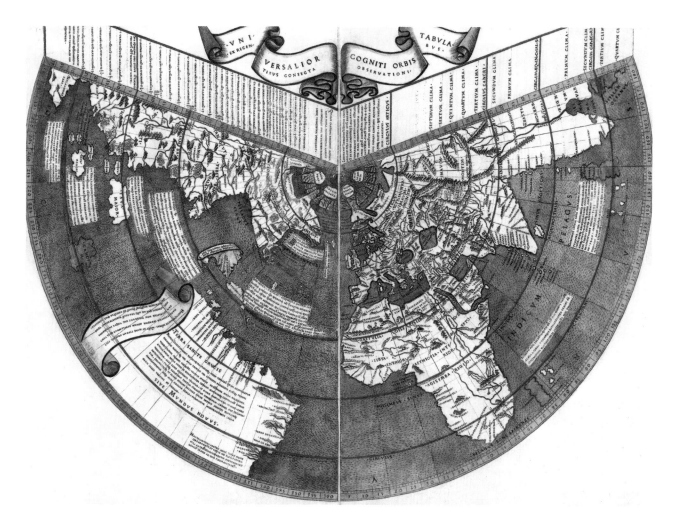

was an unusual combination of priest, explorer and cartographer. Although he joined the Benedictine Order at their monastery of St Martin at Cologne around 1506, where he studied art and astronomy, combining them to paint the monastery with a cycle of signs of the zodiac, he had previously contrived to take part in a voyage from Bristol to North America, very possibly that of John Cabot in 1497. His fame as an artist spread to Rome and he was summoned by Pope Julius II to travel there to help redecorate the papal chambers, so joining such illustrious company as Michelangelo, Botticelli and Raphael (with whom he shared lodgings for a while). It was there that Ruysch was able to indulge another passion, this time for cartography, by compiling a world map which covered all of the recent discoveries (including the arrival of the Portuguese in Sri Lanka in 1506). Somewhat austere, and lacking the sea monsters which adorned the works of his competitors, it includes lines of latitude and longitude and has a fan-like projection in which the North Pole is depicted

as a point (and not a hole, as it had been in previous maps). Most notably it includes the label *Mundus Novus* ('New World') on the Americas for the first time, although he still places Cuba suspiciously close to Asia, in deference to the continued hope that the coast of Japan and access to the riches of the Spice Islands lay within easy reach of the *Mundus Novus*. After leaving Rome (where his former room-mate Raphael had rather crowded out all the other artists), Ruysch took service with King Manuel of Portugal as an astronomer and cosmographer, making several more voyages (though to where, it is unclear), before retiring to his Cologne monastery to continue his beloved astronomical painting. He died there aged 75, wholly unaware that his future fame rested not on his artistic endeavours but on a single map, and, to some extent, to just two words he had inscribed on it.

If in search of an artist-cartographer, Ruysch might be one choice, but perhaps the most renowned in the field would be the German painter and print-maker Albrecht Dürer (1471–1528).

RIGHT
Celestial map,
Albrecht Dürer,
1515

OPPOSITE
Surviving fragment
of world map, Piri
Reis, 1513

BELOW
Model of Piri Reis
in Kilitbahir Castle,
Turkey, where he
drew his world map

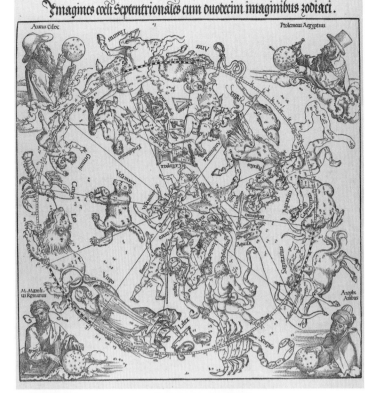

Imagines coeli Septentrionales cum duodecim imaginibus zodiaci.

The son of a Nuremberg goldsmith, Dürer was a prodigy who was already producing work of considerable talent by his late teens. Travels in the 1490s took him through Germany, the Netherlands and finally to Italy, where he imbibed the atmosphere of the Renaissance and transformed into an artist of real power, producing harmonious and detailed landscapes and energetic portrayals of the human body, while still infusing his work with a brooding sense of the old Gothic style. Over the next 40 years he crafted a succession of masterpieces, including the engraving of *The Knight, Death and the Devil*, which is one of his most haunting. His major contribution to cartography came in 1515, when, under a commission from the Holy Roman Emperor Maximilian I he created a beautiful celestial map, showing both the stars of the northern and southern hemisphere accurately placed, but with striking figures representing the constellations enclosing them. The first proper printed star map to survive, it also pays homage to eminent astronomers of the past, who are portrayed in its corners, including Ptolemy and the 10th-century Persian astronomer al-Sufi, the first to describe the Andromeda nebula.

If European merchants and explorers were often virtually indistinguishable from pirates and conquerors (a moral flexibility which goes back at least to the Vikings), the same interchangeability of role affected the Islamic world. The Turkish corsairs who plied the Mediterranean after the Ottoman conquest of Constantinople in 1453 were often independent freebooters, but just as frequently served in the sultan's fleets, and their leaders often reached positions of huge political importance. One of the most famous, and, almost uniquely among them, also a gifted cartographer was Piri Reis (*c.* 1465–1553). He cut his teeth as a junior pirate in the fleet of his uncle Kemal Re'is, who operated in the Aegean, preying on Venetian and other Christian vessels that strayed too close to Ottoman ports. By 1499 he had developed such prowess that he was promoted to *re'is* (captain) himself, with his own ship, and for the next 12 years

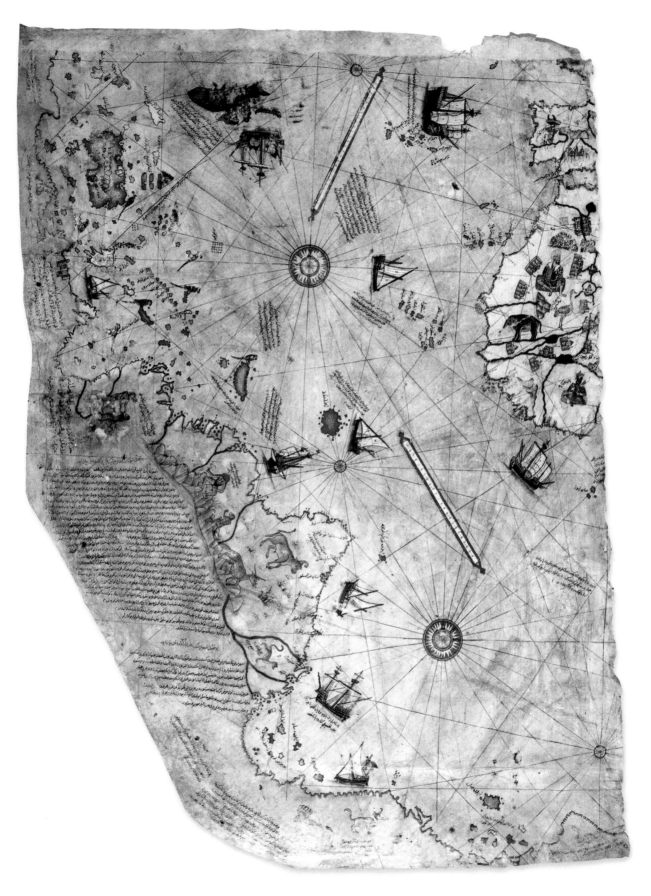

he patrolled the eastern Mediterranean on behalf of his sultan, engaging in several battles against the Venetians. In 1511 he retired to Gallipoli where, using both his personal experience of a quarter-century of voyaging and the knowledge he must have gleaned from Venetian documents that came into Ottoman hands, he compiled his very own world map.

The result was a portolan-style map, which originally measured 1.4 x 1.65 m (4½ x 5½ ft), although only about a third of it now survives. It covers the Atlantic, with parts of the coasts of France, Spain, North and West Africa in the east, and Cuba, the Bahamas and a section of Brazil to the west. Among its annotations, Piri notes how Christopher Columbus had found the Americas and handed them over to the Spanish king. He also gives a list of his sources, saying he had employed over 20 charts – including one made by Columbus himself and nine

ancient Arabic maps. Ten exquisitely detailed ships are shown criss-crossing the ocean in what was clearly a labour of love for Piri, a masterpiece which in 1517 he presented to Sultan Selim the Grim. It then disappeared into the imperial archives in Istanbul's Topkapi Palace, only to emerge in 1929 when scholars began a proper audit of its contents.

Piri also produced his own version of the western wagoneers and rutters (see p.54) in his *Kitab-I Bahriye* ('Book on Seafaring'), which he finished in 1521. Its 130 chapters each cover a port and its surrounding region and each has a chart illustrating the local landmarks and hazards, together with the surrounding topography such as hills, all clearly intended to help sea captains and pilots navigate around the area. Piri was proud enough of this that he presented it to the new sultan Suleiman I in 1525 (and made a special deluxe version for him the

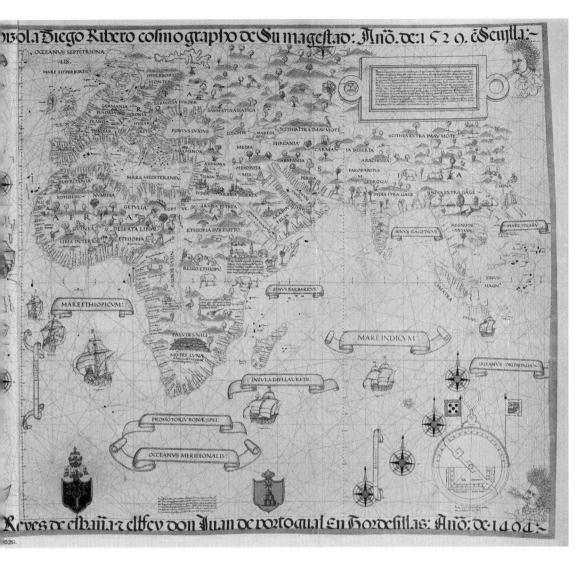

following year). By now he was back in official service, having taken part in the successful siege of Rhodes in 1522 which expelled the Knights of St John (and caused them to take up residence on Malta). By 1547 he had reached the pinnacle of his career, as an admiral and commander of the Ottoman fleet in the Indian Ocean. In 1548 he chased the Portuguese out of the strategic port of Aden, but five years later he failed to dislodge them from Hormuz, sailing out of the port with a shipload of plunder, but leaving the enemy still in command of the fort. Despite their earlier cordial relations, Sultan Suleiman was furious and ordered the aged admiral, by now in his mid-80s, to be executed by strangling, so putting an end to the life of Turkey's greatest map-maker.

For ambition, few cartographers could beat Diogo Ribeiro (d. 1533), who in the international way of his chosen profession spent most of his life known by the Spanish version of his name Diego Ribeiro after he took service with Charles I (who was also Emperor Charles V of the Holy Roman Empire) in 1518, a few years after Ferdinand Magellan. He possessed privileged information, having been on Vasco da Gama's voyage of 1502 and that of Afonso de Albuquerque in 1509, which established the Portuguese presence around Goa. By 1523 he had become official royal cosmographer and a member of the Spanish delegation which tussled with the Portuguese as to whether the line they had agreed in 1494, dividing the world between them in the Atlantic, should carry on around the globe and divide the Pacific world of the Spice Islands also (see p.201). He worked under the auspices of the Casa de Contratación in Seville, the body set up by the Spanish Crown to control all trade with the Americas and to ensure that information about the new lands did not leak to Spain's rivals. Ribeiro's contribution was the *Padrón Real*, a type of master plan of the world or, as he put it 'A universal chart containing everything that has been discovered in the world up until now'.

All Spanish sea captains returning from the Americas were required to report what they had seen to the Casa de Contratación, and adjustments could then be made to the 'universal chart'. Of the four surviving world maps made by Ribeiro during his time in Spain, the 1529 map is the most splendid, giving the most accurate geographical portrait of the world as the Spanish knew it. Meticulously drawn, with a quadrant and an astrolabe portrayed as the tools of his trade, the Spanish flag is also firmly planted on the Moluccas, asserting Spain's claim to the spice-producing region.

Four years later Ribeiro was dead, and a decade after that the first leak appeared in the Spanish information dam, although ironically with the permission of the Crown. Ribeiro's predecessor Sebastian Cabot (*c.* 1474–1557), the son of John who had first explored North America for the English Crown in 1497, had become Spain's pilot-major and

BELOW

World map,
Sebastian Cabot,
1544

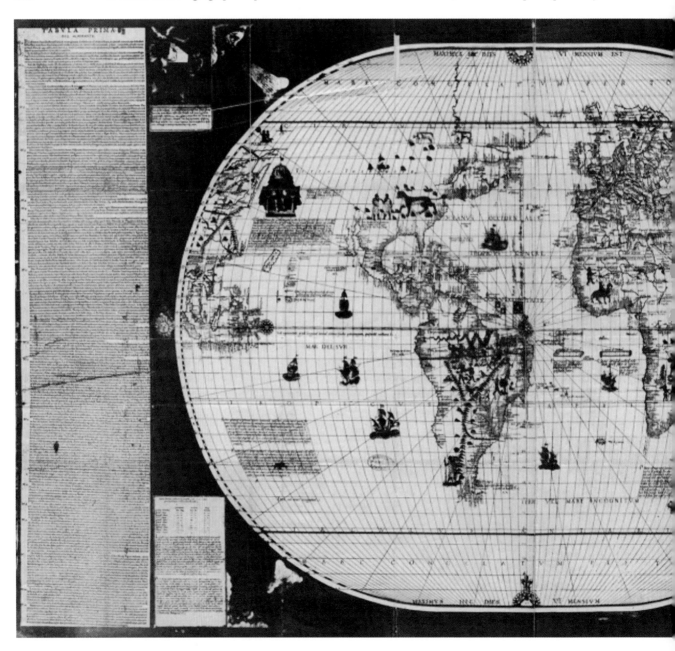

chief cartographer in 1522 (although, always the opportunist, he engaged in possibly treasonous correspondence with Venice at the same time). His voyage to South America in 1526 was a fiasco: the enticingly named Rio de la Plata ('River of Silver') on the present Argentine-Uruguayan border proved to conceal no riches; several senior officers mutinied and Cabot had them stranded on a remote island, where they are presumed to have died; another ship ran aground; and when Cabot finally returned to Seville in 1530 he was arrested, tried for causing the officers' deaths and sentenced to four years of exile in Oran in

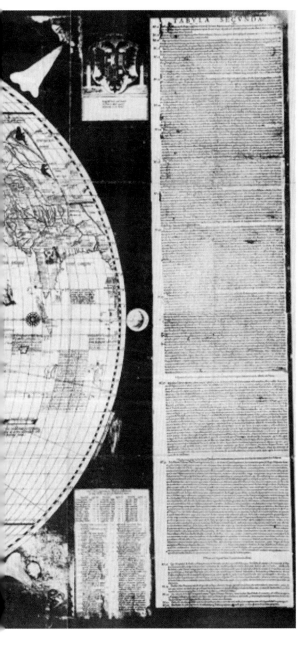

North Africa. When Ribeiro died he was recalled and restored to his former job, and in 1544 he was surprisingly given permission to have a world map printed in the Netherlands, largely based on the *Padrón Real*, which contains the fruits of the Spanish expeditions (his own ill-fated one included) over the past 15 years. Its detail on the Amazon, the Rio de la Plata and the Caribbean is precise, and he even took the opportunity to pay homage to his father in an inscription off the coast of North America.

Cabot left Spanish service in 1547 and went back to England. Negotiations with the Emperor Charles V yielded no results, and he spent the next decade as an adviser on possible English expeditions to find the North-West Passage and to the Muscovy Company (founded in London in 1553) on a hypothetical North-East Passage that might provide a short-cut to East Asia.

Though an able cartographer and inveterate explorer, Cabot's unreliability might recommend against his employment to draw our map. But his venture in the Netherlands was just a sign that efforts by the Spanish and Portuguese to try to keep information about the new discoveries to themselves were ultimately futile. World maps were produced by an ever wider range of cartographers, such as Sebastian Münster born in Ingelheim near Mainz and educated, as most of his family had been before him, in a school run by the Franciscans there. He proved an able student devouring new (and possibly theologically rather worrying to his tutors) knowledge about mathematics, geography, astronomy and languages (including Hebrew, about study of which he wrote dozens of books). By 1524 he had become Professor of Hebrew at the University of Heidelberg, where he expanded his already enormous field of interests into cartography, beginning to put together information for an encyclopedia whose ambition was breathtaking. The *Cosmographia* was to be simply a compilation of all knowledge available in the world. It took him nearly 20 years to bring it to completion, with the assistance of numerous other scholars and in the course of this he defected from Catholicism to Lutheranism during the Reformation (which took him to Basel, where he was also Professor of Hebrew). He also drew on the services of a gallery of talented artists, including Hans Holbein the Younger. One of the maps included with it, the *Tabula novarum insularum* ('Table of New Islands') in 1544 is the first to show the Americas as a discrete continent (although the North is rather squashed and referred to as the 'Terra de Cuba' or land of Cuba). Although

schematic, the wide circulation of the *Cosmographia*, which went through two dozen editions over the next century, meant that Münster became one of the most effective popularizers of the new geography. When he was laid to rest after his death in 1552, his epitaph is said to have lauded him as the 'German Strabo', the equal of the ancient geographical encyclopedist.

The torch of cartography was passed to Italy, too, where a stream of masters such as Battista Agnese (*c.* 1500–64) led a workshop in Venice that produced dozens of maritime atlases and world maps, in most of which the main landmasses are coloured a very curious deep green. Maps began to appear in other formats, too, and if in search of a truly monumental map, the Venetian Giacomo Gastaldi might be a wise choice. Beginning his career as an engineer who drew up plans of the complex system of waterways which criss-crossed Venice (and still does), from the mid-1540s he turned to producing maps with a wider ambit, in 1548 creating an edition of Ptolemy's *Geography* which included a series of regional maps of the Americas, the first to be produced in atlas form, and whose reduced format made him, in effect, the first ever cartographer to publish a pocket atlas. His fame as a map-maker grew so great that the Venetian senate, not an easily impressed body, commissioned him to produce a huge wall map on the Doge's palace between 1549 and 1553. Though that has since perished, it would have allowed the Council of Ten – one of Venice's most important ruling bodies – to reflect on the vast new discoveries made over the past six decades and how their own city, once the supreme maritime power, had largely been excluded from this bonanza. Gastaldi rounded off his career with another stunningly beautiful production: a 1561 world map which, though a masterpiece of the map-maker's art, showed both a North-West and a North-East Passage and thus routes to Asia via both the Americas and northern Russia, neither of which existed, but whose siren-like

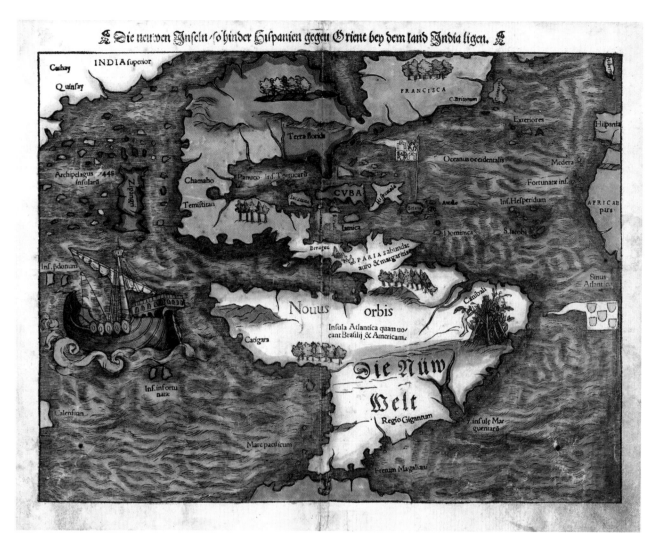

Die neuwen Inseln so hinder Hispanien gegen Orient bey dem land India ligen.

lure launched (and wrecked) dozens of expeditions over the next 300 years.

Gastaldi's life and career was roughly contemporary with one of the most colourful cartographers of them all, who proved that map-making and the pirate's life are not mutually exclusive occupations. Guillaume Le Testu (*c*. 1509–73) was born in Le Havre and formed part of an eminent school of French map-makers based around Dieppe, whose pre-eminent practitioner was Jean Rotz (*c*. 1505–60) the author of the *Boke of Idrographie* – a manuscript atlas incorporating a two-hemisphere world map – who spent several years in the service of Henry VIII of England. By 1550, Le Testu had risen to the rank of royal cosmographer, and was commissioned by King Henri II to map the coast of Brazil (with the intention of seizing land there from the Portuguese). He then accompanied the French admiral Nicolas Durand de Villegaignon to help found a French colony in the region of modern Rio de Janeiro, whose establishment in 1555 was the subject of much rejoicing, but which soon fell apart into Catholic and Calvinist factions (the latter being banished by Villegaignon), while the remaining French settlers were finally expelled by the Portuguese in 1567. Le Testu used what he had learnt though to publish the *Cosmographie universelle selon les navigateurs, tant anciens que modernes* ('The Universal Cosmography According to Ancient and Modern Navigators'), which contained six world maps, some with highly complex projections, showing his virtuosity as a map-maker. If Le Testu had stuck to cartography, all would have been well, but in the early 1570s he returned to sea and took up life as a privateer, raiding Spanish shipping on behalf of the French Crown. In 1573 he found himself off the Isthmus of Panama, where by chance he encountered Sir Francis Drake, who was engaged in the same sort of licensed piracy on behalf of Queen Elizabeth I of England. The two hit it off, and Le Testu

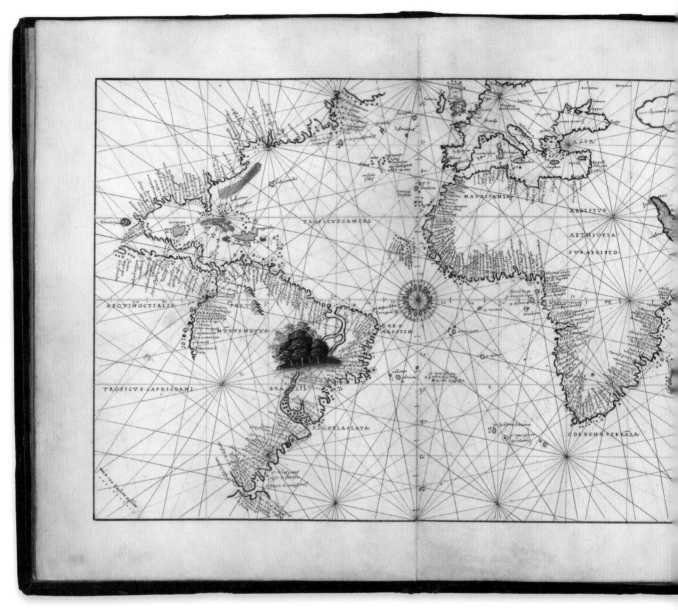

Atlantic Ocean
(left); pages
showing the zodiac
and astronomical
instrument (right);
portolan atlas,
Battista Agnese,
c. 1544

offered to join Drake in a raid on a Spanish silver mule train that was on its way to Nombre de Dios in Panama before being shipped back to Spain. Although the raid was a complete success and seized around 100,000 gold pesos, Le Testu was wounded and left behind to recuperate and to avoid slowing down the treasure-laden main group. When Drake sent back a rescue party, they found no trace of Le Testu, and it was presumed that he had been captured by the Spanish and executed. The mystery surrounding his final fate is equalled by the controversy surrounding his 1555 world map whose inclusion of the island of Java la Grande (which was, as we have seen, a regular feature of late-medieval mapping) in the place where Australia lies and the drawings of strange birds which

bear a passing resemblance to cassowaries, native to Australia, have led to suggestions that he knew of the continent from Portuguese explorers. While unlikely, the discovery in 2018 on an island off northern Australia of a coin that came from the East African merchant town of Kilwa, with whom the Portuguese were in contact (although largely by raiding), suggests trading networks of hitherto unexpected extent and that maybe, just maybe, the Portuguese sighted or landed in Australia as early as the 1520s.

That landing would have been 80 years before that of Willem Janszoon, the first Dutch explorer to reach Australia, who made landfall on the Cape York Peninsula in 1606 (see p.151). His travels and those of other Dutch navigators such as Abel Tasman were

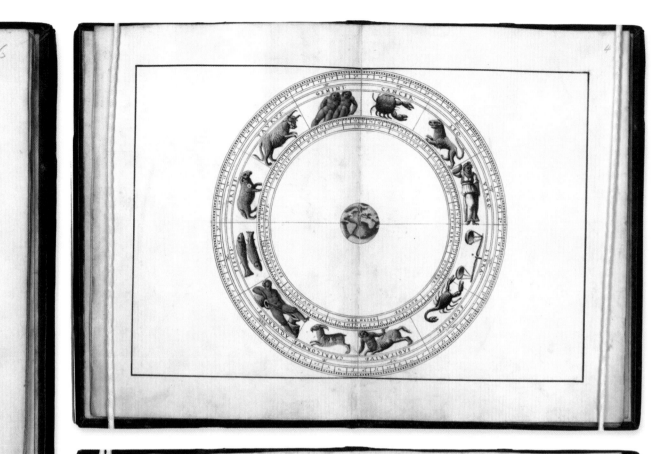

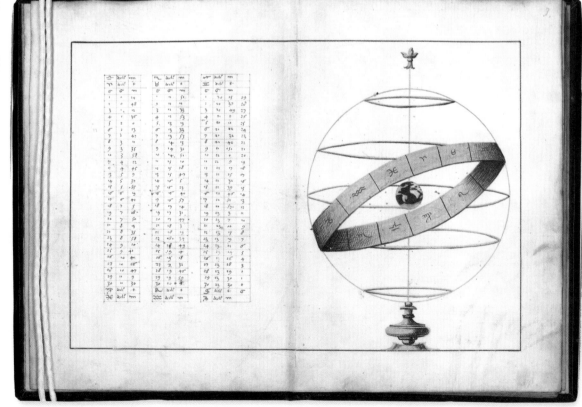

LEFT

Two different
projections
of the world,
*Cosmographie
Universelle*,
Guillaume Le
Testu, 1555

greatly facilitated by the increasing pre-eminence of Dutch cartographers, working in the tradition of Gerard Mercator (who in 1571 produced the first world atlas). Men such as Petrus Plancius (1552–1622), an astronomer as well as cartographer, who like many of his Protestant peers, fled Flanders for the safety of Amsterdam in the 1580s. Plancius became a Protestant minister and the Dutch East India Company's first cartographer. Among those for whom he prepared maps was Jan Huygen van Linschoten (1563–1611), a native of Enkhuizen in the northern

Netherlands (also the hometown of Lucas Janszoon Waghenaer, the pioneer of sea atlases, see p.55), who was one of the age's most inveterate travellers. His father had been an innkeeper, and so he was no stranger to travellers' tales, which inspired a wanderlust that took him to Seville in the service of Philip II of Spain, and then to Goa in the company of its Portuguese archbishop João Vicente da Fonseca. Van Linschoten remained there five years, assiduously gathering information from Portuguese mariners, and his own observations about local flora and fauna and Indian custom, which he collected together in his *Itinerario*, a work which fuelled the appetite of Dutch merchants for trading ventures to the east, and which allowed Plancius to raise his profile with the world map he provided for one of the volumes. Further fame came in 1589 from Plancius's collaboration with another renowned Dutch cartographer Jacob Floris van Langren on one of the first celestial globes to include first-hand information on the constellations visible in the southern sky and an even more detailed version on which he collaborated with yet another Dutch map-maker Jodocus Hondius the Elder (1563–1612) nine years later. While some of the constellations named on it, such as the Bee and the Southern Arrow, have fallen

out of fashion, Monoceros, the Unicorn, is still there on modern star charts.

Hondius established himself as one of the mainstays of the Amsterdam cartographic scene by acquiring the plates from Mercator's original atlas and continuing to publish revised and enlarged versions of them (which are known as the Mercator-Hondius atlases). He is also notable for two curious maps; one of which shows the route of the second circumnavigation of the globe by the English seafarer Sir Francis Drake in 1577–80 with an idiosyncratic projection in which the world is divided into two hemispheres, but the eastern half of North America lies in one, while the western half is sited in the other (unlike most such hemispherical maps where the Atlantic marked the division). About halfway up the coast of western North America is marked 'Nova Albion', the spot at which Drake is said to have landed (now called Drakes Bay, in California) and which he claimed for his monarch Queen Elizabeth I, but over which the English never succeeded in exerting any control. The map was published in 1590, two years after the defeat of the Spanish Armada had made Drake a national hero and elevated Elizabeth to the position of saviour of the European Protestant cause against the Catholic Spanish. It was in this milieu that Hondius published what has become known as the *Christian Knight World Map*, an otherwise standard Mercator projection world map that writhes with symbolic figures (Mundus, 'the world'; Peccatum, 'Sin'; Diabolus, 'the devil') and a Christian Knight who is seen trampling on Caro ('Lust') and about to decapitate Peccatum, who is seen as a monstrous hybrid of snake and human.

Hondius's map is almost a nod in the direction of all those medieval *mappae mundi*, which similarly drew on Christian and allegorical imagery, but they were set in the context of an increasingly modern and scientific cartography. The baton of premier map-makers gradually passed from the Dutch to the French and British, who dominated the field from the mid-17th century. The flood of information from the height of the age of exploration was slowing now, but there were plenty of lands not mapped or lightly mapped by Europeans, and Guillaume Delisle (1675–1726) contributed noteworthy maps of the French possessions in North America, the search for commissions helped by the fact that he had been tutor to the future French regent Philippe of Orléans, was appointed to the Académie Royale des Sciences at the comparatively tender age of 27, and reached the summit of the French cartographic tree in 1718 when

he was appointed *Premier Géographe du Roi*. That guaranteed him patronage and a pension. Among the many maps he produced was one that showed the area beyond the Mississippi which had been explored by the French traveller Louis-Armand, Baron de Lahontan in 1688–89. Lahontan had reported what he called a 'Longue River', which led from the Mississippi to a great range of mountains to the west. Delisle duly included this on his map, but he was sceptical and added a note, which must greatly have annoyed Lahontan, adding a note to it that the river was there 'unless the Seigneur de Lahonton [sic] has invented all of these things, which it is hard to tell, he is being the only one to have penetrated this vast land'. Delisle later became embroiled in a court case with a rival French cartographer Jean-Baptiste Nolin (1657–1708) whom he accused of plagiarizing his work by including information that he had prepared for a terrestrial globe, but not yet published. Nolin was forced to retract his maps and to pay the costs of the ensuing court case.

Employing Delisle to make our map might risk undue criticism of the patron, or expensive litigation. If Delisle was ambitious, though, the English cartographer James Wyld (1812–87) was even more so.

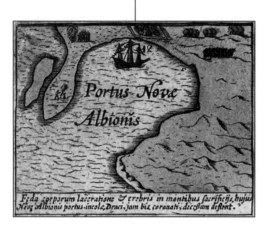

RIGHT AND ABOVE

*Vera Totius
Expeditionis
Nauticae*; and detail
of Drake's landing
site, Jodocus
Hondius the Elder,
1595

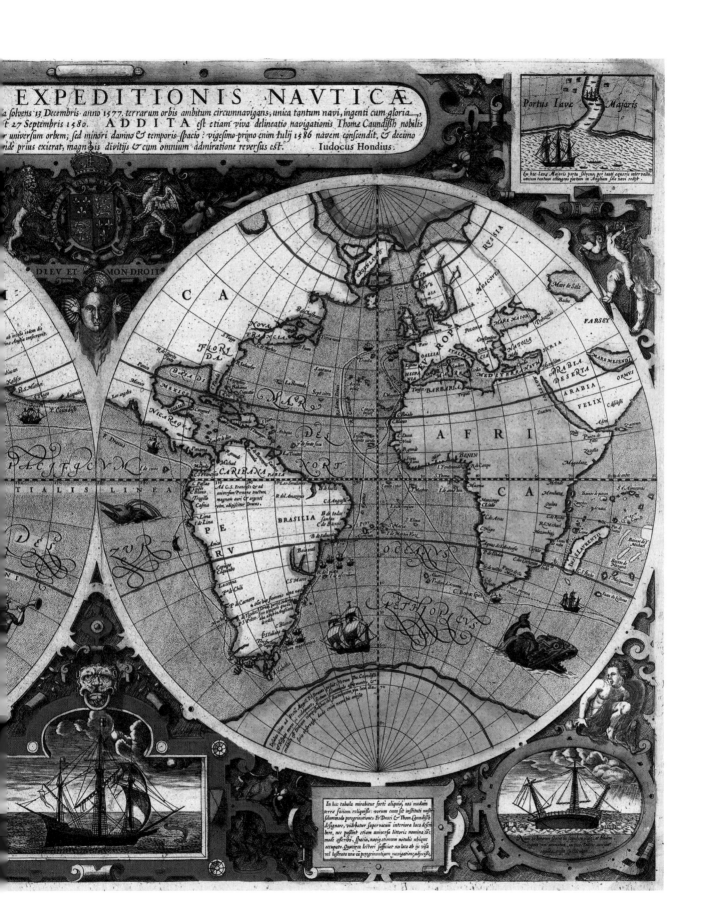

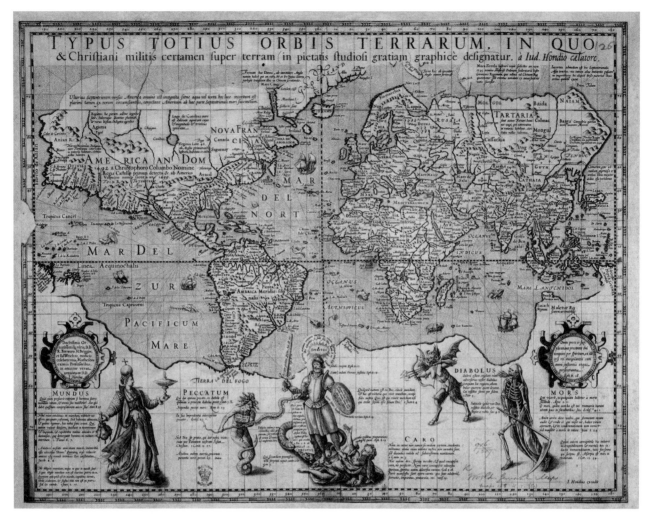

Coming, as many of his peers through history have done, from a dynasty of cartographers – his father had carried out work for the Ordnance Survey – he was steeped in map-making lore. He joined the Royal Geographical Society aged just 18, and was only 24 when he took over the family business after his father's death. His career was characterized by a keen understanding of the market and opportunistic publishing – his maps included one of the California gold fields, to take advantage of the interest roused by the Gold Rush of 1849 – and his position as MP for Bodmin from 1847 gave him an insight into, and access to, the highest reaches of decision-making. It was this that proved his downfall, when he saw the announcement of the Great Exhibition in 1851 as an opportunity for his greatest project yet. Wyld proposed that the exhibition should include a huge globe of the world, some 18 m (60 ft) in diameter, the interior of which would feature models in relief of geographical features and notable world landmarks.

To his great chagrin, Wyld was turned down by the exhibition's organizers, in part because he wished to charge a side-entrance fee (from which he would profit) but also for the very practical reason that his proposed globe was simply too large to fit inside the exhibition building.

Undeterred, Wyld negotiated with the owners of Leicester Square Gardens in central London (now Leicester Square) and arranged a 10-year lease which would give him ample time to build, fit out and profit handsomely from the globe. At first things went well. Although the lease had cost £3,000 and the building of the attraction proved expensive, not least because the interior relief of the globe required the moulding of thousands of plaster casts, the crowds queueing up to pay one shilling (and two shillings and sixpence on Saturdays) proved satisfactory, and Wyld was able to persuade notables such as Prince Albert and the Duke of Wellington to visit. The end of the Great Exhibition, however, led to a drop in visitor numbers, as fewer came from outside London and even a desperate bid to inject interest with special additions such as a scale model of Stonehenge, a stuffed polar bear and a room on the Crimean War, failed to lift them. Rival attractions such as Robert Burford's Panorama, which also fronted on to Leicester Square Gardens, and the Regent's Park Diorama also siphoned off some of the tourist trade and by 1862 the globe and its surrounding area were almost derelict. Wyld had lost control of the building to one of the proprietors of part of the square, John Augustus Tulk, and in October that year it was demolished and broken up for scrap. Wyld managed to hold onto part of the square until 1868, but was never able to revive the globe project or launch anything quite so ambitious. In a previous age, he might have inscribed dragons on his maps, or sailed uncharted seas in search of sea monsters. Instead, his chimeras were of his own making, if no less romantic for that. In our own age, where virtual reality makes images of everything possible, and maps of anything plausible, perhaps, as the last knight errant of cartography, he should be our choice.

CHAPTER 10

MIGHTY MAPS

MAPPING SUPERLATIVES

If there are numerous contenders for the title of the oldest map in existence (see Chapter 1 for the very first cartographic ventures of all), and if the newest maps are created millions of times a second as people tap in queries on their smartphones, there are still many other superlatives vying for attention in the cartographer's world.

Most maps are intended for legibility and so making them as small as possible is not generally the best idea. Many early maps were very definitely not portable, engraved on marble slabs or stone stelae, or in the form of wall paintings or painted on awkward-to-carry objects such as jars. Portolan maps were of course by their very nature portable – they were designed to be consulted aboard ship – but later on atlases became bulkier and less easy to manage.

Smaller editions of those maps which carried enough detail to be used as practical guides when travelling did, though, finally begin to appear, such as Emanuel Bowen's *Britannia Depicta* (1720), which contains 273 strip road maps showing principal routes in Britain. Much of it was copied from John Ogilby's rather weightier *Britannia*, published in 1675, but the printing of the maps on both sides of the paper reduced the bulk and made it a practicable proposition to take out on the road (and perhaps merited the rather cheeky subtitle 'Ogilby Improv'd').

Since then portable, pocket and 'handy' atlases have proliferated, although the advent of maps accessible by phone has dealt a serious blow to small-format road atlases. Far more diminutive than all of these, however, is the world map devised in

2012 by scientists working at IBM. The 22 x 11 micron map (which is, in other words, just over 1/50,000th of a metre wide) is, astonishingly, in 3D and was created using a special tool on the tip of a microscope which engraved the lines on the corner of a silicon chip in just 2 minutes and 23 seconds.

At the other end of the scale, the record for the largest atlas was held until 2012 by the *Klencke Atlas*, a positively elephantine book which measures 1.7 x 2.31 m (5½ x 7½ ft) when opened, and contains 41 massive copperplate maps within a massive bulk that takes six people to move. Presented to King Charles II on the occasion of his restoration to the throne in 1660 by a consortium of Dutch sugar merchants headed by Johannes Klencke (c. 1620–72), the atlas so impressed the contemporary diarist John Evelyn that he called it 'a vast book of mapps in a volume of neare four yards large'. Klencke was awarded for his oversized gift with a baronetcy – a hereditary knighthood – and his atlas remained in the royal collection until 1828, when it was passed to the British Museum. Klencke's monumental tome retained its title as the world's largest atlas until 2012, when it was toppled by the *Earth Platinum* atlas, which spans over 2.8 m (9 ft) when opened, contains 128

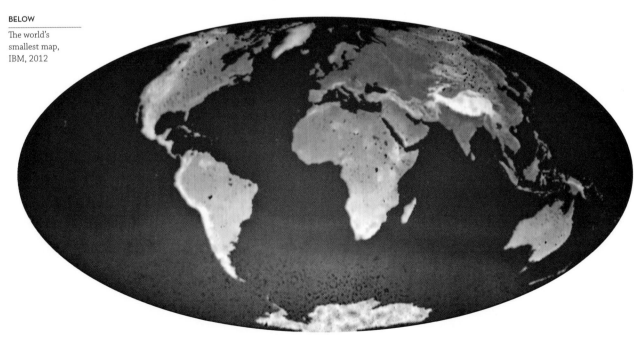

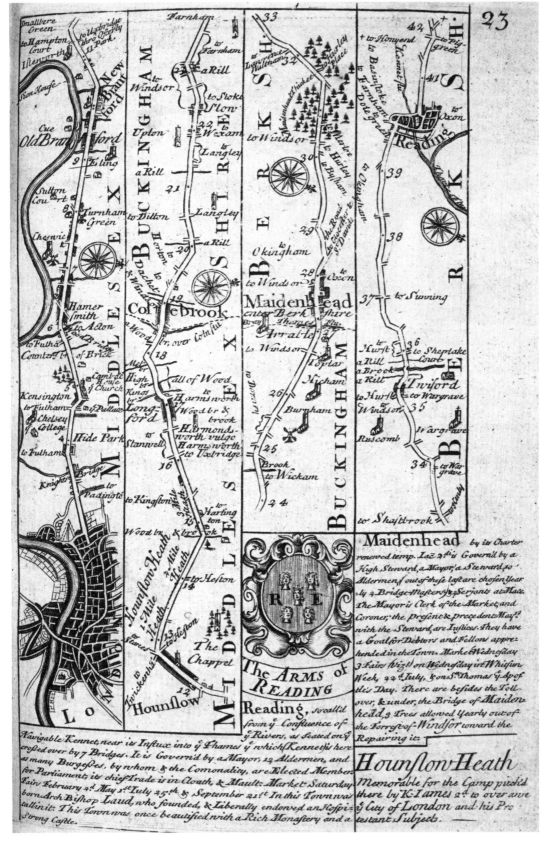

maps on 61 pages and weighs over 200 kg (440 lb), which is more than twice the weight of the average adult American male. Only 31 copies were printed – few have the right-sized shelves! – and not only the bulk, but the price tag of $100,000, puts it out of reach of the average user.

Staggering though this cost seems, it falls well short of the highest price ever paid for a map. One buyer paid more than four times this amount in 2018, handing over £430,000 for the original map of the Hundred Acre Wood drawn by E.H. Shepard for A.A. Milne's perennial favourite *Winnie-the-Pooh*, making it the most expensive map embedded as a book illustration. The highest price paid for a map at auction, however, dwarfs even this. Abel Buell's 1784 *A New and Correct Map of the United States of North America* went under the hammer at Christie's in

New York for nearly $2.1 million in 2010. Sold by the New Jersey Historical Society, which had held it since 1862, it was one of only three copies of the extremely rare map to be sold in over a century. The first map to be produced in the newly independent United States and the first to show a United States flag, its colourful creator the Connecticut silversmith Abel Buell (1742–1822) was sentenced early in his career to having part of his ear amputated for forging banknotes. He recovered sufficiently to make his fortune in minting copper coins for his home state, produced the first printing type produced in North America, and developed a sideline in the manufacture of steel coins. Somehow, though, Buell managed to squander away all these riches and he died in poverty in 1822 in the New Haven Almshouse.

Even Buell's map, however, cannot claim the title of the most expensive ever. That accolade goes to the 1507 *Universalis cosmographia secundum Ptholomaei traditionem et Americi Vespucii aliorumque lustrationes*, ('The Universal Cosmography according to the Tradition of Ptolemy and the Discoveries of Amerigo Vespucci and Others') better known as the Waldseemüller map, the 12-sheet world map created by German cartographer Martin Waldseemüller. Its status as the first map to use the name 'America' made it sufficiently an object of desire in the United States that it was purchased by the Library of Congress for $10 million in July 2001. Created by Waldseemüller and Matthias Ringman (1482–1511), it originally accompanied a work they compiled entitled *An Introduction to Cosmography* and over a thousand copies were printed. Over time, though,

these almost all disappeared – worn out or simply lost. Subsequently, scholars knew that there must have been a map, as copies of the *Introduction* itself did remain in circulation, and these referred to it, but frustratingly none seemed to have survived. One copy, however, had escaped the fate of all the others. Purchased by the Nuremberg geographer Johannes Schöner around 1515, all trace of it was lost after his death in 1547. That was until it mysteriously resurfaced in 1901, when a Jesuit priest, Father Joseph Fischer, stumbled across it while on a book-hunting expedition to Wolfegg Castle in southern Germany. What he found there was beyond his wildest expectations. As well as unearthing a rare map of Greenland – the original object of his travels – on the final day of his trip he was shown an upper room piled with books and manuscripts. One of them, bound in pigskin with two

ABOVE

Earth Platinum, Millennium House, 2012

large brass clasps, drew his attention. On opening it, he was greeted with the dedication: 'Posterity, Schöner gives you this as an offering.'

Once Fischer opened up the volume and began to scrutinize the contents, he realized it was a precious offering indeed. As well as a rare star chart by the German artist and engraver Albrecht Dürer, there was a giant world map in 12 sheets. Fischer knew the

Introduction to Cosmography well, and to his amazement the annotations on this map matched those which were mentioned in that book. The appearance of the name 'America' on one of the sheets confirmed his growing suspicions that this must be the long-lost Waldseemüller map.

This cartographic treasure, though, despite various efforts to purchase it, remained in Wolfegg

RIGHT

Universalis Cosmographia, Martin Waldseemüller, 1507

Castle, surviving the two World Wars, during which many artistic treasures perished or vanished, until, after years of negotiation the $10 million price was agreed between the Library of Congress and Wolfegg's owners. The official transfer happened in April 2007, since when the world's most expensive map has been on permanent display at the library in Washington DC. Its price is unlikely to be surpassed any time soon, unless that is someone finds somewhere in a dusty archive one of those maps – such as a Roman-era version of Ptolemy's mapping – which it's hypothesized might have existed, but which vanished centuries or even millennia ago.

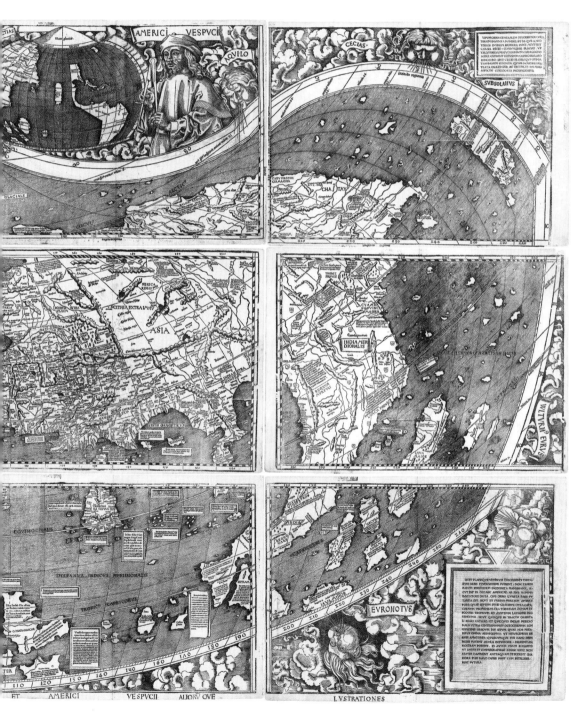

CHAPTER 11

A MAP IN HAND

THE PURPOSES TO WHICH MAPS HAVE BEEN PUT

The map has been planned, the information gathered, a patron secured, the cartographer employed. The map has been surveyed, drawn and distributed. Some maps, though, have an afterlife which makes their significance far greater than their drafters can ever have imagined.

In some cases this is because they chronicle a voyage or exploration, or map a region whose later significance gave even greater weight to the cartographer's work. Maps lend authority to the possession of land, or at least to claims to possess it, and have done ever since the Nuzi map, four millennia ago in Mesopotamia, named the owner of a field (see p.7). Written charters and other legal agreements or international treaties may state that such and such a portion of territory belongs to one or other power, but the visual representation of this on a map seems to have an almost mystical hold. Display it cartographically, and it is so.

BELOW

North Atlantic Ocean, *Atlas Miller*, Pierre and Georges Reinel and Lopo Homem, 1519

Medieval borders were a muddle, and nowhere more so than in Europe, where the overlapping claims of feudal suzerainty meant that one individual could hold land from several lords (and even in extreme cases hold land from a feudal superior who in turn held land from him in a different district). William IX, Count of Poitiers from 1153 to 1156 was the first son of King Henry II of England, but also owed allegiance to King Louis VII of France for his Poitevin lands (which had come into English hands through Henry's marriage to Eleanor of Aquitaine in 1152), though any moral and political dilemmas were somewhat mitigated by William's passing away aged just three. Great lords could also be little ones. The Hundred Years' War eventually did break out between England and France in 1337 after Edward III stubbornly refused to swear an oath of allegiance to Philip VI of France for his lands in Aquitaine (including Bordeaux) and only ended in 1453, with the English in possession of just Calais. Any serious attempt to resolve this through mapping, even had there been the will or the technical capacity to do so, would have been doomed to failure.

As central governments became more powerful, bureaucracies more capable and widespread, and cartography more sophisticated, the options available to rulers who wanted to assert their claims through maps grew. The projection of European power outwards into new lands, in Asia, Africa and in particular the Americas from the late 15th century, both raised the issue of mapping these territories (some of them, in Mexico and East Asia in particular,

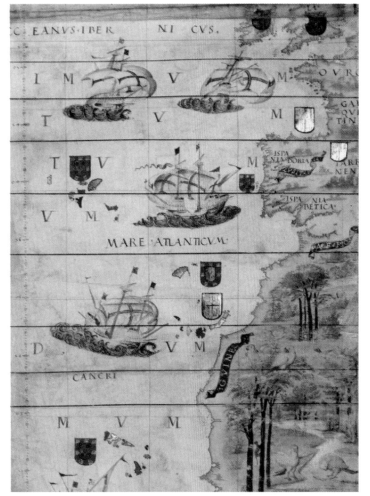

ABOVE

View of Seville,
Sanchez Coello,
16th century

had long had their own cartographic traditions) and of resolving disputes between the colonizing powers as to where the boundaries between them should lie.

Perhaps the first international dispute to be resolved by reference to maps was that between Spain and Portugal as to where the dividing line between their respective territories should be drawn after the discovery of 'New Worlds' by Christopher Columbus in 1492. The arbiter whom the Spanish and Portuguese chose to determine this was the Papacy. In one sense this was logical: ever since the 1450s the Papacy had promulgated the 'Doctrine of Discovery', initially aimed at regularizing the Portuguese explorations around the west coast of Africa. In 1455 Pope Nicholas V issued the papal bull *Romanus Pontifex* ('Roman Pontiff'; such documents are simply named after the first few words contained within them), in which he granted King Afonso V of Portugal the right to 'invade, search out, capture and subdue all Saracens and pagans whatsoever ... and to reduce their persons to perpetual slavery' along a long stretch of the west coast of Africa.

Columbus's voyages, which opened up a new area for exploitation by the Spanish to match Portugal's advances in Africa, was followed by vigorous lobbying by both nations for a papal determination of where their respective zones of influence should end. The Spanish were rewarded on 4 May 1493 with the papal bull *Inter Caetera* ('Among Other Things') which granted them 'all island and mainlands found and to be found, discovered and to be discovered towards the west and south, by drawing and establishing a line ... one hundred leagues towards the west and south from any of the islands commonly known as the Azores and Cape Verde'. As a salve to religious sensibilities, and just to be on the safe side, the bull excluded any territories which were in the possession of 'Christian princes' and it also enjoined and encouraged the Spanish to convert any peoples they found to Christianity. Ferdinand and Isabella of Spain could be well satisfied that vast new realms were now open to them and, just as importantly, that interlopers from Portugal could be kept out. Understandably, the

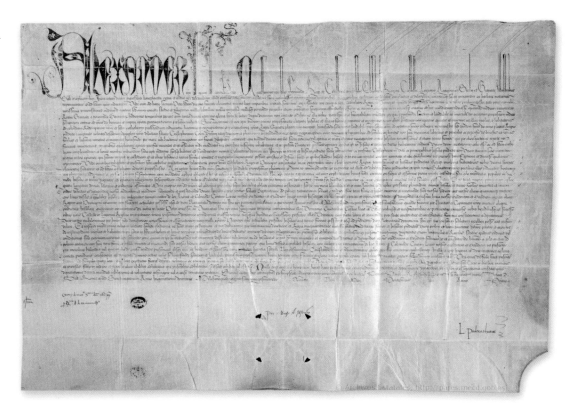

Portuguese were not entirely happy with this outcome, claiming that the 1479 Treaty of Alcáçovas, which had granted all lands south of the Canaries to Portugal (at a time nobody in Europe was aware that anything much of significance lay to the west), meant that all of Columbus's discoveries and all of the vast new domain claimed by the Spanish Crown was, in law, actually Portugal's property.

Bypassing the Papacy this time, the Spanish and Portuguese negotiators agreed a new line, 270 leagues west of the Azores, which gave Portugal some confidence that its trade routes around Africa would not be impinged upon by Spanish adventurers, and left the Spanish reassured that the Portuguese would keep out of the New World. It turned out that King João II of Portugal had the better side of the bargain struck by this new Treaty of Tordesillas, since in April 1500 the Portuguese navigator Pedro Álvares Cabral (c. 1467–1520) landed in Brazil, the eastern portion of which lay comfortably to the east of the agreed line. It may have been a coincidence but there were whispers at the time, and suggestions since, that the Portuguese knew all along that the terms of Tordesillas would leave them with at least a share of the new lands across the Atlantic.

The treaty line is marked in dramatic fashion on the *Cantino Planisphere*, a map whose origins lie in a piece of 16th-century espionage. Other rulers had

their own ambitions to secure some part of the riches falling to Lisbon and Madrid from their new empires, or at least to get a better sense of their extent. Ercole I d'Este, Duke of Ferrara, was a true Renaissance ruler and patron of the arts (and in particular music: his cappella, boasting the finest singers in Italy, was the envy of other rulers and he managed to snag the services of Josquin des Prez, the most prestigious composer of the age). In 1502, he despatched an agent, Alberto Cantino, to Lisbon with instructions to find out as much as he could about the new lands Portugal and Spain had been busily slicing up between them. It was a risky assignment as the penalty for revealing information about the lands across the Atlantic was death. Even so, Cantino managed to make contact with an informant who provided him firstly with details of a Portuguese expedition to Newfoundland led by Gaspar Corte-Real the previous year, but, more importantly, handed over (for the price of 12 ducats) a copy of a world map showing Portugal's holdings in South America. Only the second map to show the New World's coastlines in any kind of detail, it highlights that of Brazil in a garish green (matching the parts of West Africa and the Malay Peninsula – also key parts of the growing Portuguese global empire). More tellingly, it shows the Tordesillas line, a deep red scar running vertically down the Atlantic, bisecting South America just west of where

Brazil juts out into the ocean. This, clearly, was a document originally drafted by someone very close to the court, aware of the political sensitivities of the demarcation line (not that, as the century wore on, the Portuguese kept too strictly to it, and they quite happily occupied large parts of what is now Brazil, which lay far to the west of the line).

The map, though, possessed one glaring flaw, in that it did not (as the terms of the Treaty of Tordesillas also failed to do) extend around the Poles to show where the dividing line between Spanish and Portuguese should lie in the eastern hemisphere. It soon dawned on cartographers and kings alike that the area where an extension of the Tordesillas line might run through lay right in the middle of the Spice Islands, the source of incredibly rare and exotic commodities such as pepper, clove, nutmeg and mace, from which the Portuguese were profiting handsomely. This had not been a problem at the time of Tordesillas. Only in 1511, when the Portuguese captured Malacca and began to push eastwards, did it become apparent that the area to its east could prove at least as valuable an economic proposition as the entire Americas. It was in part as a counter to Portuguese expansion in the area that Ferdinand Magellan embarked on the voyage that would ultimately result in the first circumnavigation of the globe (although not by him, as he died during a skirmish with local people on the island of Mactan in the Philippines). Even so, the arrival of a Spanish fleet in March 1521 set off a flurry

of diplomatic manoeuvring, including the employment by Spain of a Portuguese cartographer Diogo Ribeiro (see p.173) who produced a map locating the Spice Islands firmly to the east of the hypothetical extension of the Tordesillas line, and hence within the Spanish sphere. Only in 1529 did Charles V give up the Spanish claim, as he needed

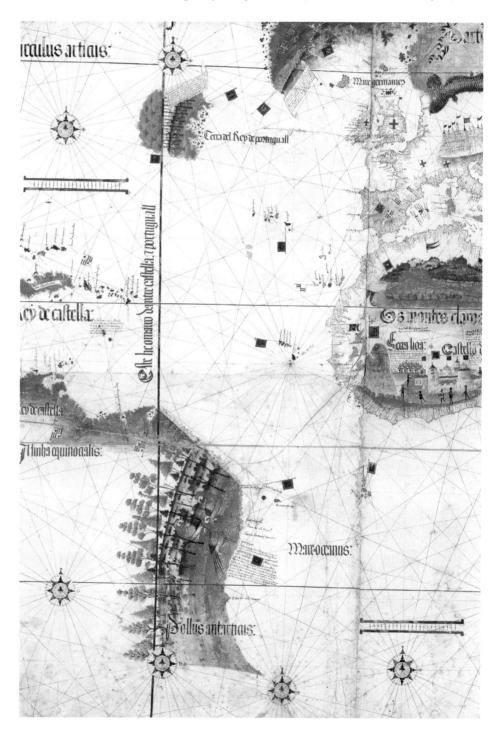

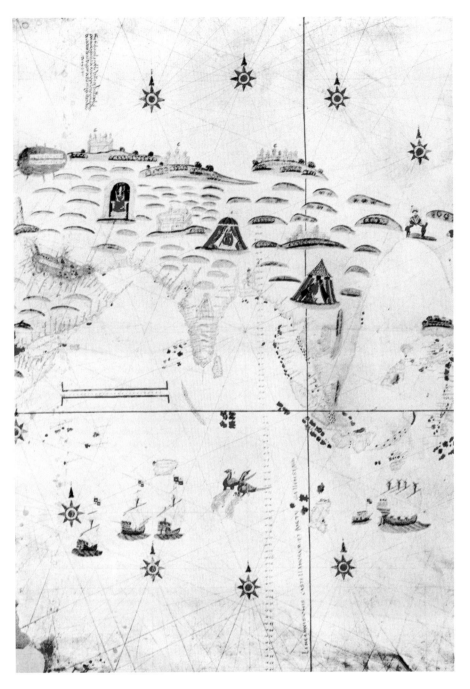

Cartography continued to lie at the heart of European expansion, with maps being surveyed and produced as a means of asserting ownership. Occasionally they were used, as at Tordesillas, to resolve disputes between the imperial powers, but in one case they actually sparked an almost uncontrollable rush to occupy territory. By the late 1870s Europeans had occupied much of the coastline of Africa, initially in the west where they established forts as conduits for the transatlantic slave trade, beginning with Elmina (in modern Ghana), founded by the Portuguese in 1482 (and eventually captured by the Dutch West India Company in 1637), and extended into North Africa as Ottoman rule there decayed in the early 19th century. They had not however penetrated too far into the African interior where the difficult terrain and hazy knowledge of the river systems, which did provide a way in, hampered any European push inland.

Just as at Tordesillas, it was the European powers' suspicions of each other that sparked another ratchet upwards in their colonization efforts. Although the English, French and Portuguese, whose colonial holdings were the largest on the continent, other countries, and in particular Germany, felt excluded. Portugal principally controlled Angola and Mozambique, France was pre-eminent in the north and west,

ABOVE

Map of Asia with an 'ante-meridian' to demarcate the Portuguese sphere of influence (west of the red line) from the Spanish, Nuño García de Toreno, 1522

Portuguese support to prosecute a war against France and England, and so he agreed to the Treaty of Zaragoza, which formally extended the Tordesillas line and affirmed that the region in dispute lay on the Portuguese side. With no hint of irony, Ribeiro was once again employed to map the occasion, this time lauding how it showed the world 'divided into two parts according to the capitulation between the Catholic Kings of Spain and King John of Portugal which they made at Tordesillas in 1494'.

and Britain's interests centred in the south and east, although with a significant presence in West Africa, around what is now Nigeria and Ghana. In 1884–85, the redoubtable German chancellor Otto von Bismarck (1815–98) called a conference in Berlin, ostensibly to resolve competing imperial claims to African territory and in particular to the Congo Basin, which the French maintained should belong exclusively to them, but with the scarcely concealed additional motive to carve out some kind of German presence in Africa.

The French advances had been in part intended to head off those of King Leopold II of Belgium (r. 1865–1909), who was creating a private empire under the auspices of the International Congo Society. Based on the extraction of rubber, this involved the imposition on the indigenous population of a regime of almost unimaginable brutality (local officials amputated the hands of plantation workers who failed to fulfil their quotas). In 1880 a French expedition under Pierre de Brazza (1852–1905) claimed the region around what is now Brazzaville, while both Britain and Portugal sought to press counter-claims in the region. The British in turn felt pressured by the burgeoning French expansion eastwards from Congo, which threatened to cut the hoped-for continuous ribbon of British-controlled territory from South Africa via Sudan to Egypt (which Britain had in effect occupied in 1882 after a nationalist revolt against the regime of the Khedive Tewfik led to an anti-Christian riot in Alexandria, and the despatch of British gunboats and troops to restore order).

To resolve the escalating spiral of claims, Bismarck invited delegations of 13 European nations, plus the United States to a conference at Berlin, which opened on 15 November 1884 and dragged on for over three months, until the end of February the following year. As well as resolving to end the slave trade within Africa (where, even after its abolition by European powers, it remained in operation in areas not controlled by them), it also confirmed Leopold in his occupation of the Congo, where conditions were so bad as to be tantamount to slavery, and which, with his rule internationally sanctioned, the Belgian king in August 1885 declared to be the 'Congo Free State'. Crucially, the Berlin Conference also enshrined the principle of 'effective occupation'. This laid down that

Cartoon of the Berlin Conference, *Chronicle*, 1884

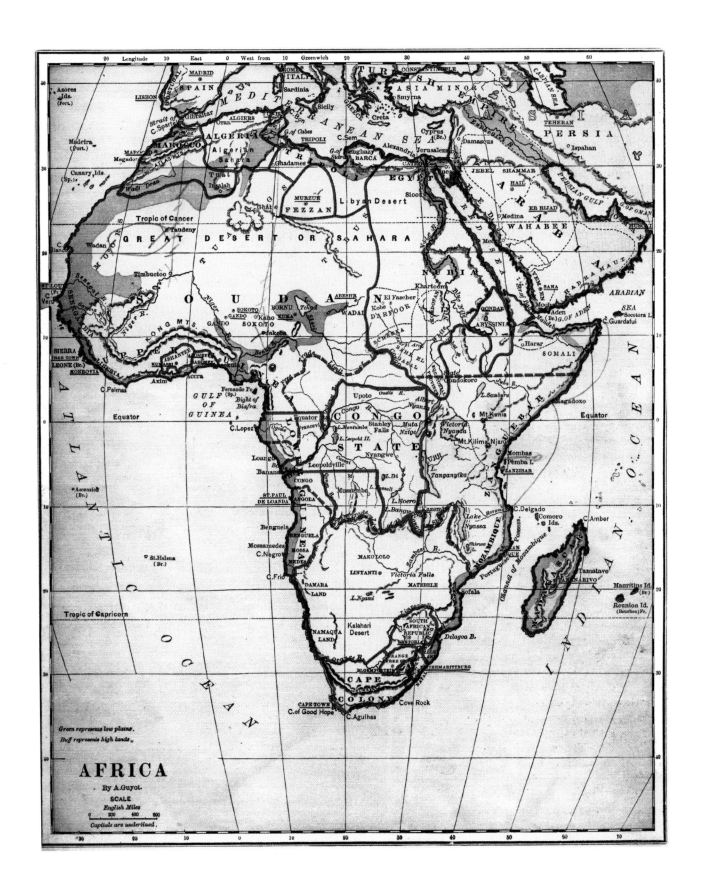

AFRICA

By A.Guyot.

SCALE

English Miles

200   400   600

Capitals are underlined.

Green represents low plains.
Buff represents high lands.

Plate 45.

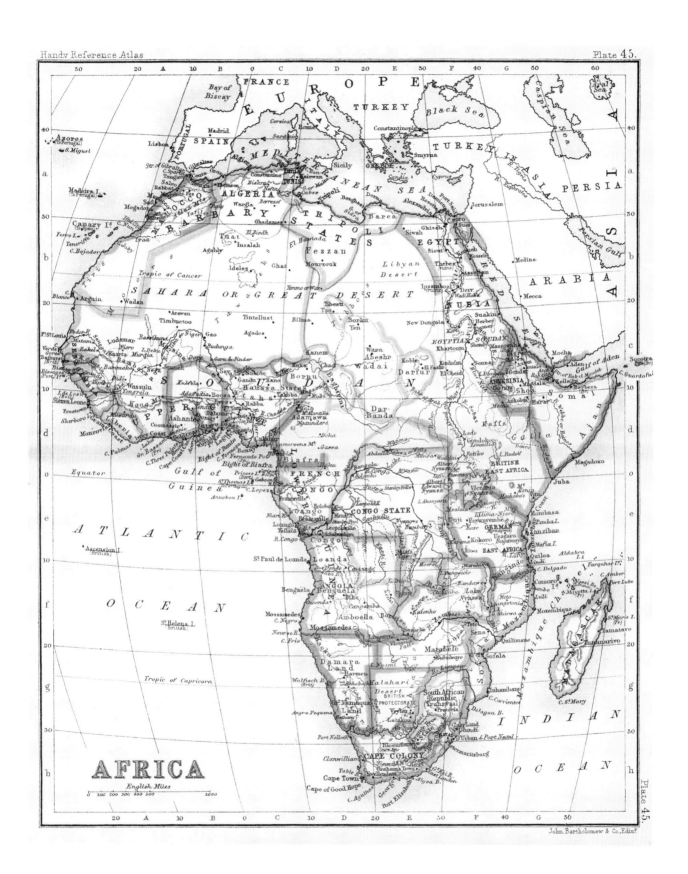

AFRICA

English Miles

0   100 200 300 400 500   1000

John Bartholomew & Co., Edin^r

Plate 45.

PREVIOUS PAGE, LEFT

Africa before the Berlin Conference, *Guyot's New Intermediate Geography*, Arnold Guyot, 1882

PREVIOUS PAGE, RIGHT

Africa after the Berlin Conference, *Handy Reference Atlas of the World*, John Bartholomew, 1893

a European state could only lay claim to an area of Africa in which it had a real presence, with an organized administration and forces to defend its position. It could not, in other words, simply rely on signing treaties with local rulers who signed away their rights (whether they possessed the power to do so or not, and whether they were tricked or cajoled into doing so). Despite the principle being explicitly limited to coastal lands, which were almost all in any case already occupied (and of which Germany had none), it was interpreted by France and Britain in particular to mean that the possession of coastal bases also brought legal control of the hinterland behind them.

The result of the conference was to inflame colonial competition for Africa rather than to calm it. The Portuguese issued the *Pink Map* joining up their territories in Mozambique and Angola by claiming a linking strip going through what is now Zambia and Zimbabwe, land which the British vigorously insisted should be theirs. The French pressed eastwards, leading to a confrontation at Fashoda in Sudan in 1898, where an expedition led by Jean-Baptiste Marchand occupied a fort on the Nile and found itself in a tense confrontation with Lord Kitchener's Anglo-Egyptian force fresh from victory against the Mahdist Islamist rebels at Omdurman. It was again realpolitik that intervened, as the French foreign minister Théophile Delcassé ordered a withdrawal back to Congo as the price for securing British support against the new common enemy, Germany.

Out of the 'Scramble for Africa', which by 1898 left only Ethiopia and Liberia independent of European rule, Germany did gain its long-hoped-for colonial empire. In 1884 the German East Africa Company was set up and by the following year

RIGHT

The Upper Nile from Korosko to Fashoda, at the time of the Mahdist War, *Field Marshal Lord Kitchener, His Life and Work for the Empire*, 1916

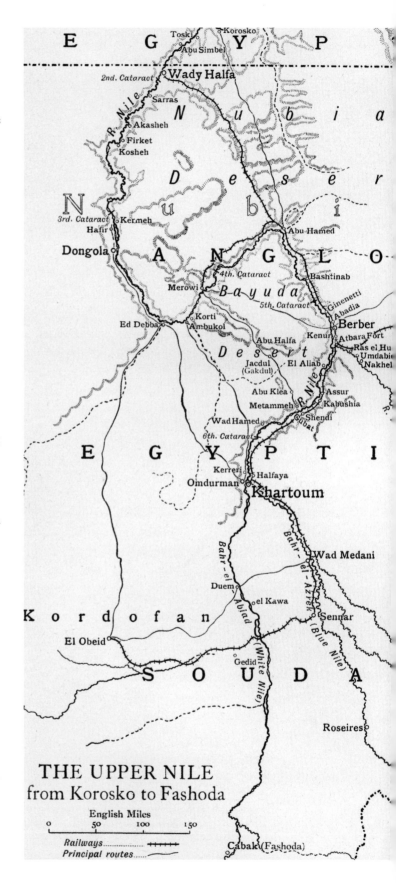

THE UPPER NILE
from Korosko to Fashoda

LEFT

Illustration of
the Anglo-French
Convention of
1898, *Le Petit
Journal*, April 1899

Le Petit Journal

SUPPLÉMENT ILLUSTRÉ

DIMANCHE 9 AVRIL 1899

LA CONVENTION FRANCO-ANGLAISE
M. Paul Cambon et Lord Salisbury

Nama, Herero and other indigenous peoples, resulting in a genocidal extermination campaign by the German military, which killed almost 80 per cent of the Hereros between 1904 and 1908.

Germany was assured its 'place in the sun', as foreign minister Bernhard von Bülow characterized it with deceptive quaintness in 1897, but the consequence of the Berlin Conference for Africans had been a catastrophic loss of independence, as the maps of the continent in 1882 and 1893 show (see pp.204–05). In trying to prevent a spiralling land grab, the conference had in played a great role in accelerating the 'Scramble for Africa', a colonial knot-tying that was only to be unravelled in the 1960s.

If the Berlin Conference and the redrawing of the map that arose from it evoke bitterness in Africa, even more raw emotion was raised by another set of lines, whose imposition (or attempted imposition) in the Middle East still has the power to create aftershocks in the 21st century. The Asia Minor Agreement was the archetypal 'line drawn in the sand', a monument to imperial arrogance. More generally known as the Sykes-Picot Agreement, it was negotiated by Sir Mark Sykes (1879–1919) on the British side, and François Georges-Picot (1870–1951) for the French. Both Britain and France were keen to head off growing German influence in the decaying Ottoman Empire (and in particular to stymie the project for a Baghdad to Berlin railway that would bind it tightly in Germany's economic embrace).

Britain had already encouraged a revolt by Arab leaders in Iraq, Palestine and Syria against Ottoman rule, enticing Abdullah and Faisal, the sons of Sherif Hussain of Mecca to join their cause. Yet British promises of support for Arab independence soon proved hollow. Almost as soon as Sykes and Picot had their first meeting in London in November 1915, the plans to create an Arab state centred around Lebanon, which the French regarded as firmly in their sphere of influence, and Syria, on which the Paris government also had designs, were dropped. Instead, the two negotiators carved up the Middle East with no regard to previous pledges, and little either for the historic allegiances or contemporary aspirations of the region's population or its leaders. As the map of the agreement shows, Britain kept control of most of modern Iraq, while France was handed Lebanon and

had established a presence in Tanganyika (the mainland portion of modern Zanzibar). By the end of the decade this new German empire had expanded into Urundi (Burundi) and Ruanda (Rwanda). In West Africa, meanwhile, the German explorer Gustav Nachtigal, who had branched out from his position as physician to the bey (ruler) of Tunis to engage in several expeditions in Chad and the Kordofan region of Sudan, was sent by Bismarck to plant the German flag in Cameroun and Togo. Germany also annexed what is now Namibia by the tried-and-trusted colonial expedient of negotiating agreement with local chieftains – the European side of the 'bargain' in this case being the adventurer Adolf Lüderitz, who succeeded in persuading the Berlin government to declare the area a German protectorate in August 1884. German South-West Africa, as it became known, would become the site of protracted resistance to European rule by the

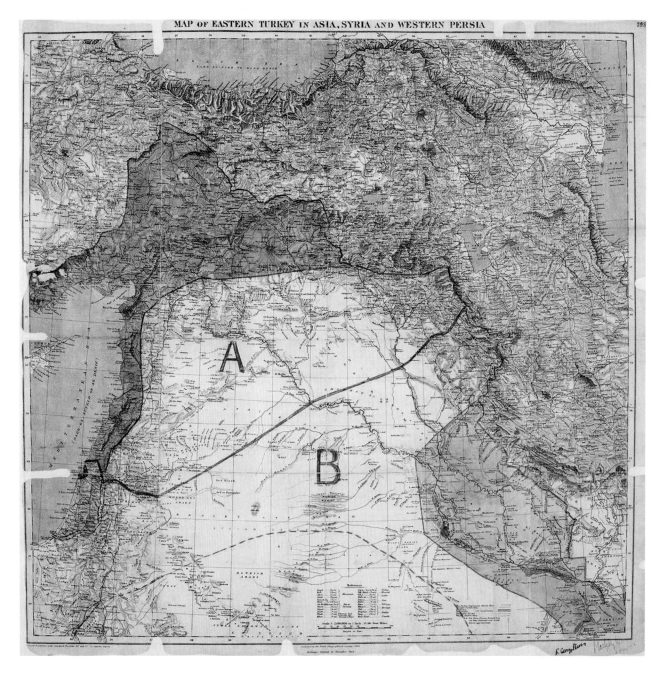

ABOVE

Map of Eastern
Turkey, Syria and
Western Persia, Sir
Mark Sykes and
François Georges-
Picot, 1916

the northern part of Syria (the two countries'
allocated areas marked in solid blue and red). A rather
vaguer area in which the respective European powers
were to be pre-eminent without absolute control were
marked as 'Area A' (in Syria, which was to be in the
French orbit) and 'Area B' (in western Iraq and Jordan,
which fell to the British). Palestine remained largely
unresolved: Haifa and Acre were allocated to Britain,
but the bulk was to be governed by an international
committee, an arrangement that proved satisfactory
to nobody and which was ended when Britain was

awarded a League of Nations mandate over the whole
of Palestine in 1922.

The agreement was supposed to remain a secret:
after all Britain still needed the active military
support of the Arab leaders who were participating
in an uprising against the Ottomans (in which the
army officer T.E. Lawrence, later immortalized as
'Lawrence of Arabia' was playing a colourful part).
The whole project was scuppered, however, because
the agreement also included the annexation by
Russia of part of Armenia, and in the aftermath of

the overthrow of the Tsar by Lenin's Bolsheviks in November 1917, the new revolutionary government leaked its terms. Matters were further complicated by the promises which the British prime minister had made in the Balfour Declaration the same month that Britain would 'view with favour' the establishment of a Jewish homeland in Palestine, thereby flatly contradicting what Faisal and Abdullah had understood would happen.

A different carve-up of the region in the end occurred, with Palestine and Iraq being awarded to Britain by the League of Nations to hold as 'mandates', and Syria and Lebanon coming under French rule on the same basis. The theory was that they would be governed by the mandated powers on behalf of the League, but in practice this varied very little from full-blooded colonial rule. Before long, opposition to the new rulers was growing (fuelled in great part by resentment at the diplomatic manoeuvring of Sykes-Picot) and major revolts broke out against the British in Iraq in 1920 and in the Jabal al-Druze region of French Syria in 1925. During the Iraqi uprising, Winston Churchill, then the Secretary of State for War, ordered the unleashing of a bombing campaign by the RAF against the rebels and, infamously, promoted the use of poison gas to subdue the uprising. In the end the nationalist rebels gained their longed-for independence, as Iraq was granted it in 1932, Lebanon in 1943 and Syria in 1946. For them, one line in the sand had proved as bad as another.

If the British had used maps in the construction of their empire, they played a key and often destructive role in the dismantling of imperial rule. The deceptively straight lines which the colonial powers drew across Africa in the aftermath of the Berlin Conference took no account of the realities on the ground and often scythed through the lands of indigenous groups, leaving parts of them stranded on the other side of a legal barrier which they had had no say in erecting. Matters were even more complicated in Palestine. The Balfour Declaration, which offered the prospect of British support for a

Jewish homeland, had encouraged migration to Palestine, where the Jewish population, which had been around 85,000 in 1922, reached almost 450,000 by the start of the Second World War. Tensions between these incomers and the existing Arab inhabitants, who feared (as it turned out, rightly) the demographic tide turning against them, sparked sporadic violence, including large-scale riots in 1920 and 1929 when Jewish properties were attacked. In 1936, the Peel Commission recommended that a Jewish state be established, based around Tel Aviv, but Zionist claims for a larger share of the Holy Land could not be satisfied by such a partial measure. The Second World War brought a temporary pause to the growing conflict, but the aftermath of the Holocaust, which both increased sympathy by those arguing for a Jewish state and also the numbers of refugees from Europe reaching Palestine, reignited a campaign by Jewish guerrilla groups against the British mandate.

By 1947, it was clear that the British government was losing the will to remain in the region, its resources, both diplomatic and economic, sapped by

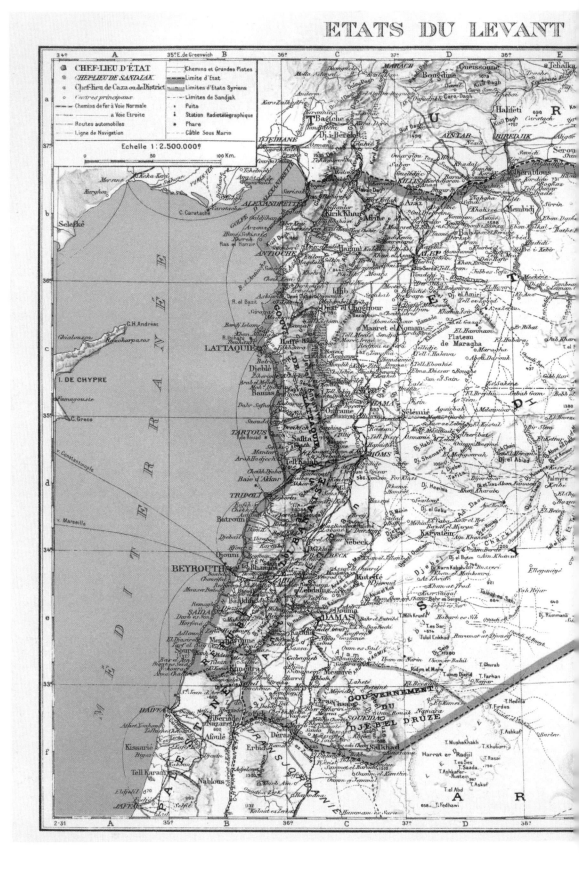

ETATS DU LEVANT

MANDAT FRANÇAIS

DAMAS

1 El Tékié
2 Hamidié
3 Hôpital
4 Ecole de Médecine
5 Gare du Hedjaz
6 Egl. des Jésuites
7 Egl. des Lazaristes

0	500	1000	2000 m.

BEYROUTH

0	500	1000	1500	2000	1500 m.

1 Mosquée Dabagha
2 Palais de Justice
3 Halles
4 Eglise St Georges
5 Université St Joseph
6 Hôpital Français
7 Champ de Courses

Édité par L'Illustration.

the Second World War, and aware that it could satisfy neither party, Arabs or Jews, fully, and that its continuing holding of the mandate was causing its international prestige to ebb away. Britain decided that the best solution was to simply hand back the problem to the United Nations, in effect the successor to the League of Nations, which had inherited responsibility for the mandates. In May 1947 the United Nations Special Committee on Palestine (UNSCOP) was set up, which sent rapporteurs to Palestine to take evidence from the contending sides. The result was a report in early September which recommended separate independent Jewish and Arab states (although a minority of the committee proposed a federal union). Arab leaders, however, felt that their interests had been ignored and rejected the plan, while Jewish Zionist leaders accepted the majority proposal, which was formalized by the Ad Hoc Committee on the Palestinian Question that was set up to implement the plan.

The map shows a tenuous Jewish state actually cut into three segments by the proposed Arab state south of Ramla and east of Haifa, while an Arab enclave south of Jaffa looked more precarious still. Jerusalem was to be retained as a zone under international administration, because to either partition it or award it to either the Jewish or Arab state seemed too incendiary a move.

The Ad Hoc Committee map and the belief that UNSCOP's proposal had created a settled environment for the two new states proved ephemeral. On 14 May 1948 the British withdrew their last forces from Palestine and on the same day the Jewish leadership under David Ben-Gurion declared the State of Israel. War immediately erupted with the new state's Arab neighbours, Lebanon, Syria, Iraq, Transjordan and Egypt, who sent troops pouring over the border. An initial four weeks of bitter fighting was followed by a series of ill-kept truces and renewed combat which only finally ended with armistices in February and March 1949. The Israeli army, formed around the Haganah and other Zionist military organizations which had fought the British, had by far the better of the war and Israel ended up in possession of nearly 80 per cent of the old British mandate. Jordan, in turn, pre-emptively occupied the West Bank of the Jordan and the eastern part of Jerusalem, while Egypt took the Gaza Strip. The Palestinian Arabs were left with nothing and hundreds of thousands of them fled to refugee camps where many of their descendants remained into the 21st century. The UNSCOP draft had proved to be one

of a succession of maps which turned out to be cartographic mirages, at each stage of which the hoped-for peace and the potential territory to be ruled by an Arab or Palestinian state grew more exiguous.

The division of Palestine by map was at least done on the basis of years of survey and consideration of how to draw a line between the warring communities. In contrast, British India was sundered in two by cartographic fiat. Just as in Palestine, decades of opposition to British rule had sapped London's will to remain, and it was evident by 1947 that greater political autonomy would not satisfy the aspirations of Indian nationalists and that independence would have to be granted. Complicating matters was the vigorous campaign by the All-India Muslim League, led by Muhammad Ali Jinnah (1876–1948), which lobbied for a separate state for India's Muslim population, arguing that their interests could never be fairly represented in one that encompassed the whole of British India, in which they would be forever condemned a minority in a broadly Hindu population.

Despite last-ditch attempts by veteran Indian nationalists such as Jawaharlal Nehru (1889–1964) and Mahatma Gandhi (1869–1948) to preserve a one-state solution, the British government acceded to Jinnah's demands and made preparations for the division of India. In June 1947 they chose Cyril Radcliffe (1899–1977), who had been a civil servant in the wartime Ministry of Information, to determine where the partition between India and Pakistan (as the new Muslim state would be known) should lie. It was a last-minute decision and its implementation bore all the hallmarks of near panic. There was no time to carry out new surveys to determine which areas near the proposed border had Muslim- or Hindu-majority populations and the boundary commissions established to make decisions on Bengal and Punjab, two of the most contested areas, were paralyzed by squabbles between their equally balanced Hindu and Muslim membership. The commissions were forced to work with census returns which were decades out of date and Radcliffe did not help matters by taking a hands-off approach in which he scarcely engaged with the fine detail of the decisions made.

The process was doomed to failure, but its failure proved to be a catastrophic one. By the time Radcliffe's final report was published, two days after the independence of India and Pakistan had taken effect, hundreds of thousands of people were already on the move. The flight accelerated when many villages along the line found they were not on the side of the line that they had expected to be. Over 15 million people fled

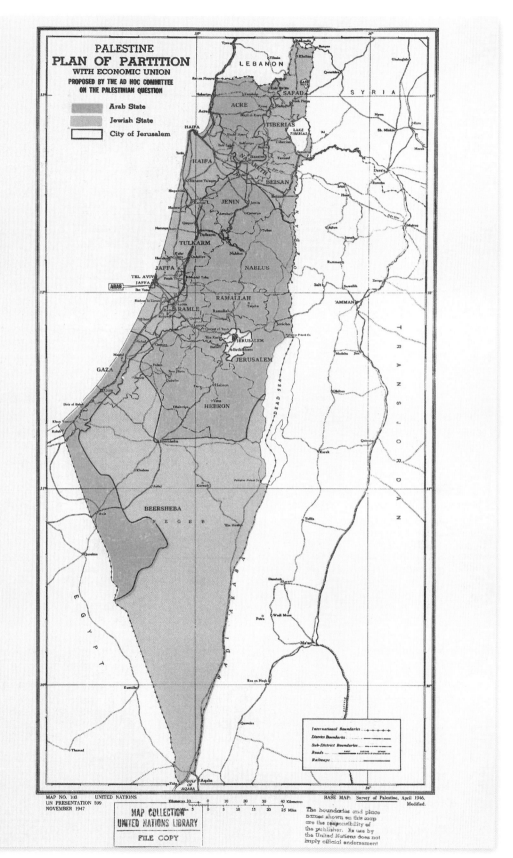

PALESTINE
PLAN OF PARTITION
WITH ECONOMIC UNION
PROPOSED BY THE AD HOC COMMITTEE
ON THE PALESTINIAN QUESTION

Arab State
Jewish State
City of Jerusalem

LEBANON

SYRIA

TRANSJORDAN

EGYPT

DEAD SEA

GULF
OF
AQABA

MAP NO. 103   UNITED NATIONS
UN PRESENTATION 599
NOVEMBER 1947

BASE MAP: Survey of Palestine, April 1946.
Modified.

International Boundaries
Districts Boundaries
Sub-District Boundaries
Roads
Railways

The boundaries and place
names shown on this map
are the responsibility of
the publisher. Its use by
the United Nations does not
imply official endorsement

LEFT

*Palestine: Plan
of partition with
Economic Union
proposed by the
Ad Hoc Committee
on the Palestinian
Question*, UN
Geospatial
Information
Section, 1947

their homes in one of the largest mass exoduses in history, and around a million died as gangs of vigilantes hunted down and slaughtered those of a different religion. Whole trainloads of refugees were massacred and by the time the violence had subsided, relations between Pakistan and India were permanently damaged, a situation aggravated by tensions over the state of Kashmir. These were complicated by the actions of its maharajah Hari Singh (1895–1961), who had decided to preserve his own domain as a third independent state in the Indian subcontinent. In theory he had every right to do so: the British had never ruled the whole of India directly, and much of it was controlled by a patchwork of princely states which remained independent, as long as they did not impinge upon essential British interests. In 1947, the independent princes were given the choice of opting to become part of India or Pakistan or remaining as mini-states in their own right. Most of them acceded to less than subtle pressure from the new Indian or Pakistani governments or accepted the reality that they simply could not survive on their own. Not so Hari Singh. He soon, though, faced a revolt among his Muslim subjects in the west of Kashmir, an invasion by Muslim Pashtun tribesmen and a counter-invasion by Hindu and Sikhs from the Punjab, and the prospect that Pakistan would simply step in and annex the whole of his kingdom. Suitably cowed, the Maharajah signed the Instrument of Accession

to India in October 1947, provoking the long-feared intervention by Pakistan, which invaded from the west and sparking the first of three invasions over Kashmir (the others being in 1965 and 1971), sporadic skirmishing over the Line of Control agreed between India and Pakistan in 1949, and a state of permanent animosity between the Delhi and Islamabad governments. The legacy of Radcliffe's line was long-lasting and poisonous.

By the 1990s, cartographers must have believed that their role in delineating border shifts within Europe was over. Long gone were the seismic upheavals at the end of the First World War, when the dissolution of the Austro-Hungarian Empire gave rise to a much-reduced Austria, a separate Hungary and the new state of Yugoslavia, as well as adjustment to the borders of Italy, the achievement of independence from Tsarist Russia by Finland

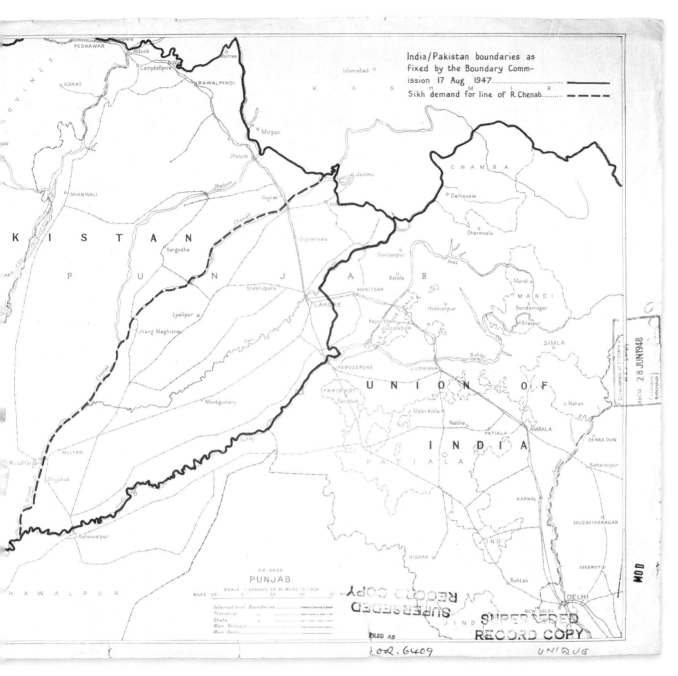

India/Pakistan boundaries as
fixed by the Boundary Commission 17 Aug 1947............
Sikh demand for line of R.Chenab...........

and Poland and the cession back to France of Alsace – which Germany had annexed after the Franco-Prussian War in 1870–71. The turmoil after the Second World War, when Poland was literally moved hundreds of kilometres to the west by taking a chunk out of Germany and losing its eastern marchlands to Russia, also seemed a distant memory. The reunification of Germany as its eastern half, liberated from its role as a Soviet satellite state when communist regimes throughout eastern Europe collapsed in 1988–90, joined West Germany to form a united federal republic, was followed within two years by the dissolution of the Soviet Union itself into its 15 constituent republics, now independent states.

These changes, though, happened along established borderlines and without widespread fighting. Yugoslavia would be different. Constructed in 1918 out of a hotchpotch of Slavic ethnic groups – largely Catholic Slovenes and Croats, Orthodox Serbs and Macedonians, and with significant Muslim populations in Bosnia and

ABOVE

Map showing the
northern section of
the Radcliffe Line,
including Kashmir,
London War Office,
1947

Kosovo – the cauldron of nationalities was kept from boiling over by the firm hand of Marshal Josip Tito (1892–1980), Yugoslavia's communist autarch, who was a veteran of the struggle against Germany in the Second World War. His political canniness also involved keeping the ambitions of the various communities confined to carefully controlled competition within the Communist Party, while forbidding overt expressions of nationalist feeling.

Tito's death on 4 May 1980 changed everything. Although Yugoslavia struggled on for a further decade and even seemed to weather the storm of the collapse of communist regimes elsewhere, voices within its constituent republics arguing for a better deal for their own ethnic groups grew ever more strident. One man, Slobodan Milošević (1941–2006), who rose to prominence in the Communist Party's Belgrade branch, argued that Serbs were being given a raw deal. In 1987, he inflamed nationalist feeling with a speech on the field of Kosovo Polje, site of Serbia's historic defeat by the Ottoman Empire exactly 600 years before (after which the medieval state of Serbia was extinguished). In it he argued that Kosovo, with a largely Muslim population, should have its status as an autonomous component of the Serbian republic revoked.

Relations between Serbia and the other Yugoslav republics deteriorated dramatically, and by January 1990 the consensus which had long held the country together collapsed during the 14th, and final, Congress of the Yugoslav Communist Party.

On 25 June 1991 Slovenia declared its independence. The brief 'Ten-Day War' followed when the Federal Yugoslav Army advanced into Slovenia, but facing resistance from Slovene territorial forces, rapidly withdrew. The conflict in Croatia was far worse, beginning with attacks by Serb nationalists in the Krajina region and escalating into a full-scale war as what was left of the Yugoslav army, allied with Serb militia, occupied much of Eastern Slavonia, reducing towns such as Vukovar to rubble. The fighting, which cost over 20,000 lives, died down early in 1992, but by then an even bloodier civil war had erupted in Bosnia-Herzegovina, where a three-way struggle between Bosnian Muslims, Croats and Serbs saw atrocities on a level not seen in Europe since the Second World War. The activities of the Serb forces in particular, whose nearly four-year siege of the capital Sarajevo left around 14,000 dead, and the massacres by Serb militias of large numbers of Bosnian Muslim civilians trapped in the enclave of Srebrenica, led to accusations of genocide.

The tide turned in 1995 as the Croatian army intervened, Bosnian Muslims and Croats patched up an alliance that had fractured during the early part of the war, and NATO airstrikes on Serb positions brought Milošević to consider that the cost of war now outweighed the price of peace. The leaders of the contending parties were flown to the US Airforce base at Dayton, Ohio, a location chosen deliberately for its isolation (so that the leaders, including Milošević, Franjo Tudjman of Serbia and the Bosnian Muslim president Alija Izetbegović could not grandstand in front of press conferences in between negotiating sessions). Sequestered from the outside world they were put under considerable pressure by the United States to come to an agreement. Hours of argument, offers and counter-offers led to the final Dayton Agreement map (shown on p.218). The Bosnian Serbs could be satisfied that their share of the territory had grown from 46 per cent, which they occupied before Dayton, to 49 per cent (although largely by dint of acquiring tracts of mountainous territory in the east

BELOW

Map of the Kingdom of Yugoslavia, 1922

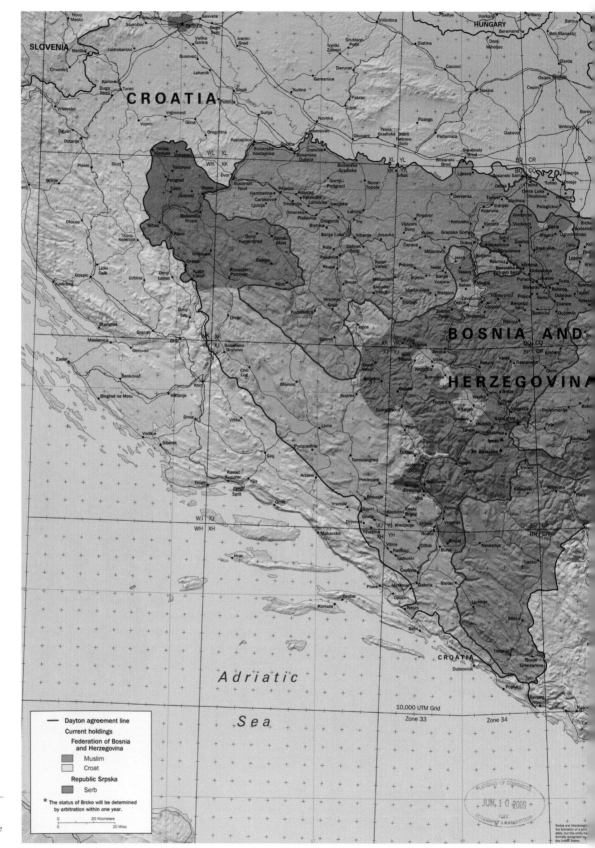

RIGHT

Dayton Peace
Accords map, US
Central Intelligence
Agency, 1996

of Bosnia at the expense of giving up Sarajevo). The Bosnian Muslims got most of Sarajevo, strategic strips of eastern Bosnia, and grew their share of the republic from 28 to 30 per cent. The Bosnian Croats lost land, including in particular Donji Vakuf, which they had fought to hold, but outnumbered and under pressure, they gave in.

The Federal Republic which the Dayton Agreement established, divided between a largely Serb component in the east and a Croat-Bosnian Muslim one in the west, struggled to escape from the supervision of the United Nations and the European Union, threatening at times to enact a miniature version of the dissolution of Yugoslavia and a re-run of its stage of the Yugoslav Civil War, in which over 100,000 people had died. For all its faults, all sides agreed that ripping up the Dayton Agreement map would lead to disaster and so its lines, which in truth had pleased no one, largely held nearly 30 years later.

Disputes over borders continue to be a source of tension between states into the 21st century, and there are somewhere over 100 open border disputes between members of the United Nations, some of which flare up into open warfare, as did that between Armenia and Azerbaijan over the disputed territory of Nagorno-Karabakh in September 2022 (rekindling a war which had first broken out in 1991 amid the dying embers of the Soviet Union). The annexation of Crimea from Ukraine in 2014 was characterized by Russia as part of a long-standing territorial dispute between Moscow and Kyiv, although that of the four border oblasts of Luhansk, Donetsk, Kherson and Zaporizhia in September 2022 after a full-scale Russian invasion did not even have the fig leaf of a pre-existing dispute to cover the first state-level annexations by force in Europe since the Second World War.

In Africa, the drawing of lines at the time of the Berlin Conference and drive to African independence from the late 1950s left many of the infant nation-states with borders whose deceptively straight lines masked very real problems. Ethnic groups straddled the borders and historic claims which had mattered little when both sides were occupied by the same colonial power, suddenly came to be of existential importance when two new and proudly assertive countries had to deal with the unresolved issues. Ethiopia, which had resisted European colonization (apart from a brief Italian occupation in 1936), found itself enmeshed in a border dispute with Eritrea, which Italy had gradually annexed between 1869 and 1889 and retained as a colony until it was placed under British military administration in 1943 following the Italian surrender to the Allies. It was then subsumed into Ethiopia in 1952, a decision sanctioned by the United Nations over the heads of the Eritreans, which led to the foundation of the Eritrean Liberation Front (ELF) in 1961. This and a splinter faction, the Eritrean People's Liberation Front (EPLF), which eventually became the dominant nationalist faction, fought a more than 30-year war against the Ethiopian government, securing most of Eritrea's territory by 1977 – although a government offensive the following year pushed them back –and in 1991 seizing the rest as the Marxist government in Addis Ababa fell after the collapse of the Soviet Union, its long-time sponsor.

In a referendum in 1993 Eritrean independence was confirmed, but that still left the border between it and Ethiopia ill-defined, particularly in the region of the town of Badme. Clashes between the two erupted in early May 1998, and despite a temporary cessation of hostilities in March the following year, peace talks failed, and Ethiopian forces pushed further into Eritrea. By May 2000 they occupied more than a fifth of the country. The peace which was signed between the two countries in Algiers in December 2000 referred the matter to the United Nations, whose Ethiopia-Eritrea Boundary Commission based at the Hague called on no less a map-maker than the head of the UN Cartographic

Section to scrutinize maps and agreements between the various parties, including the Ethiopian empire and the Italian colonial authorities which went back to the early 20th century. Colonial treaties from 1900, 1902 and 1908 were pored over and interpreted – not an easy task when the original maps themselves were ambiguous and the watercourses which defined sections of the frontiers were badly marked. Things proceeded relatively smoothly until in 2003 Ethiopia disputed part of the commission's determination in the eastern sector, leading the UN to decree that if both parties did not accept the commission's recommendations by November 2007, then those recommendations would in any case become binding.

In 2012, fighting erupted again along the border and the two sides traded accusations of supporting rebel movements against the other. Only in 2018 did peace and a resolution to the border question seem in prospect, when a new Ethiopian prime minister Abiy Ahmed announced that the Ethiopians were giving up all claims to the disputed areas, including the long-contested town of Badme. If maps had been the cause of a century of border conflict, the lines of the frontier on this one seemed finally settled.

There seems little prospect, however, that the long tradition of calling on map-makers either to assert possession of territories through mapping, or to create or interpret maps in an effort to resolve international dispute will end. As well as the renewal of conflict between Azerbaijan and Armenia, the backwash of Russia's invasion of Ukraine in February 2022 touched Central Asia, where Moscow's influence remained strong even after the Soviet Union's collapse. In mid-September that year border guards from Kyrgyzstan and Tajikistan clashed along a section of the border that was not properly demarcated as the Kyrgyz accused the Tajiks of encroaching on their territory. Over 100 people were killed in a week of fighting before a ceasefire restored calm. Yet this dispute is unresolved and seems likely to flare up again, particularly as it is worsened by

From the confluence of the Mareb and the Mai Ambessa to Point 11, the boundary line follows the Mareb.

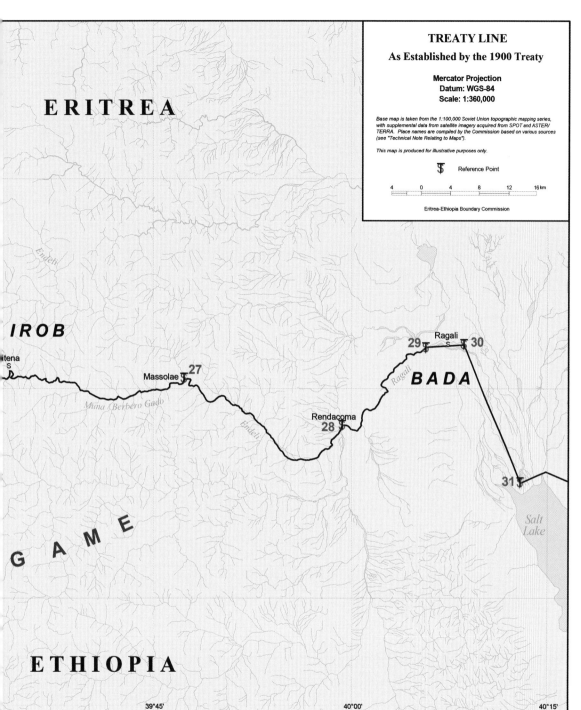

ERITREA

IROB

itena
S

Massolae 27

Mina (Berbero Gado)

Endeli

Endeli

Rendacoma
28

Ragali
29 S 30

Ragali

BADA

31

Salt
Lake

GAME

ETHIOPIA

39°45'   40°00'   40°15'

TREATY LINE

As Established by the 1900 Treaty

Mercator Projection
Datum: WGS-84
Scale: 1:360,000

Base map is taken from the 1:100,000 Soviet Union topographic mapping series, with supplemental data from satellite imagery acquired from SPOT and ASTER/TERRA. Place names are compiled by the Commission based on various sources (see "Technical Note Relating to Maps").

This map is produced for illustrative purposes only.

Reference Point

4   0   4   8   12   16 km

Eritrea-Ethiopia Boundary Commission

LEFT

Treaty Line,
as established
by the 1900
Italian-Ethiopian
Treaty, Ethiopia-
Eritrea Boundary
Commission

arguments about control of a resource which is becoming ever more scarce and precious: water.

For the foreseeable future, therefore, mapmakers will continue to be forced into the role of peacemakers and maps will continue to have the potential to ignite conflict.

CONCLUSION

In any business someone pays, someone purchases and someone profits. The map that has been carefully planned must be paid for, distributed, purchased (its maker hopes) and then found useful enough that the customers will want to buy more. In the 21st century, those customers must subscribe more or click more as mapping becomes increasingly a digital phenomenon and their ability to create or modify their own maps without the intervention of a cartographer raises the question of whether the age of the map – at least as a physical object – is finally at an end.

Most maps through history have had a patron, been commissioned by someone, or, as the map-making process became an industry, have been produced with an eye on the market. We will probably never know quite who decided to create the Çatal Höyük fresco map but it, and similar large-scale ancient cartographic creations, involved an investment in time in return for a pay-off in the fulfilment of ritual or the gaining of prestige. The *Turin Papyrus* in around 1150 BC clearly had a more practical purpose – the mapping of mineral resources in Egypt's Eastern Desert (see p.19) and was instigated by the pharaoh himself or someone close to him.

Ventures such as the various Roman itinerary maps, like the *Antonine Itinerary*, or whichever map formed the basis of the *Peutinger Table* (see p.47), or the cadastrations which mapped out land holdings for each new Roman settlement, all required the support of the imperial or at least provincial administrations. In the Middle Ages, at least in Europe, patronage for maps was more spasmodic, though elaborate productions such as the *Hereford Mappa Mundi* were costly in terms of the time and materials taken to produce them. We rarely have accounts of what they did cost (though one *mappa* mentioned in the accounts of the monastery of Klosterneuburg specified that the map had cost 30 florins to produce, a huge amount for the time).

There was nothing like a cartographic 'industry' until the 15th century, by which time the Spanish and Portuguese Crowns were formally sponsoring map-making and, later seeking to monopolize it through institutions such as the Casa de Contratación in Seville. Among them was Cardinal Raffaele Riario, who received a chart compiled by Grazioso Benincasa in 1482, though slightly less elevated folk were by now commissioning atlases, such as the Genoese doctor Prospero da Camogli who ordered one from Benincasa in 1468 (which happened to

BELOW

Map of Westmorland and Cumberland, Christopher Saxton, 1576

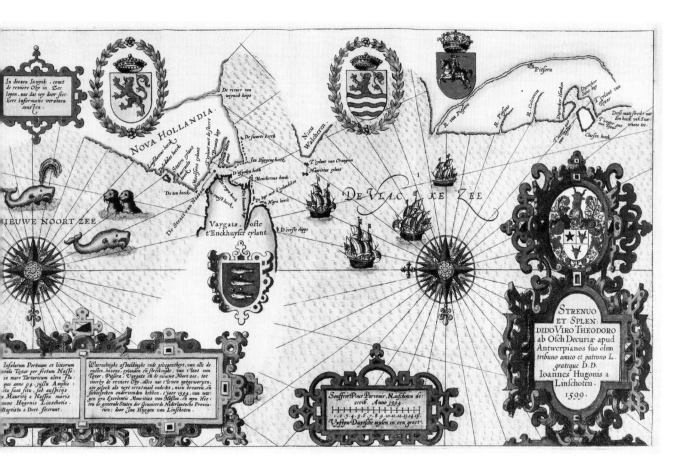

include the first appearance on maps of the Cape Verde islands, discovered by the Portuguese just a dozen years earlier). In this respect Italy benefited from the tradition of patronage which had grown up in the arts more generally, where contracts with fees between artist and patron were commonplace.

High-ranking and preferably royal patronage was vital. The *Catalan Atlas* compiled in 1375 by Abraham and Jafudà Cresques was a specific royal commission (see p.82), and prominent churchmen, too, were presented with maps to whose production they would have provided an element at least of the costs. Without such backing the production of large-scale works was haphazard and fraught with difficulty. Christopher Saxton (*c.* 1540–1610), who created an epic series of county maps of England and Wales between 1573 and 1579, enjoyed the patronage of the lawyer Thomas Seckford (1515–87), whose impressive portfolio of offices included Master in Ordinary of the Court of Requests. Through him Saxton came to the attention of Lord Burghley, Elizabeth I's chief minister, but even then, cost pressure resulted in many important coastal counties (the main point of the survey from the Crown's point

of view being to give an accurate map of areas which might be subject to foreign invasion) being mapped at a reduced scale. Rather than direct payment, Saxton was awarded a 10-year monopoly on printing his maps from July 1577. Even in their largesse, patrons could be parsimonious.

In the Netherlands of the 17th century, map-making thrived due to the heady mix of a thrusting new commercial culture, the growth of bourgeois patronage networks and sheer curiosity about the world in a population that understood the sea was the route to power and prosperity. Men such as Jan Huyghen van Linschoten (see p.182), whose pathfinding voyages to the East Indies did much to open the eyes of his countrymen to the profits to be had there and to the weakness of the Portuguese monopoly, had access to a dynamic and ambitious elite in his hometown of Enkhuizen. These circles included well-connected men like François Maalzon (1538–1602), a local physician, who was an adviser to Prince Maurits, the Captain-General of the Dutch Republic and mastermind of their successful rebellion against the Spanish. Maalzon also helped select Jan Huygen as the leader of a voyage to search out the

ABOVE

Map from *Travel Account of the Voyage of the Sailor Jan Huyghen van Linschoten to the Portuguese East India*, 1601 edition

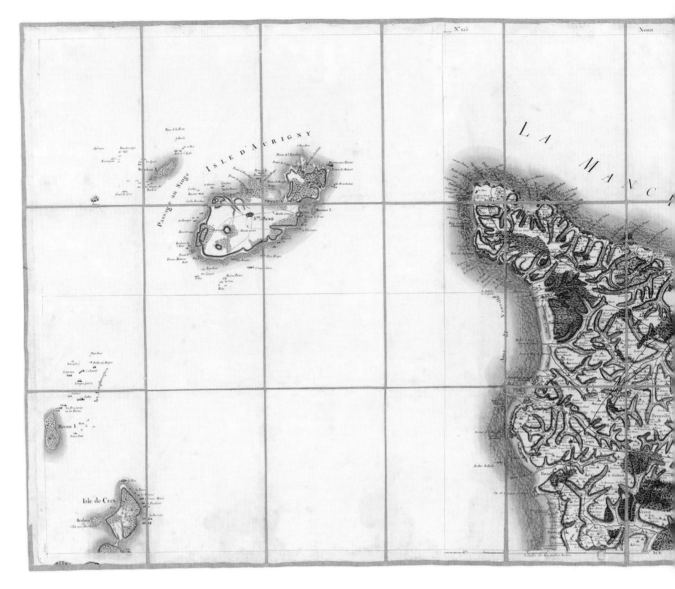

ABOVE

Detail of the
Cotentin Peninsula,
*Carte générale de
la France*, Cassini
Family, 1758

North-East Passage, a hypothesized route over Russia
to East Asia in which the Dutch vested great hopes.
He also knew Berend ten Broeke (known as
Palludanus), whose home in Enkhuizen acted as a
salon and networking site for travellers and scholars
(his album *amicorum* or guest book has over 1,900
names mentioned in it). Van Linschoten was also
acquainted with the chart-maker Lucas Janszoon
Waghenaer who thanked him in his 1598 *Enchuyser
Zee-caert-boeck*. It was connections such as these that
secured Jan Huygen both a place on a voyage to China
sponsored by the East India Company and a 10-year
privilege (an early form of copyright) on his *Itinerario*,
an account of his various voyages.

The map of France produced by the multi-
generational effort of the Cassini family from 1643

(see p.34) is a clear demonstration that the large-scale
surveys needed to produce modern scientific maps
could not be supported by an individual. Apart from
the costs of the instruments themselves the surveyors
had to be kept in food and lodging for many months.
For just that of Brittany in 1721, the cost came to
12,000 livres in a year, while César François Cassini
de Thury (1714–84) told Louis XV in the 1750s that
to complete the survey of France would cost 40,000
livres a year. In Britain, too, map-making experienced
a process of consolidation. Just before the
establishment of the Ordnance Survey in 1766, its
future mastermind William Roy (1726–90) submitted
a plan, estimating that a national survey would cost
£2,778 (equivalent to roughly £375,000 today). And if
the cost of surveying was bad enough, that of printing

the maps could be staggering and explained why, by the 18th century, cartographers handed their work over to publishers, rather than trying to bring the map to market themselves. The engraved copperplates were among the most expensive items: a plate measuring 20 x 28 cm (8 x 11 in) weighed about 5 kg (11 lb) and given the cost in France could be up to 3 livres a pound, this soon mounted up. The engravers had to be paid, and their work was painstaking and time-consuming: the plates for Lord Anson's *A Voyage Round the World* (finally published in 1748), which gave an account of his four-year-long circumnavigation of the globe, took a further two-and-a-half years to produce. Maps were expensive and they could not be hurried.

All this cost meant that the prices being charged for maps escalated so much that in 1688 the French government passed an ordinance stamping down on the then prevalent practice of forcing customers to buy a whole atlas when what they really wanted was just a single sheet – nonetheless prices charged to customers still escalated from 5 to 6 sous for a map in late 17th-century France to three times that amount early the next century. Print-runs were relatively small, generally between 500 and 1,000 maps, and trade was not always brisk. When Guillaume Delisle died in 1726, his widow was left holding a stockpile of 18,000 maps, which she estimated as 25 years' worth of sales. In the absence of a rich patron such as Philippe, duc d'Orleans (1674–723), who hired Guillaume Delisle as tutor to the heir to the throne and began a tradition of awarding titles such as *Géographe du Roi* to favoured cartographers, map-makers turned to other ways to raise funds. Some tried subscription. The Carte de France used it to escape from its perennial funding crisis through the establishment in 1756 of a subscription system by which all 173 sheets of the projected map could be had for 500 livres (as opposed to the 720 livres cost if bought piecemeal). Unfortunately for the project, only 203 subscribers ever stumped up. In Britain the map publisher and cartographer John Senex (1678–1740) was more successful, attracting 1,047 subscribers to his *New General Atlas* in 1721. Around a quarter of

Naves e China et Iaua velis ex arundine
contextis et anchoris ligneis.

Schepen van China en Iava met rietten
serleij en houten anckers

ABOVE AND RIGHT

Pages from
Itinerario, Jan
Huygen van
Lischoten, 1596

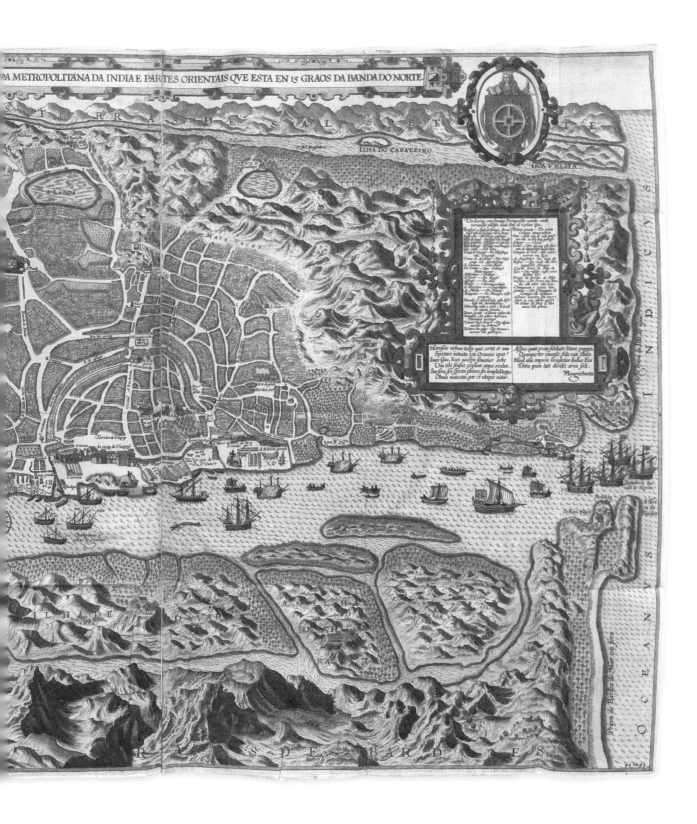

RIGHT

The Americas,
*Atlas bestehend
in auserlesenen
und allerneuesten
Land-Chartern über
die gantze Welt,*
Johann Baptist
Homann, 1707

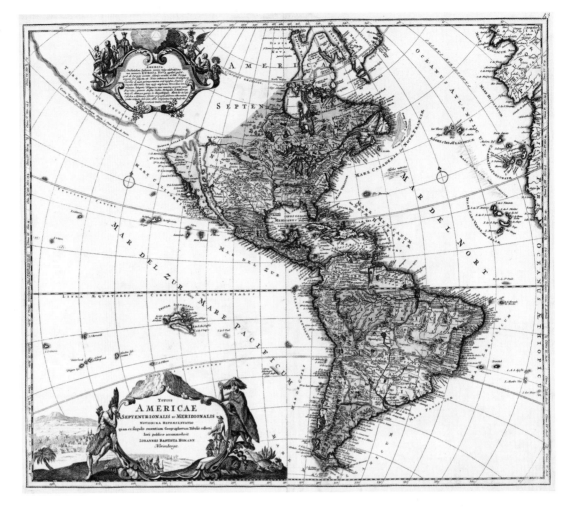

whom were humble craftsmen and yeomen, suggesting that the appetite for maps was not limited to the higher echelons of society.

The final solution was the establishment of large-scale publishing companies such as the Homann family firm, founded in 1702 by Johann Baptist Homann (1664–1724), which launched its century-and-a-half of cartographic successes with *Atlas bestehend in auserlesenen und allerneuesten Land-Chartern über die gantze Welt* ('Atlas Comprising the Selected and Very Latest Country Maps of the Entire World') in 1707, followed by the awarding of the accolade of *Kaiserlicher Geograph* (royal geographer) in 1716. By the middle of the century it was probably the premier map-publishing outfit in Europe, although time, commercial missteps and increasing competition from France and Britain meant it finally fell out of fashion, out of the hands of the original family in 1813, and then out of business in 1852 when all its plates were sold. In Britain, the trade was characterized still by individual cartographers and

entrepreneurs, such as Thomas Jefferys, whose map of New Hampshire (1761) was the first comprehensive one of that colony, but whom the cost of major new surveys of English counties such as Bedfordshire and Oxfordshire (1769) bankrupted. Larger companies now took over, such as John Bartholomew & Co, founded in 1826 by John Bartholomew Senior (1805–61), whose son and successor John Bartholomew Junior, notably, engraved the map that appears in Robert Louis Stevenson's *Treasure Island*, and George Philip (1800–82), who established George Philip & Son in 1834.

The 20th century saw such companies become larger until finally the inevitable happened with the consolidation of publishing houses from the 1970s and then the impact of digital publishing and smartphones, which hit physical map publishing particularly hard. Google Maps launched in 2005, gradually overtaking all competitors until its position in the eye of the average internet user became virtually unassailable. As computer software and smartphones grew ever more sophisticated and powerful, users increasingly had the ability to summon up a map at will, and, if prepared to spend a little more time and a few more clicks, even to customize it with the location of their favourite coffee shops or as a base on which to draw the frontlines of the Russia–Ukraine conflict. It seemed finally, as the second quarter of the 21st century approached, that the long career of the map as an item produced by trained specialists and with a defined physical form was over. We no longer need cartographers, doomsayers might pronounce, or, more optimistically, we are all cartographers now.

Both views have their merits, and both contain an element of truth. The basis of mapping is the collection, compilation and presentation of information about the world in graphic form. The information in Google Maps does not exist in isolation and has been collected in some form of survey (aerial or in the time-honoured means of going on foot, or on moped). The projections shown on digital maps are variants on those developed through the ages, and the decisions on what to show and how to show it are exactly those faced by cartographers, their publishers and patrons through the ages. Someone still needs to conclude that a map is needed and why, to pay for it, to collate the information, decide what to show and then deliver it to the customers. That some of these stages are quicker (almost instantaneous in the delivery to the digital map consumer) makes them no less real. That map users can now customize their maps is a boon rather

than a threat, though the barrier to entry of the huge cost of assembling a digital database such as Google maintains, raises troubling questions about who controls the information, and how it might be manipulated without the end-user being aware. However, these are perhaps no more than contemporary versions of the challenges faced by the map-makers who wanted to know more about the latest discoveries in the Americas, but encountered obstruction by the Spanish and Portuguese authorities who wished to maintain at least a partial veil of secrecy.

If anything, maps are more ubiquitous than they have ever been, available to almost anyone with internet access and providing a near universally understood means of approaching the geography of our planet, of depicting thematically the challenges facing it, and of navigating with ease around it. In our search for the ultimate cartographer, perhaps the answer is that everyone now is one – and in our search for the best map, perhaps the solution is that we hold it in our hands.

LEFT

Digital map of
Blenheim Palace
and Bladon Park,
Oxfordshire, UK

FURTHER
RESOURCES

Books

Bagrow, Leo *History of Cartography,* Revised edition, edited by R.A. Skelton (London 1964)

Barber, Peter and Board, Christopher *Tales from the Map Room: Fact and Fiction about Maps and their Makers* (London 1993)

Barber, Peter and Harper, Tom *Magnificent Maps: Power, Propaganda and Art* (London 2010)

Brooke-Hitching, Edward *The Phantom Atlas: The Greatest Myths, Lies and Blunders on Maps* (London 2016)

Brotton, Jerry *A History of the World in Twelve Maps* (London, 2012)

Brown, Lloyd A, *The Story of Maps* (London 1951)

Delano Smith, Catherine and Kain, Roger J.P. *English Maps A History* (London 1999)

Dilke, O.A.W., *Greek and Roman Maps* (Baltimore, 1998)

Harper, Tom, *Maps and the 20th Century: Drawing the Line* (London 2016)

Harper, Tom and Bryars, Tim *A History of the 20th Century in 100 Maps* (London 2014)

Haywood, Jeremy *To the Ends of the Earth: 100 Maps That Changed the World* (London 2006)

Hewitt, Rachel *Map of a Nation: A Biography of the Ordnance Survey* (London 2011)

Parker, Philip *Atlas of Atlases* (London 2021)

Rapoport, Yossef *Islamic Maps* (Oxford 2020)

Talbert, Richard *Ancient Perspectives: Maps and Their Place in Mesopotamia, Egypt, Greece and Rome* (Chicago, 2012)

Woodward, David & Harley J.B (Series Editors) *The History of Cartography,* volumes 1 to 6 (Chicago, 1987 to 2020)

Websites

The History of Cartography (Online versions of Woodward & Harley series):
   press.uchicago.edu/books/HOC/index.html

Imago Mundi, The International Journal for the History of Cartography:
   maphistory.info/imago.html

Map History, cartographic gateway from former British Library map librarian:
   maphistory.info/index.html

Cartography Unchained, essays on cartographic history before 1600:
   cartographyunchained.com

The Chart Room, links to images of antique maps:
   wildernis.eu/chart-room

The Map Room, large collection of historical maps and atlases:
   maproom.org/index.html

Bibliothèque Nationale, searchable map index from France's National Library:
   gallica.bnf.fr/html/und/cartes/cartes?mode=desktop

Old Maps Online, large collection of online historical maps:
   oldmapsonline.org

My Old Maps, wealth of articles on key maps in the history of cartography:
   myoldmaps.com

National Library of Scotland, over a quarter of a million hi-res zoomable images of the British Isles and beyond:
   maps.nls.uk

INDEX

CREDITS

Collection/Alamy; 106–07 CPA Media Pte Ltd/Alamy; 107r Central Intelligence Agency (United States Government work); 108t ©Warwickshire County Council Collections/Bridgeman Images; 108b The National Archives of the UK; 109 Science History Images/Alamy; 110t ©The Trustees of the British Museum; 110b funkyfood London - Paul Williams/Alamy; 111 Gianni Dagli Orti/Shutterstock; 112t Boaz Rottem/Alamy; 112b Luisa Ricciarini/Bridgeman Images; 113 Hermericus (public domain); 114 Ivy Close Images/Alamy; 115 Bibliothèque nationale de France; 116 ©British Library Board. All Rights Reserved/Bridgeman Images; 117t VDWI Automotive/Alamy; 117b MShieldsPhotos/Alamy; 120 ©British Library Board. All Rights Reserved/Bridgeman Images; 121 Universal History Archive/Getty Images; 122 View Stock/Alamy; 123 Library of Congress, Geography and Map Division; 124 Library of Congress, Geography and Map Division; 125 EU/BT/Alamy; 126 Fine, Oronce. Noua, Et Integra Uniuersi Orbis Descriptio. [Paris?: Orontius Fineus, 1531] Map. https://www.loc.gov/item/2005630228/,World Digital Library; 127 Wellcome Collection (CC BY 4.0); 128 The History Collection/Alamy ; 129 ©MAPS IN MINUTES™ (2015). All rights reserved.; 130–31 Alvaro German Vilela/Alamy; 132–33 Alvesgaspar (public domain); 134t Nationaal Archief Nederland (public domain); 134b–135 The Picture Art Collection/Alamy; 136 AF Fotografie/Alamy; 137 ©British Library Board. All Rights Reserved/Bridgeman Images; 138–39 ©British Library Board. All Rights Reserved/Bridgeman Images; 140–41 Alvesgaspar (public domain); 141r Bibliothèque nationale de France; 142 Balkanique (public domain); 143r Ordnance Survey; 143 gbimages/Alamy; 143b Jane Tregelles/Alamy; 147 Plank (public domain); 148 Ray007 (public domain); 149 DEA PICTURE LIBRARY/De Agostini via Getty Images; 150 The Picture Art Collection/Alamy; 151 The Picture Art Collection/Alamy; 152–53 Geagea (public domain); 154 State Library, South Australia; 155 James Ford Bell Library, University of Minnesota; 156t Peripatesy (public domain); 157 Library of Congress, Parallel Histories: Spain, the United States, and the American Frontier; 158–159 Geographicus Rare Antique Maps/Wikimedia Commons (public domain); 160 GRANGER - Historical Picture Archive/Alamy; 161 Everett Collection Historical/Alamy; 162–63 The Picture Art Collection/Alamy; 163r The History Collection/Alamy; 164–65 Debivort (CC BY-SA 3.0); 168 Album/Alamy; 169 Geography and Map Division, Library of Congress; 170t Harris Brisbane Dick Fund, 1951, Metropolitan Museum of Art, New York; 170b fotopanorama360/Shutterstock; 171 Heritage Image Partnership Ltd/Alamy; 172–73 Science History Images/Alamy; 174–75 The Picture Art Collection/Alamy; 176t Florilegius/Alamy; 176b ©University of St. Andrews Library/Bridgeman Images; 177 Science History Images/Alamy 178–79 Library of Congress; 180 Bibliothèque nationale de France; 181 Bibliothèque nationale de France; 182r Science & Society Picture Library/Getty Images; 183 The Print Collector/Print Collector/Getty Images; 184–85 Library of Congress; 186 ©British Library Board. All Rights Reserved/Bridgeman Images; 187t Broichmore (public domain); 187b GRANGER - Historical Picture Archive/Alamy; 190 Reprint Courtesy of IBM Corporation ©. Photo: A. Knoll, D. Pires, O. Coulembier, P. Dubois, J. L. Hedrick, J. Frommer and U. Duerig, 'Probe-based 3-D Nanolithography using Self-Amplified Depolymerization Polymers' Advanced Materials, Advanced Online Publication in the scientific paper, 23 April 2010. Copyright Wiley-VCH GmbH. Reproduced with permission.; 191 ©British Library Board. All Rights Reserved/Bridgeman Images; 192 ©British Library Board. All Rights Reserved/Bridgeman Images; 193 Jonathan Hordle/Shutterstock; 194 Library of Congress, Geography and Map Division; 198 Photo ©Photo Josse/Bridgeman Images; 199 Album/Alamy; 200 Zuri Swimmer/Alamy; 201 Alvesgaspar (public domain); 202 CPA Media Pte Ltd/Alamy; 203 Chronicle/Alamy; 204 Florida Center for Instructional Technology, Courtesy the private collection of Roy Winkelman; 205 Antiqua Print Gallery/Alamy; 206–07 Classic Image/Alamy; 207r INTERFOTO/Alamy; 208 Niday Picture Library/Alamy; 209 Bettmann/Getty Images; 210–11 Antiqua Print Gallery/Alamy; 213 UN. Geospatial Information Section; 214 World History Archive/Alamy; 215 ©British Library Board. All Rights Reserved/Bridgeman Images; 216 Central Intelligence Agency (United States Government work); 217 Colin Waters/Alamy; 218 Library of Congress, Geography and Map Division; 220–21 Decision Regarding Delimitation of the Border between the State of Eritrea and the Federal Democratic Republic of Ethiopia, Eritrea-Ethiopia Boundary Commission, 13 April 2002. Accessed via haguejusticeportal.net; 222 Photo ©Christie's Images/Bridgeman Images; 223 AF Fotografie/Alamy; 224 Bibliothèque nationale de France; 225 Oranjblud (Ordnance survey/UK government, public domain); 226–27 Universiteitsbibliotheek Utrecht; 228 Library of Congress, Geography and Map Division; 229 Bridgeman Images

About the Author

Philip Parker is a historian with a particular interest in the role of maps, and the ways in which we can use them to uncover history. He is the author of the *DK Eyewitness Companion Guide to World History* (2010), *History of the World in Maps* (2015), *History of Britain in Maps* (2017), *A–Z History of London* (2019), *History of World Trade in Maps* (2020), Small Island: *12 Maps that Explain the History of Britain* (2022) and *The Atlas of Atlases* (2022) and was the General Editor of T*he Great Trade Routes: A History of Cargoes and Commerce over Land and Sea* (2012). He is also a specialist in late antique and early medieval history and wrote *The Empire Stops Here: A Journey Along the Frontiers of the Roman World* (2010) and *The Sunday Times* bestseller *The Northmen's Fury: A History of the Viking World* (2015). He studied History at Trinity Hall, University of Cambridge and International Relations at Johns Hopkins School of Advanced International Studies Bologna Center. He previously worked as a diplomat, the editor of a travel magazine and as a publisher running a list of historical atlases and illustrated history books, and lives in London.

Acknowledgements

Just as the making of a map involves a host of people other than the named mapmaker, so a book about the making of maps has needed the time and skills of a team of whom the author is but one. I would like to thank especially Richard Green, Publisher at Ivy Press, for commissioning the title and to Laura Bulbeck for her heroic efforts in keeping the book (and author) on track. Thanks also to Caroline Earle for copy-editing, Victoria Lympus for proof-reading and Ben Ruocco for the page design, all of whom shaped the book you hold today. Finally, thanks to my family for their perennial good humour and tolerance of yet more authorial months hunched over medieval and early modern maps.

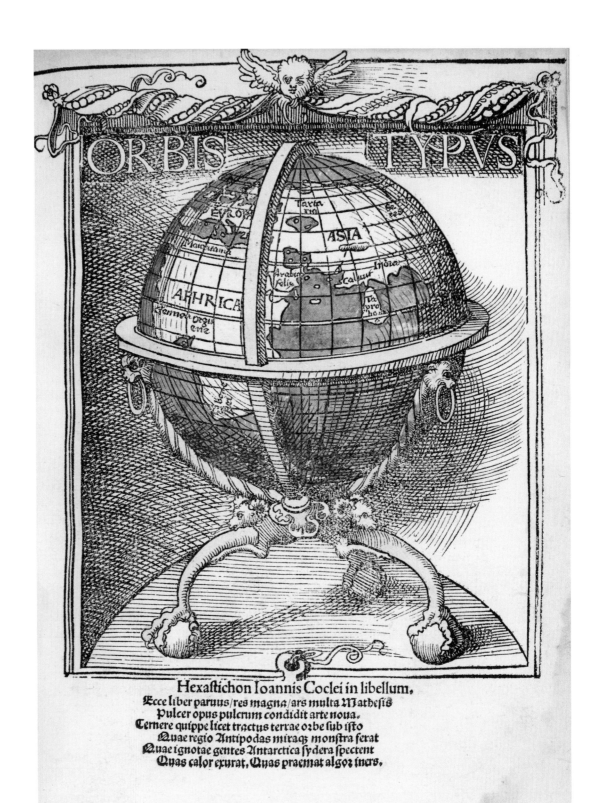

Hexaſtichon Ioannis Coclei in libellum.
Ecce liber paruus/res magna/ars multa Mathesis
Pulcer opus pulcrum condidit arte noua.
Cernere quippe licet tractus terrae orbe ſub iſto
Quae regio Antipodas miraꝗ monſtra ferat
Quae ignotae gentes Antarctica ſydera ſpectent
Quas calor exurat, Quas praemat algor iners.